Anonymous

Toronto Normal School Jubilee Celebration

Biographical Sketches and Names of successful Students 1847 to 1875

Anonymous

Toronto Normal School Jubilee Celebration
Biographical Sketches and Names of successful Students 1847 to 1875

ISBN/EAN: 9783337111212

Printed in Europe, USA, Canada, Australia, Japan

Cover: Foto ©ninafisch / pixelio.de

More available books at **www.hansebooks.com**

1847-1897

TORONTO NORMAL SCHOOL

JUBILEE CELEBRATION

(October 31st, November 1st and 2nd, 1897)

BIOGRAPHICAL SKETCHES AND NAMES OF
SUCCESSFUL STUDENTS 1847 TO 1875

TORONTO:
WARWICK BRO'S & RUTTER,
1898.

PREFACE.

The Toronto Normal School was instituted by the late Dr. Ryerson for the purpose of training teachers for Public School work. In fact, it was an integral part of the system of education which he recommended after having visited the schools of Europe and the United States, under the direction of the Government, with a view to legislation of a comprehensive character for the schools of Ontario. An experience of fifty years in the development of this system (the Normal School included) has clearly shown the wisdom of his conclusions and its adaptation to the social and municipal institutions of the country.

There was no feature of the system of education founded by Dr. Ryerson which had a more important bearing upon Elementary and High School education than the establishment of the Toronto Normal School. For many years it was the only educational seminary at which the training, qualifying a man or woman for the profession of teaching could be obtained. It was always a Normal School, even in the modern sense of the term, for every subject which the student was expected to master was also considered in a pedagogical sense. Much can be said in favor of this early feature of our Normal School, and no doubt, were it not that the High Schools of Ontario attained to such pre-eminence, the literary courses, originally established in the Normal School, would have been continued to this day.

During the last half-century, a great multitude of students graduated from the Toronto Normal School, all of whom felt that they were indebted to its curriculum and staff for a certain mental stimulus which was of great value to them in after life. And so it occurred to some of the earlier students that an opportunity should be given them of doing honor in some public way to their Alma Mater. Out of this desire laudable and kindly in the highest degree, arose the Jubilee Celebration, which it is the object of this volume to record. The opportunity was an admirable one to let the Province see how the old students appreciated the services of some of the great men who, nearly half a century ago, were connected with the educational work of the Province. They were all great teachers—men of magnetic personality and thoroughly in sympathy with the teacher's work. It was meet that their names should be revered by their students and held in grateful remembrance by the country which they served. Their portraits in the school room where they taught will remind successive generations of teachers, of the honor that has been done them, while the impetus they gave to scholarship and education will go on, it is hoped, increasing with the wealth and growth of the country.

Not the least gratifying circumstance in connection with the Jubilee was the presence of two of its first graduates, Dr. E. H. Dewart and Dr. J. H. Sangster: the one a distinguished divine of the Methodist Church, and the other a former Principal of the School, but more recently a physician in active practice. The story of their early difficulties to acquire an education is best told in their own words. It is to be hoped their example will be imitated by many of their fellow-Canadians.

The large attendance of old students indicated the respect in which the Normal School is held by the graduates of former years. Every function in connection with the celebration appeared to be enjoyed to the fullest degree, the only regret in the case of many being that public duties would not allow them to give as much time to the exercises as they desired.

TORONTO, 1897.

CONTENTS.

		PAGE
I. SERMON.	Rev. E. H. Dewart, D.D.	1
II. UNVEILING OF PORTRAITS:		10

    Thomas Jaffray Robertson, M.A.   David Fotheringham.
    J. Herbert Sangster, M.A., M.D.   Rev. R. P. McKay, M.A.
    Rev. HenryW. Davies, M.A., D.D.   Charles A. Barnes, B.A.
    Past Headmistresses of the   Mrs. Nasmith.
      Girls' Model School.   Miss Mary Caven.
    Past Headmasters of the Boys'   David Ormiston, B.A.
      Model School.   Charles A. Hodgetts, M.D.

III. REMINISCENT SPEECHES: 23

    Mrs. Catharine Fish ; William Carlyle ; David Ormiston, B.A. ; Rev. Mungo Fraser, D.D. ; Mrs. G. Riches ; Joseph H. Smith ; A. S. Allan.

IV. REPORT OF CONVERSAZIONE.   40

V. EDUCATIONAL ADDRESSES: 41

    A Brief Sketch of the Toronto Normal School.   Thomas Kirkland, M.A.
    The School of the Twentieth Century.   James L. Hughes.
    Protestant Education in Quebec.   S. P. Robins, M.A., LL.D.
    Where do we stand, Educationally, as compared with Fifty Years ago?   J. Herbert Sangster, M.A., M.D.

VI. REPORT OF BANQUET.   83

VII. BIOGRAPHICAL SKETCHES: 89

    Rev. Egerton Ryerson, D.D., LL.D. ; Hon. Adam Crooks, M.A., LL.B. ; Hon. Geo. W. Ross, LL.D. ; J. G. Hodgins, M.A , LL.D. ; Alex. Marling, LL.B. ; John Millar, B.A. ; Thomas Kirkland, M.A. ; Wm. Scott, B.A. ; A. McIntosh ; Margaret T. Scott ; R. W. Murray ; May K. Caulfeild ; T. M. Porter ; Mary M. A. Meehan ; Jeannie Wood ; Alice Stuart ; Hattie B. Mills, B.A. ; Sara Ross ; Eugene Albert Masson ; A. C. Casselman ; Sydney H. Preston ; Thomas Parr ; Wilhelmina Mackenzie ; Louisa H. Montizambert ; Kate H. Mitchell ; Mary E. Macintyre ; Ellen Cody.

VIII. NAMES OF STUDENTS WHO ATTENDED THE NORMAL SCHOOL FROM 1847 UNTIL 1875 AND RECEIVED CERTIFICATES ; ALSO ALL AVAILABLE BIOGRAPHICAL NOTES 100

IX. MEMBERS AND EX-MEMBERS OF THE STAFF.   199

X. COPY OF THE JUBILEE PROGRAMME   202

[vii.]

THE TORONTO NORMAL SCHOOL JUBILEE CELEBRATION.

I.

The Jubilee Celebration was inaugurated by Divine Service in the Metropolitan Church, Toronto, on Sunday evening, October 31st, 1897. It was conducted by the Pastor, Rev. R. P. Bowles, M.A., B.D., assisted by Revds. John R. Phillips, R. P. McKay, M.A., and by Rev. E. H. Dewart, D D., who preached the sermon. The centre pews of the church were reserved for members of the Convention, among whom were the Committee of Management, the present Normal and Model School staffs, inspectors of schools from different parts of the Province, teachers from the city and from the country, and a number of ex-students of the Normal School, some of whom are members of other professions, while others have retired from professional work.

SERMON:
THE TRUE ELEMENTS OF INDIVIDUAL AND NATIONAL PROGRESS AND STABILITY.

Rev. E. H. Dewart, D.D.
(A Student of the 1st Session).

"And wisdom and knowledge shall be the stability of thy times, and strength of Salvation: the fear of the Lord is his treasure."—*Isa. 33 : 6.*

Memorial Commemorations.

The commemoration of important events has been practised from the earliest times of which we have any account. In the Old Testament we find many interesting illustrations of this usage. Jacob erected a stone pillar and called it Beth-El—the house of God—where he saw the vision of angels and received Divine revelations. After the passing of the Jordan, Joshua set up twelve stones to be a memorial of that event, so that when the children should ask their fathers,

"What meaneth these stones?" they could tell them of what the Lord had done for Israel. After a victory over the Philistines, Samuel set up a memorial stone and called it "Ebenezer," saying, "Hitherto hath the Lord helped us." The Feast of the Passover was a perpetual memorial of a great deliverance.

In more modern times people have commemorated great battles which gave national deliverance from threatened subjugation: the beginnings of important movements that were fruitful in blessings; the work of patriots who lived noble and useful lives and removed evils that had oppressed the people; and events that affected personal and family life for good.

Such commemorations are not foolish or unfruitful. All that is good in our present civilization is the outgrowth of seed sown in the past. In reviewing and commemorating such events as I have mentioned, we may catch something of the spirit that inspired the brave deeds that call forth our admiration. We may gather lessons from the past to nerve and guide us in the conflicts of the present. And a more intelligent appreciation of the rich inheritance to which we are heirs should prompt us to live more worthy of our great privileges and opportunities.

An Event Worthy of Commemoration.

The common disposition to place a high estimate on things that possess outward features that attract attention often causes us to underestimate forces that operate more quietly. But the event we celebrate on this occasion, though it belongs to the latter class, is eminently worthy of being held in grateful remembrance by the people of this country of every class and creed. The establishment of a Normal School for the training of teachers for our Public Schools was the opening of a fountain at which many thirsty souls, whom circumstances had previously shut out from such a privilege, were permitted to slake their thirst for knowledge. I can testify from personal experience and observation that the students at the earlier sessions were nearly all of this class. I shall never forget how the announcement of the opening of the Normal School in Toronto, which I incidentally saw in a newspaper, fell on my path, in the backwoods of the county of Peterborough, like a beam of light from Heaven. I had tried, sometime before that, to make an arrangement to go to another educational institution and had failed, and was very much disappointed. I read the announcement over and over. It seemed almost too good to be true, but it seemed to be just what I required. I wrote to Dr. Ryerson, and received an encouraging answer. So I started for Toronto and tramped one hundred and twenty miles through the November snows. Like another pilgrim we read of, I found hills of difficulty and sloughs of despond before I reached the celestial city. But though footsore and weary, I trudged on and never thought of turning back. A kind welcome from Dr. Ryerson and Mr. Robertson, the Head Master, made me forget all the fatigue of the journey.

But the Normal School was not a mere local fountain of knowledge. It has been a living spring that has sent forth streams of salutary influence over the whole country, increasing the intelligence and quickening the intellectual life of successive generations of our youth. We must not measure the value of the institution simply by the benefits it has conferred upon teachers. To change the figure, they carried the torches they lighted at its fires to illuminate many a remote place. They did not learn, what they learned for themselves, but for the youth of the country, whom they were to teach. The value of the results, like that of all results in the sphere of mind and thought, cannot be tabulated, or weighed in any commercial balances. When we speak of the large number of teachers trained in our Normal Schools during the last fifty years, and the great increase in the number of schools and pupils, we only touch some outward and visible signs of progress. The most important results are the improvement in the efficiency of the teachers and the schools, and the great influence for good that has been exerted on the character and life of our people, by the diffusion of knowledge and the mental training of the young.

Higher than the work of parliaments, and next in importance to the work of the Christian churches, which teach the great truths of our Holy religion, I am disposed to rank the work of our schools and colleges, which prepare the coming men and women of our country for the duties of citizenship. The people of our country are largely what the churches and schools have made them. We should not allow either sectarian or political prejudice to prevent us from candidly recognizing the great debt we owe to those who founded and those who developed and built up the educational system that has done so much for our country. It is well known that the school system of Ontario has in a great degree inspired and moulded the systems of the other provinces of our Dominion. (Dr. Ryerson was a trustee of this Metropolitan Church.)

A Period of Growth and Progress.

The period that has elapsed since the opening of the Normal School in this city embraces the greater part of Queen Victoria's long reign, which has been so recently celebrated throughout the British Empire, and therefore includes most of the same events. It is a period characterized by change and progress in all departments of human thought and action. There have been wonderful discoveries in science and inventions in the mechanical arts, which have lessened labor and conduced to the comfort of human life. Steam and electricity have to a great extent annihilated distance and brought distant countries near together. Countries that had been for ages inaccessible, have been thrown open to the missionary labors of the churches. In the sphere of legislation there have been great political and social reforms which removed evils that formerly oppressed the people. There has been a steady growth of civil and religious liberty which has broken down the barriers to progress and given increased power to the people. Agencies and institutions for the promotion of social reforms and the relief of want and suffering have been greatly multiplied.

In the churches there has been a decline of sectarian feeling and a growing spirit of union, which tends to make the denominations more like different divisions of the "one army of the living God." There is a more general conviction than ever before, that the great object of religion is to produce unselfish benevolence and righteousness in all the conduct of life. There is also a fuller recognition of the place and power of woman, and greater practical interest by the churches in the religious education of the young.

The World is not Growing Worse.

I cannot agree with those good people who believe the world is growing worse. "The good old times," of which we hear so much, were times in which credulity, injustice and oppression flourished. We cannot go very far back in the history of the past till we reach a condition of things that would be deemed intolerable in these times of light and liberty. There is a great contrast between then and now:

"Learning then was Fortune's favor, to the poor by fate denied ;
  Now, the gates of Truth and Knowledge unto all stand open wide ;
And the poor man's boy, with only honest heart and active brain,
  May evince his native kingship and the highest place attain.

Ignorance, Injustice, Folly, linger still while myriads wait,
  Till the valleys are exalted and the crooked paths made straight ;
But the direst ills and follies which becloud the world to-day
  Are but shades of darker evils that have almost passed away.

Rough and steep the path of progress ; slowly earth's oppressions die ;
  Yet the world is rising higher as the burdened years go by.
Truth and Righteousness unconquered, in this warfare shall prevail ;
  This the God of Truth has promised, and His word can never fail."

The Text Corrects a Popular Fallacy.

Without attempting any formal exposition of the text I have read, we may take these words as affirming that knowledge and wisdom are the true elements that give salutary growth and stability to the character of individuals and nations. Like many other Scripture truths, this utterance is at variance with a prevailing sentiment among men of the world, as to what is the chief good. There is a broad difference between the heavenly and the earthly, the divine and the human standards of value and honor. Among men who judge all things from an earthly standpoint outward things, such as the applause of the world, the increase of wealth and material prosperity, are esteemed and sought after, as if they were the chief things of life. But in the sight of God, a right spirit, righteousness in character and conduct, are regarded as the supreme things.

In the world men are honored who have displayed physical courage—men are honored who can trace their pedigree through a long line of titled ancestry, though they may have done nothing great or good themselves—men are honored who have acquired great wealth, however they may have gained it—men are honored who possess great intellectual gifts, even though they "wade through slaughter to a throne and shut the gates of mercy on mankind." But God's heroes are distinguished by different qualities. He ranks highest on the honor roll of heaven who bears life's burdens most patiently, who uses the talents committed to him most faithfully, and who does the greatest amount of unselfish work for the glory of God and the good of his fellow-creatures. The words of the Master are: "If any man serve me, him will my Father honor." In the Old Testament we find a similar truth: "They that be wise shall shine as the brightness of the firmament, and they that turn many to righteousness as the stars forever and ever."

We have seen the truth of this great Scriptural principle of the inferiority of the outward and material to the moral and spiritual, illustrated in the sphere of our own observation. We know it as a historic fact that a nation may possess a rich inheritance, and all the elements of material prosperity, and yet be known as a country where ignorance, superstition and political serfdom hold unbroken sway. We must never forget that it is "righteousness that exalteth a nation." Some of the greatest empires in history have crumbled into decay and perished, because they had not the conserving salt of moral integrity. So also we know that a man may gain riches and outward prosperity, while all that is noble and generous in his better nature is dying out, and he is becoming harder and more selfish. The case of the church at Laodicea is a striking illustration. In their own esteem they were "rich and increased with goods and had need of nothing;" but in God's sight they were "wretched and miserable, and poor and blind and naked." Oh! for a prophet's voice to ring out above the din and clamor of the mammon-worship of our times the great truth spoken by our Lord, that "a man's life consisteth not in the abundance of the things which he possesseth."

The Value of Knowledge.

Both reason and Scripture testify to the value of knowledge and the evils of ignorance. The fact that God has endowed us with faculties of observation and reflection and has spread around us fields of knowledge for the exercise of these faculties shows that it is the purpose of our Creator that we should gather knowledge and be intelligent beings. What we call the sciences are simply the facts we have observed in the works of the Creator, placed in orderly relations to each other. As light to the eye, as music to the ear, as food to the body, so is the knowledge of the works and word of God to the mind. To widen the gauge of our knowledge of truth, to strengthen and develop the faculties with which our Maker has endowed us, to climb steadily upward to loftier heights of mental and moral elevation from which we can survey with broader and clearer vision the grand and beautiful and true in God's universe, is the duty, the interest, and the glorious privilege of all. If we fail to grow in knowledge, we must fail in accomplishing the great ends of life. There might as well be no truth or beauty in Nature, if we do not develop any capacity for appreciating all that is revealed in her vast and varied resources. Many have eyes but see not, and never have apprehended the sublime truth of the Hebrew Psalmist, that "the heavens declare the glory of God and the firmament showeth His handiwork." To such people we may fitly propose the Poet's question:

"O how canst thou renounce the boundless store of charms," etc.

The Scriptures tell us "for the soul to be without knowledge is not good," and Hosea represents God as saying: "My people are destroyed for lack of knowledge." Ignorance misleads and enslaves. Knowledge emancipates and sheds light on the path of life. Ignorance prevents mental growth and lessens happiness. It limits the power of usefulness, and breeds superstitious credulity. The deepest moral degradation is generally found associated with ignorance.

Religion Essential to True Education.

We must, however, never forget that, in educating men and women for useful citizenship and the complex duties of life, Knowledge alone is not sufficient. Religious character and religious principles are needed to govern the conscience. This is what is meant by the wisdom and the fear of the Lord of which the prophet speaks. The views of men concerning life will determine their ideas as to the kind of education the young should receive. Those who have low views of man's place in the scale of being, and who think of life mainly as an opportunity of gaining wealth and the pleasures of sense, will have a correspondingly low conception of education, and will regard it merely as a sharpening of the mental faculties for the secular business of life. But those who regard man as a being made in the divine image, with an immortal and spiritual nature, to glorify God and enjoy Him forever, will esteem education as a preparation to fit him for his high duties and destiny as a child of God and an heir of immortality. Moral integrity and Christian faith must be united with intellectual acuteness and intelligence.

Faith in the great truths of our holy religion is the foundation of moral obligation. I know that many disparage religious beliefs, and deny the essential relationship of religion to right conduct. But right beliefs are the roots from which right actions grow. If we believe the Scriptural truths, that there is a holy all-seeing God to whom we owe love and obedience—that we are accountable beings, who shall be judged according to our works—that as God is our Father all men are our brothers to whom we owe brotherly kindness—that our personal experience of the saving mercy of God qualifies and obligates us to be witnesses for God and heralds of His grace to others, it will hardly be denied by any one that the belief of such truths is eminently adequate to influence and determine character and conduct.

We need religious faith for the motives it supplies and the strength and consolation it affords in all the great emergencies of existence. Out on the great battlefields of life there are fierce conflicts to be fought, heavy burdens to be borne, and arduous work to be done; and it largely depends upon the use that we make of the early years of life, in acquiring useful knowledge and building up worthy character, whether the result shall be victory or failure.

Religious Teaching in the Schools.

There is probably not much difference of opinion among Christian people as to the importance of religious education. We all believe that moral and religious training is as essential as the acquisition of knowledge and the culture of the intellect to qualify for a right discharge of our duty as citizens and Christians.

It is in regard to the best way of achieving this result that differences exist. I heartily believe in surrounding our schools and colleges with moral and religious influences, so far as this can be done without violating the conscientious convictions of parents or pupils. I have never been able to see any good reason why the great truths of religion, which we profess to hold in common, could not be taught in common to all Christian children. But I am not in sympathy with all that is said in some quarters in favor of religious or theological teaching in the Public Schools. In their zeal for religious teaching, some are willing to break up our whole system of united education and substitute a system of denominational schools. I believe any such scheme would greatly lessen the efficiency of our schools, without increasing their religious power. I cannot but think that united education, fellowship in school life between those who are to work together in the future as fellow citizens, is more patriotic and Christian than any system of division. It seems to be assumed by those who advocate theological teaching in our schools that the children must grow up without religion, unless their plan is adopted. Such an assumption ignores the work of the Christian churches. There are the regular services of the churches, Sunday Schools for the young, an abundant supply of suitable religious literature, and the influence of Christian homes, all aiming at the same object. Are all these to be disparaged and ignored in the interest of a theory? As a matter of fact nineteen-twentieths and more of the Godly Christian men and women in the different churches did not receive their religious knowledge in the schools, but through other Christian agencies. I have never seen any satisfactory evidence that the children educated in church schools display a higher type of moral character than those educated in national schools.

The loudest demand for theological teaching in the schools generally comes from those who want to have the peculiar doctrines of their creed taught, rather than the common principles of the Christian religion. At least it is significant that the plea for so-called "voluntary schools," is on the sectarian line, and not for united Christain teaching. I do not deem it uncharitable to say that there is generally more "churchianity" than Christianity in their demands. When Christians are drawing closer together, when minor differences have ceased to be magnified, and when the spirit of Christian union and liberality is abroad, this is not the time to encourage any schemes of sectarian division, inimical to the unity of our educational system.

The Times Require Sound Education.

The education of the coming men and women of a country is always important, but the circumstances and tendencies of the present time invest the question of the sound education of both head and heart with special interest. We are laying the foundation of our national life, and by the lives we live and the work we do at this formative period of our history we largely determine what the future of our country shall be. The change and progress that have taken place in the past are prophetic of important work to be done in the coming time, which will need good men and true to do it successfully. The work of the church and of the state must be done with a wise recognition of the requirements of the times in which that work has to be done. Whether we like it or dislike it power is going down to the common people, and if we would avoid disaster they must be educated to exercise that power wisely and soberly. Error and heresy are rife. There are theories of agnosticism, materialism, and anti-supernatural rationalism in the air, which, in whatever they differ, all tend to reject or ignore the inspiration and authority of the Holy Scriptures. The prevalence of such teaching requires a type of Christian who, without bigotry or intolerance, will intelligently and earnestly contend for "the faith which was once delivered unto the saints."

There are important social and political problems to be solved in the coming years. Different remedies are presented by different theorizers as their panacea for the ills that affect humanity. They do not reach the seat of the disease. Brethren, the only efficient remedy for these ills is the practical application of the principles of the religion of Christ in all the relations of human life.

A Defence of Individualism.

Some social reformers of our day disparage individualism and talk as if society as a whole may, in some way that is not very clear, be uplifted by the Church or State. But society is made up of individuals, and it is just what the character of the individuals who compose it make it. There can be no such thing as a holy church made up of unholy members. No nation can occupy a high place in the scale of Christian civilization, if its people are ignorant and demoralized. If the members of a church are converted and consecrated men and women, that church will be a powerful agency in the promotion of every moral and social reform. If the people of a nation are intelligent and virtuous, that nation will be distinguished by progress and stability, and shall not fail to be a force for truth and righteousness in the world. The Apostle Peter, when speaking of the Christian graces, says, "For if these things be in you and abound, they make you that ye shall neither be barren nor unfruitful in the knowledge of our Lord Jesus Christ." As the disciple of Him who preached to the woman of Samaria at Jacob's well, we cannot afford to despise efforts for the salvation of the individual. There is no way of elevating nations or communities except by uplifting the individuals of which they are composed. All the great reforms that have blessed the world were begun by individual souls, who were inspired by some high purpose. We have societies enough and to spare. The greatest need of the world to-day is more men and women who will be living epistles, illustrating the truth and power of religion in all spheres of human life. We want them in the pulpit—men of keen intelligence, broad charity and sincere piety. We want them in our political and judicial offices—men of incorruptible integrity and true patriotism. We want them as editors of our public journals—men of broad unsectional views, who will realize the sacredness of their work as educators of public opinion. We want them in the marts of trade and commerce—men of unswerving uprightness, to whom wealth will be a means of usefulness, and not a mere instrument of selfish gratification. We want them in our Sunday Schools and Public Schools—men and women who feel it to be a grand and sacred thing to direct the first awakenings of intellectual life and influence the destiny of immortal beings. We want them everywhere—men and women who shall ennoble the lowly toil of daily life by the faith and patience with which their work is done. Only by God's saving grace can we become vessels unto honor having our spirit unto holiness. Brethren, "the harvest truly is great, but the laborers are few." You who are yet young, who are to carry the banners, which some of us must soon lay down, have the inspiration of hope, as well as of gratitude, in your work. Remember, you best serve your country and your God by living useful unselfish lives. Let your motto be: "Not slothful in business, fervent in spirit, serving the Lord." Though apparent failures may discourage at times, no true work done for Christ and humanity shall ever be in vain. In due season you shall reap, etc. "Therefore, my beloved brethren, be ye steadfast, unmovable, always abounding in the work of the Lord; for as much as ye know that your labour is not in vain in the Lord:"

> Work for the good that is nighest
>   Dream not of greatness afar ;
> That glory is ever the highest
>   Which shines upon men as they are.
>
> Work though the world may defeat you,
>   Heed not its slander and scorn ;
> Nor weary till angels shall greet you
>   With smiles through the gates of the morn.
>
> What if the poor heart complaineth,
>   Soon shall its wailings be o'er ;
> For there, in the rest that remaineth,
>   It shall grieve and be weary no more.

II.

UNVEILING OF PORTRAITS.

The ceremony of unveiling the portraits of past Principals of the Normal School, past Head Mistresses of the Girls' Model School, and past Head Masters of the Boys' Model School, took place in the Principal's lecture room, on Monday afternoon at 2 o'clock, in the presence of a large number of visitors. Hon. Geo. W. Ross, LL.D., Minister of Education, occupied the chair and delivered an address in which he outlined the history of the Toronto Normal School and welcomed all those who had responded to the invitation of the Committee.

The portrait of Mr. Robertson was presented by the students of the Normal School many years ago; those of Dr. Sangster, Dr. Davies, the Head Mistresses of the Girls' Model School, and the Head Masters of the Boys' Model School, were presented by the Education Department.

THOMAS JAFFRAY ROBERTSON, M.A.

David Fotheringham.
(Inspector, Public Schools, South York).

Thomas Jaffray Robertson, the first Head Master of the Toronto Normal School, was born in Dublin, Ireland, in March, 1805, and was the youngest son of Charles Robertson of the same place, Miniature Painter.

He was educated at the Frinaiglian Institute in Dublin, and entered Trinity College of that city, but through illness was unable to take his degree. Proof of fidelity and success in his studies at Trinity is to be found in the prizes awarded to Mr. Robertson while there, and now in possession of his eldest son.

In the years 1827 and 1828 he held the position of Classical Teacher in the Frinaiglian Institute. After which he passed into the Irish office of Education; and in May, 1832, was appointed an Inspector of the National Schools, which involved a good deal of travelling.

In 1838 Mr. Robertson was appointed Senior Assistant to the General Superintendent of the National Schools, and soon after this appointment married Amelia, daughter of Richard Nelson, Solicitor of Dublin.

In July, 1845, Mr. Robertson was promoted, provisionally, to the office of Chief Inspector of National Schools of Ireland, the Commissioners of National Schools observing in the minutes of their proceedings that " Mr. Thomas J. Robertson having had long experience in the business " of School Inspection, and shewn the requisite knowledge and discre- " tion which are required for the due performance of the duties of such " an office be appointed to carry the foregoing plan into effect at such " time and under such regulations as the Board may hereafter prescribe."

In December of the same year (1845) Mr. Robertson was confirmed in the office of Chief Inspector.

In 1847 Dr. Ryerson appears to have applied to the Commissioners of Education of Ireland asking them to select a person qualified to take the Head Mastership of the Normal School in Toronto ; for in a letter still in the possession of his family, and dated July 1st of that year, the Secretaries of the Commissioners notify Mr. Robertson that, in accordance with such application, the Commissioners had selected him to fill that position.

Accepting this appointment, Mr. Robertson soon after crossed the Atlantic in a sailing vessel, and reached Toronto early in September, 1847.

The Normal School was first opened in the Old Government House, corner of King and Simcoe Streets, Mr. Robertson for a time occupying with his family a suite of rooms on the second floor.

The old Parliament Buildings were at that time used as a lunatic asylum.

Early in 1852, if not in 1851, it became necessary to vacate Government House, as Toronto was to become the seat of Government ; and, as the new Normal School buildings were not completed, the Temperance Hall, on Temperance Street, was occupied for a time.

Mr. Robertson of course entered the new buildings, when they were completed, and continued his services in them till another removal was made to the building in rear of that now called the Education Department, and known as the Model Grammar School. This continues to be the home of the Normal School at the present date.

During the winter of 1865-6, Mr. Robertson's health failing him, he was granted leave of absence ; and this was renewed in the summer following ; but he never recovered, and died on the 26th September, 1866, after a service of nearly twenty years, during the formative period of our public school system.

In addition to his duties as Head Master of the Normal School, Mr. Robertson acted for some years as Inspector of Grammar Schools throughout Upper Canada.

In appearance Mr. Robertson was tall, erect and well filled out. His favorite pastime was yachting ; and, during the months that were open for that exercise, he wore the bronzed and breezy face of a sturdy sailor ; and though he sometimes told his students in his familiar moods that a gentleman could be told by the size and general gracefulness of his hands and fingers, some fancied that he would have preferred to be tried by his own standard in the winter season rather than in the dog-days.

Thirty-one years after Mr. Robertson's demise, his widow at the ripe age of 85 still survives her husband; and all the children remain, and are loyal Canadians on the stock of the sturdy Irish thorn. They are the following:—Thomas Jaffray Robertson, Barrister-at-law, resident at and ex-Mayor of Newmarket, to whom the writer is largely indebted for the present exact and satisfactory outline of his father's career.

Amelia M. Bristol, widow of the late Dr. Bristol, Napanee, Ont.

Llewellyn H. Robertson, of Toronto, Real Estate Agent.

Clementina Appelby, wife of R. S. Appelby, of Oakville, Ont., Barrister-at-law.

Frederick C. Robertson, Chief Auditor of The Pullman Palace Car Co., Chicago.

Isabel Lewis, wife of O. R. Lewis, Q. C., Toronto.

Did time permit, some interesting incidents of Mr. Robertson's life could be given. One at least may be mentioned. While discharging the duties of Inspector in Ireland, he had to travel through some out-of-the-way places, and in one of these he was taken for a Process-Server, an officer for whom the Irish people entertained a holy horror, and was only saved from serious maltreatment by the timely intervention of the Roman Catholic priest of that place. This, Mr. Robertson took pride in saying, was only a sample of the generosity, hospitality and consideration shown uniformly by the clergy of that church, as well as those of other churches, while travelling through Ireland.

The nature and merit of Mr. Robertson's services as first Head Master of the Toronto Normal School do not enter into the scope of the monograph asked from the writer. But it may be said, he was a stalwart who had little to do with the fine distinctions of psychology and child-study, but much to do with the foundation principles of grammatical analysis and synthesis, the immutable laws of the phenomena of physical geography, and the erection of a clearly defined skeleton of ancient and modern history on which, at their leisure, his students could build the full, symmetrical story of man's life, labors and progress on the earth.

Mr. Robertson's strong, rugged character and direct ways stamped themselves on many of his students who, to this day, testify that he confirmed, if he did not originate in them, sturdy, energetic, thorough-going ways and methods that still stand the survivors in good stead, among the many devices now popular for making the royal road to learning less masculine, less a road of effort and overcoming, and more a road of theorizing, of wooing and sugar-coating.

The impress of this bold, fearless educator as a pioneer in Normal School work still stands out as a stimulus to bold, energetic, thorough-going methods in educational and national efforts for Canadian progress.

J. HERBERT SANGSTER, M.A., M.D.

Rev. R. P. McKay, B.A.
(A Student of the 25th Session).

It is my privilege and pleasure to unveil the portrait of a man whom I always esteemed, and to whose influence I am indebted.

There are two elements in education that are indispensable—without which a man can neither be educated nor be an educationist. 1. He must use his own powers, be they great or small. He must not be simply a rehearser of the results of other men's labours—reaping where others have sown. He must learn to use his own powers of observation, and induction and imagination. He must think for himself. The primary use of the results of other men's thoughts, as far as education is concerned, is the development of that power of independent effort within ourselves. 2. He must in the second place be capable of severe and continued application. Great efforts can alone produce great results. That is the universal law, even of the greatest minds. We must pay the price. He that saveth his life shall lose it, has an application wider than simply the spiritual.

Dr. Sangster has these two qualifications. That is seen both in the quality and quantity of work he has done. I well remember how his students used to speak about him as a prodigy in these respects. How in addition to his professional work, he snatched time to acquire an extensive knowledge of Botany, Chemistry, and Medicine. How he prepared books on Algebra, and Arithmetic, and Chemistry, and Natural History, which books were for a time used as text books in our schools, and did their part in the development of that splendid system of education of which the country is so justly proud.

Dr. Sangster not only worked himself, but I can testify that he made his students work. I can well remember how he used "to pile Ossa on Pelion and never relent," while the students sometimes despaired. But I am quite sure that the example of his own indefatigable application led many a student to similar effort such as they otherwise would not have put forth.

I should like to add another quality essential in an educationist. Dr. Sangster kept before his students a high moral purpose. Never did I forget the farewell address Dr. Sangster gave the class at the end of the session. When he solemnly impressed upon us the responsibilities of the teaching profession, the influence for good or evil we were to have in the lives of children—the necessity for watchfulness as to the details of life, and especially the necessity of keeping the heart pure if the words and actions were also to be pure. That address remained with me a living power, and it is a pleasure to be able to express it in Dr. Sangster's presence.

Comparisons are invidious, but all are agreed that Dr. Sangster has earned the right to be enrolled as one of the leading educationists in this Province, and it is with peculiar pleasure I now unveil this, his portrait.

REV. HENRY W. DAVIES, M.A., D.D.

Charles A. Barnes, M.A.
(Inspector, Public Schools, Lambton No. 1).

It affords me the greatest possible pleasure to be present with you on this very important occasion to celebrate with you the half-century jubilee of the establishment of this Normal School. As I understand it, Sir, this school was established in 1847, but the corner stone of this present structure was laid on the 2nd of July 1851, by Lord Elgin, who was at that time Govenor-General of Canada. On that occasion the Noble Lord gave expression to the following :—" It gives me unfeigned pleasure to know that the youth of this country who are destined in their maturer years to meet in civil life on terms of perfect civil and religious equality, are receiving an education so well fitted to qualify them for the proper discharge of the important duties of life, and also associated under such conditions as are likely to promote the growth of those Christian graces, mutual respect, forbearance and charity." And Sir, I believe the same spirit has actuated those who have been responsible for the work carried on within these walls during the past fifty years. I believe the teachers have endeavored to inculcate into the minds and hearts of the students the principles enunciated by Lord Elgin : so that they should go forth in the different pathways of life saturated with the principles of good citizenship, and carrying with them the essential qualifications for making life a success. They should go forth bearing those influences which are calculated to raise a type of manhood and of womanhood whose very lives would be a benediction to others and a credit to those teachers who trained them. They should go forth to carry on the busy work of life, and show by life and character that the training received within these walls had been of inestimable value in the development of a high type of Christian citizenship. How important therefore, that we, as teachers and educators should realize the responsibility that rests upon us, that we should remember, that the boys and girls in our public schools, the young men and the young women in our high schools, our normal schools, our colleges and universities, will soon be out into the broad, busy world, engaged in its conflicts, and that upon the face, heart and soul of these pupils and students will lie the reflected image of the teacher. How essential that we should be thoroughly equipped for our work, that we should be thinkers and not machines, that we should be men and women of original ideas, lofty purposes, and sure and steady aim, rather than the fossilized relics of past ages.

Again, I have said that I am glad to be with you to-day, but notwithstanding the pleasure and enjoyment which I experience in being present with you, there are traces of sadness and sorrow mingled with it. I look around me and ask myself the question, " Where are those who were my classmates and my associates in this Normal School years ago " ? I see a few of them here to day. Many of them are scattered here and there over this continent, carrying on the great work of life, and some lie yonder in the cemetery of the city from which I come, and some I doubt not in the cemetery of this city, and some here and there in the different parts of this province; they have finished their labors and have gone home to the great school above where the Lord Jesus Christ Himself shall preside ; where the universe shall be the curriculum of study and eternity shall be the time for graduation.

Again, I see before me some of those who were teachers when I was a student in the Normal School. I see the present Principal and Vice-Principal, who stand shoulder to shoulder engaged in the great work of training and educating the young people of this Province, and sending them forth to be a blessing to the country in which they live, but I look in vain for the face and form of him who at that time occupied the position and assumed the responsibilities of the Principalship. The flood of years of which Bryant speaks has taken him too, and I look back in my memory and I call to mind the many acts of kindness that I received from the Rev. Dr. Davies. I call to mind his genial smile and his pleasant countenance as often I went to his private room for advice, for assistance and for instruction. And as I perform the duty that devolves upon me to-day, by request of your committee, I do it with pleasure mingled with sadness and regret. As I unveil the portrait of the Rev. Dr. Davies, a portrait painted in enduring colors to typify the imperishable worth and the imperishable renown of its original, I trust it may remain for ages to come where we place it to-day within these walls. And as we look upon it in the future, may we all be reminded of the genial nature and personal worth of him, who for nearly a quarter of a century occupied the high, honorable and responsible position of Principal of this Normal School. Sir, I cannot say more, my heart tells me of many things which I cannot find language to express to you to-day, but ere another half century shall come and go, doubtless you and I and many others in this assembly to-day shall have passed on into the great future that lies before us. Others will rise to take our places and to carry on the work of life and to perform duties similar to those performed by us to-day. But I trust the portrait which I have this day unveiled will ever remain as a memorial of this gathering and as a tribute to the memory and personal worth of him who for so many years performed good and noble service in connection with this Normal School.

MRS. DORCAS CLARK AND MISS M. ADAMS.

.⁂ .⁂

Mrs. Nasmith.
(A former pupil of The Girls' Model School).

.⁂ .⁂

Mrs. Dorcas Clark occupied the position of Head Mistress of the Girls' Model School, Toronto, from January, 1852 until June, 1865, and during that time, by her energy and capability, she helped largely to build up the reputation which the institution so deservedly enjoys. She was one who combined, in an unusual degree, those womanly virtues which adorn the quietest life with those qualities which go to make a successful teacher. Full of ambition for her pupils, she inspired them with her own enthusiasm, and nothing pleased her more than to know of their success either in school or in after life. In her time, Toronto University had not opened its doors to women; they could not even attend a High School; had it been otherwise, there is no doubt that some of her scholars would have won honors in these institutions, for she gave freely of her time and strength, both before and after school hours, to bring her backward pupils up to the required standard, or to help her ambitious ones to higher attainments. Having herself encountered and overcome difficulties in preparing for teaching, she was well able to encourage those in like straits, and delighted to tell how, in the many occupations of a busy life, she yet found time to fit herself for her beloved profession.

Energetic in disposition, she yet was gentle in her discipline, easily winning the affection of her pupils, and governing largely by love. Severe rebukes were seldom needed; to most of her charge a word of reproof was enough.

Her teaching was not confined to the school curriculum; she taught her pupils respect for authority, regard for the feelings of others, and absolute sincerity in word and action. She taught them the dignity of labor; lenient with many faults, she was intolerant of idleness, reckoning it the blackest sin of the school-room. Many other moral lessons she taught, as well by her life as by her words; crowning all with the lesson from the wisest of men, that "The fear of the Lord is the beginning of wisdom."

In the thirty and more years that have gone since she left Toronto and the Model School, her scholars have been scattered to all parts of the world: and some, the brightest and sweetest, have journeyed to that "undiscovered country," but she still lives, not claiming yet a total respite from labor, but enjoying the consciousness of a life spent for the good of others, and realizing that "not happiness apart from service, but the happiness of added service, is the highest reward of one who serves faithfully."

Her scholars look back with pleasure to the years spent under her care, and more than one would offer her, in her western home. their tribute of loving regard, taking for their own the words of Whittier:

> "They part; but in the years to be
> "Shall pleasant memories cling to each,
> "As shells bear inward from the sea
> "The murmur of the rhythmic beach.
>
> "And one shall never quite forget
> "The voice that called from dream and play,
> "The firm but kindly hand that set
> "Her feet in learning's pleasant way."

Miss Adams began to teach in the Central School, Hamilton, at a very early age: she won there the affection of her scholars and the regard of her fellow-teachers; but it was in the Toronto Model School that she earned her highest honors and was recognized as amongst those at the head of the profession. Conscientious almost to severity, she looked for the same upright dealing in her class and thus established among them a high standard of honor. Expecting the best from her pupils, and letting her expectations be known, she naturally obtained from them proportionate results. These results were apparent in the exceptional standing of those of her pupils who passed into the Normal School, also at the sessional examinations. By her fellow-teachers, Miss Adams was held in the highest regard; she was always ready to assist them to the utmost of her power, and proved herself a true friend in any difficulty; and her good judgment in dealing with the perplexing questions which at times confront every teacher, was acknowledged by all. Though only occupying her position for the comparatively short period of three years her influence remained; and the lessons of patience, perseverance and self-denial that she taught, more by example than by precept, have been potent in moulding the characters of some of Toronto's noble women to this day.

The following letter from Mrs. Clark, the first head mistress of the Girls' Model School, now residing in San Francisco, was read by the Secretary, Mr. Scott:—

To the teachers and friends of education assembled to commemorate the fiftieth anniversary of the opening of the Toronto Normal School, please present the *true, heartfelt,* loyal greetings of an ex-student on the far distant shores of the Pacific.

When the portraits of past principals are unveiled, I shall be with you in spirit, my plaudits mingling with those of the confraternity in ascribing honor to the first principal, Thos. J. Robertson, who was at the head of affairs when I was a student in the years 1849-50.

Since I left Canada, I have been associated with learned men and famed educators, but have not seen Mr. Robertson's equal—as a systematizer, as an original thinker, as a humanist, as a disciplinarian, while in executive ability, he stands peerless

To his classes Mr. Robertson was an inspiration. On sultry afternoons he would glance at the students, select the languid, faint-hearted, homesick members, and invite them to take a sail with him after lecture hours. (Mr. Robertson was a skilful yachtsman.) On or before sunset he would land them safely, and escort them to his residence, where Mrs. Robertson would receive them with tender, motherly courtesy, and assisted by her two charming daughters, regale them with tea, cakes and exquisite music. After careful escort to their several homes, they were enjoined *not to study that evening,* but to retire at once and sleep soundly. Who can estimate the worth of such fatherly attention and protecting care?

I herewith desire to present to any member of Mr. Robertson's family that may be present my grateful, loving remembrance and deep, tender sympathy. May the Lord make His face shine upon them, and be very gracious to them.

On reaching this coast, my credentials from the Toronto Normal School introduced me to the leaders in the school department of San

Francisco, who at once ranked me with the highest class of educators, bestowing on me gratuitously a first-class State certificate and a life diploma. Of course, I was fully aware of the fact that all these marks of respect were not personal, but arose from their desire to do honor to the institution of which I was for the time a representative.

So I will pray for the prosperity of the Toronto Normal School. 'For my brethren and companions' sakes, I will now say, peace be within thee.'

Yours respectfully,
DORCAS CLARK.

MRS. CULLIN.

Miss Caven.
(A former pupil of The Girls' Model School).

I have been asked to say a few words in remembrance of Mrs. Cullen, third Head Mistress of the Girls' Model School. She was a woman of prepossessing and dignified appearance. In repose her face had a very thoughtful almost a severe expression, but who, of those who knew her, does not love to recall that face when a smile broke over it.

Mrs. Cullen possessed great strength of character, but this only made more conspicuous her amiability, her benevolent and sympathetic disposition, and all the gentler qualities of her nature. As a teacher she had much ability and achieved great success. She was characterized by her knowledge, zeal and patience: her patience indeed seemed inexhaustible. In a very striking degree, she was considerate of the feelings of her pupils. No one—not even the most timid or the dullest—was afraid to attempt an answer to a question, to ask an explanation or to confess ignorance of any subject; and her sympathy with those who failed in winning honors forbade anything like boastfulness on the part of successful pupils.

Mrs. Cullen was indeed an ideal to many a girl who passed through the Model School. As little children we admired her gracious, dignified manner; and as we passed into her division and got to know her well, we felt the beauty of her character. Hers was a silent influence but powerful and persuasive, and it is not too much to say that Mrs. Cullen's influence was a great factor in moulding the character of many a Model School girl. To-day all her old pupils must rejoice to see this tribute of respect paid to her memory.

MESSRS. LOWEY, McCALLUM, FOTHERINGHAM AND CARLYLE.

David Ormiston, B.A.
(A former teacher in the Boys' Model School).

Fellow graduates of the Toronto Normal School it is with pleasure I meet you here on this occasion, when words of kindly remembrance are said of those who ably and skilfully managed the affairs of work of the Normal and Model Schools during the first years of their existence and also after they had come to their full stature in the educational machinery of our country.

The authorities of the Normal School very soon discovered that the work undertaken by them—the training of teachers for successful work in our schools—could not be accomplished unless there was a public or common school where the teachers in training could see a school conducted in a proper manner and also be allowed to take a part in the teaching and have their work criticized and their mistakes pointed out by competent teachers. Hence, in February 1848, the Model School was opened with Mr. Lowey as the first Head Master, a teacher from one of the eastern counties, who was supposed to be the best qualified for the position at the time: a man of kindly disposition and agreeable manners who would doubtless have been a success in the new work, but before the end of the year he was called away by death, leaving his work, one might say, just commenced.

Mr. Archibald McCallum, a graduate of the Normal School was selected to take his place and became the second Head Master, and for ten years he honorably filled that situation and was well known and greatly loved and esteemed by all the old students of the Normal School. He loved his work and was never more happy than when surrounded by a crowd of his pupils. A man of great tenacity and persistency in accomplishing what he undertook and considered to be right, but yet so unwilling to give offence or hurt the feelings of others, that at times he appeared to yield, but only for a little until he could accomplish the desired end without alienating the sympathy or affection of those he felt constrained to oppose. Then, too, many of us remember how often a kind word from him cheered us as we, feeling thoroughly disheartened and wishing we were again at home engaged in the quiet duties of rural life, came out of one of the Model School class rooms, where for half an hour we had been endeavoring to teach a class of forty boys, each of whom was, from past practice, fully prepared to give us all the annoyance he could and not break the regulations of the school.

As one of his assistants for a time, I had a good opportunity of knowing his firm adherence to truth and duty, and his readiness at all times, to assist anyone striving to obtain knowledge. For ten years he successfully presided over the School and was in 1858 selected by the Board of Education of Hamilton to take charge of the Central School there, the largest and best public school in the Province, and ultimately became Inspector of Hamilton schools, which position he filled until his death—at a comparatively early age. I have no doubt his close application to his duties while at the same time spending many hours in close study to obtain a University degree and accurate knowledge in advanced subjects, undermined a naturally strong constitution and somewhat shortened a useful life.

The third Head Master was appointed in May 1858, and I am glad to say is still among us engaged in school work, Mr. David Fotheringham, who has this afternoon given us such a concise and accurate historical sketch of the greatly esteemed first Principal of the Normal School. He, too, is a Scotchman or more correctly an Orkney man, possessing the characteristics of the inhabitants of these small northern Isles, one of which is determination to succeed in whatever he undertakes. He, as might be expected, was a graduate of the Normal School, and was, at the time of his appointment to the head mastership, an assistant in the Model School. He was a strict disciplinarian and was sure to have the school where he presides in first-class order. I sometimes thought he was just a little too strict to have every small matter of detail carried out. For some reason he did not remain long in this position but resigned to take a situation elsewhere, with the intention, like so many of his countrymen, of studying for the ministry. But from this he was turned on account of ill health, and after teaching for a time he became, in 1871, Inspector of Public Schools in North York, a difficult position which he filled so well, that a few years ago on the death of Mr. Hodgson, Inspector of South York, Mr. Fotheringham was appointed to the vacancy, and he now presides over the destinies of the schools all around this fine city. And sir, though I have never visited those schools, from my knowledge of the man and his determination to have all things done rightly and in order, I am sure the school houses and schools in that riding stand among the best of the land, and it is my sincere wish that he may long be spared to inspect these schools. May his portly figure never grow less.

And now a word about the fourth Head Master, Dr. James Carlyle, a relative of the celebrated Chelsea Seer, whose name will be honored and revered as long as the English language is read. He, too, is a Scotchman, but if not born, he was at least educated and trained in Canada, hence a true Canadian. A man of fine appearance, and for many years a faithful, painstaking teacher and educationist. While attending the Normal School in 1854, he, his brother William and myself boarded at the same place and tried to be helpful to one another. On the resignation of Mr. Fotheringham in 1858, Mr. Carlyle was selected by the Chief Superintendent for the position, which he held for thirteen years with advantage to the school, honor to himself and satisfaction to the department, as was shown by his being placed as Mathematical Master in the Normal School. He filled this position till 1893, when, owing to failing health, he had to resign and retire to private life. He began the practice of medicine, for which he had prepared himself while performing his arduous duties in the Model School. And I am sure we all very much regret that he is not able to be here and take part in these jubilee exercises of the Normal School which he loved so well.

MESSRS. HUGHES, SCOTT AND CLARKSON.

Chas. A. Hodgetts, M.D.
(A former pupil of the Boys' Model School).

" Sweet memory wafted by thy gentle gale,
Up the stream of " Time " I turn my sail
To view the haunts of long lost hours."

And what more delightful to an "Old Model Boy" than to recall the happy hours spent under his old masters in those halls when to study was a pleasure, and kindness won our young hearts and holds them still. Truly, happy memories cluster around the names of James L. Hughes, Wm. Scott and Charles Clarkson, and many are the hearts which beat with affection towards these masters of our earlier years, for

"Lull'd in the countless chambers of the brain"

are the good impressions which they made.

Beginning alike their studies in rural schools, when they laid the foundations for the educational superstructures which are now actively identified with some branch of educational work in the Province; passing through the Normal School they each in turn became masters in the Boys' Model School.

The name of James L. Hughes was not so familiar in the homes of Toronto in April, 1867, when he was appointed second assistant master, as it is now. From that date, however, his career has been one of marked success. He became Head Master of the school in July, 1871, and resigned it in May, 1874, to accept the position he now occupies of Inspector of Public Schools for the City of Toronto. During the twenty-three years of his inspectorship, the expansion of the public school system has been great, while the standard in all respects is such that we may safely say he has made "Model Schools" of all under his supervision, and thus tens of thousands of all classes in the community have every reason to love and respect him—none, however, rejoice more at his success than do his "Old Model Boys," in whose hearts he holds an enduring place, won by his kind words of encouragement, his warm personal influence, shown in the studies of each and all of us, and the influence for good he has had upon our characters and lives.

The career of William Scott, B.A., has been equally successful as that of his immediate predecessor, though possibly in a less public manner. Appointed to the Model School in October, 1869, he acted as assistant master for five years, was then promoted to the Head Mastership in May, 1874, and occupied the position until August, 1882, when he was appointed to the Mathematical Mastership of the Normal School, Ottawa. He returned from that city to occupy his present position as Vice-Principal in the Normal School here. The honorable and important appointment Mr. Scott now holds has been won by perseverance and careful attention to detail. Thoroughness has ever characterized his life and work, and pupils, be they young or old, have each alike felt the example of his life and work as influences for good, and we feel sure the standard of our future teachers will be higher, their manhood more enriched and ennobled by being brought under his influence.

Charles Clarkson, B.A., began his studies in the Normal School in 1866, and was appointed Head Master of the Model School in September, 1882, and resigned in December, 1886. At present he occupies the position of Principal of the Seaforth Collegiate Institute, where he finds greater scope for the exercise of his scientific attainments. Ever kind and sympathetic in manner to his pupils, he too has the confidence, esteem and well wishes of many an "Old Model School Boy."

Though the boys of the "old school" are scattered wide in every zone, filling almost every calling in life, surrounded with the responsibilities and cares of mature years, they one and all unite in the wish that their old masters may long be spared to the cause of education, and trust in their latter years not the least bright spot in memory's exhaustless mine may be the one clustering around The Model School and their old boys, whose esteem and affection they will ever hold and when sinks life's setting sun may the enlightened souls of masters and scholars alike be found where perfection of knowledge is only attainable.

"Parvum non parvæ amicitiæ pignus."

III.

REMINISCENT SPEECHES.

The Reminiscent Speeches were made in the Public Hall of the Education Department, on Monday afternoon, commencing at three o'clock, Hon. Geo. W. Ross, LL.D., Minister of Education, acted as chairman. Great interest was taken in the meeting by those present, as much of the heretofore unwritten history of the school was presented in a very natural and apt manner. The speakers were selected by the committee so as to represent the whole of the early period in the history of the school.

Mrs. Catharine Fish.
(A former teacher in the Girls' Model School)

It gives me great pleasure to be here to-day on the invitation of your committee to give a few reminiscences of my connection with the Toronto Normal School.

The Good Book teaches us to "Offer unto God thanksgiving and praise," and as I take a retrospective view of the years in which I was connected with this institution, I realize truly the lines have fallen to me in pleasant places, and, in the knowledge here acquired, I had a goodly heritage, which has been a benediction to me and mine in later years.

So many things come clustering in my mind, I know not to which I should give utterance. I think of the pure, noble and generous Christian, Dr. Ryerson, who conceived and then so worked as to bring those conceptions to a glorious issue, viz., the founding of our Provincial Normal and Model Schools, and our great system of National Schools.

Then my mind calls up the highly cultured and earnest teacher, the first Head Master of the Normal School, T. J. Robertson—also the kind-hearted and sympathetic Archibald McCallum. These have passed to receive their reward—their works do follow them.

One other name connected with the institution in my day was the genial, whole-souled friend of us all, Dr. Ormiston, now of California.

> As the rose doth its fragrance impart
> To the basket in which it is laid,
> Whether wrought of pure gold or of braid;
> So, receiving wise men in thy heart,
> Thou shalt find, when their persons depart,
> That their wisdom behind them hath stayed.

With Mrs. Clark I had the happinness of opening and for some years teaching in the Girls' Model School. On my retiring, two new teachers were engaged. Dr. Ryerson, in speaking of the fact to me, playfully remarked, " You see it takes two to fill the vacancy."

Mrs. Clark is living in California, enjoying a ripe old age, her passion for teaching still upon her. She conducts a large Bible class every Lord's Day. My lot in life has been cast in many places, and in my wanderings I have met many of our pupils, filling important positions in the home and in the country.

Others of my co-laborers in this school have risen to distinction in the literary and scientific world, occupying positions of responsibility and trust. Some I am happy to greet at this auspicious hour.

I often now wonder how I had the courage to apply for the situation, never having had any experience in teaching, and being comparatively young in years. Well do I remember with what trembling at first did I behold our Chief, coming in with some of the foremost men and women in the work of education in other lands, but I soon learned to trust these as my best friends. The old Doctor had a fondness for mental arithmetic, and often he would ask me what was the lesson for the hour, then would kindly say, " Would you mind giving us a little mental arithmetic?" We were all, I think rather fond of our work in this department, and it was a source of much criticism at our public examinations, by some university students and others, who confidently asserted those questions could not be performed in the head without having been previously worked out and committed. The girls were too clever for them in that line.

Many changes, and, I presume, improvements have taken place in the buildings as well as in the manner of conducting the work of the Institution since those days: all of which I have noted with great delight, never having lost my interest in these things, and surely have I proved true another saying of the late Dr. Ryerson's, "No matter if the young ladies do not teach many years in the school-house, they have to be teachers all their lives, and if we can educate the mothers of our country, we shall have accomplished much that we desire." When our children come to us with the much-talked-about homework, naturally the mother is appealed to for help, and happy is that mother and those children if the needed help can be obtained. Nothing makes me feel so young as to be with and try to help the youth around me to be happy by being useful and good.

All education, I think, should aim at preparation for life work. To my mind, after the ordinary English branches have been mastered, every child should be taught that which he feels will best fit him for his future. Home training for the girls, I am afraid, is sadly neglected in these days. If mothers would have their daughters capable of presiding over and making happy the inmates of homes of their own, they should see to it that while mental culture is not neglected, practical home work should go hand in hand with it. You will readily perceive mine has been a practical life, not an ideal one. So should every life be to be happy, filled up with work— intellectual, moral or physical, or a little of all, helping to make the world better than we found it.

Then should we have a practical and pleasing illustration of the words of the wise man:

"She openeth her mouth with wisdom, and in her tongue is the law of kindness."

"She looketh well to the ways of her household, and eateth not the bread of idleness."

> Where are our early lessons,
>   The teachings of our youth,
> The countless words forgotten,
>   Of knowledge and of truth?
> Not lost! for they are living still.
> As power to think and do and will.
>
> Where is the seed we scatter,
>   With weak and trembling hand,
> Beside the gloomy waters,
>   Or on the arid land?
> Not lost! for after many days,
> Our prayer and toil shall turn to praise.
>
> Where, where are all God's lessons,
>   His teachings dark or bright?
> Not lost! but only hidden,
>   Till in eternal light
> We see, while at His feet we fall,
> The reasons and result of all.

Emily H. Stowe, M.D., writes from Redwood, Lake Joseph, Ontario, on October 26th, 1897:

With feelings of deep regret I inform you that unforseen events have occurred that will prevent my return to Toronto until after the date appointed for the jubilee. I should very much have enjoyed being present on that auspicious occasion. As one of the early students my remembrance covers a lapse of time marked by many changes for the better in our educational system.

It is with much pleasure that I contemplate what the Normal School has done for the women of Canada.

She was the first to open the doors to woman's higher education; first to recognize equality in the ability of the sexes to compete in the halls of learning, and first to establish a system of co-education. All hail to our Provincial Normal School! She has built our national education on a basis of justice and equity, silently projecting a force that has ultimately opened the higher institutions of learning—our universities, colleges and law schools.

Again expressing my sincere regret for absence on so great an occasion as the jubilee of so revered an institution as the Provincial Normal School.

I am, with regret,

Yours sincerely,

EMILY H. STOWE, M.D.

William Carlyle.
(Inspector, Public Schools, Oxford).

In giving reminiscences of the Normal School, I must of necessity be personal. My remarks shall centre around three gentlemen: Thomas Jaffray Robertson, Principal; the Reverend William Ormiston, Master, and Mr. S. P. Robins, Teacher, then in the Provincial Model School, and also in the Normal School, now Principal of the McGill Normal School, Montreal.

I attended two sessions, the 10th, 1853, and the 14th, 1855. Then a young, verdant lad from the farm, with a year's experience of teaching in a rural school, and seeking light, I entered the Normal School. I had been given a letter of introduction to Mr. Ormiston by another Scotchman who had met the former in the county I lived in, and assisted him in demolishing two opposing disputants in debate on the Clergy Reserve question, then rampant in the public mind.

Mr. Ormiston had electrified his newly-made acquaintance as well as his opponents with a torrent of eloquent denunciation and fervid invective. The latter was a friend of my father's household, hence the introduction which proved the prelude to a protracted intercourse with a man whom I soon recognized as a true friend and benefactor, and in many respects to me the most wonderful man I ever met.

With Mr. Robertson, one of the first cultured minds, I, as a lad, enjoyed the privilege of meeting, I did not suddenly cultivate acquaintance. His teaching of English Grammar was a revelation and an inspiration to me. But for weeks I avoided him, never during the greater portion of my first term exchanging a word with him save in answering his class questions. That massive forehead with curly black locks, something of the head of a Dickens, that swarthy complexion, those black eyes sheltered beneath shaggy brows that knit and lowered upon one with a mixture of disdain and suppressed threatenings, a mirthful twinkle, notwithstanding, glinting out of their corners, constituted for me a very uncertain study; while the beard and a heaviness in the lower portion of the face rendered easily possible the darkening of that already dark face, with a scowl filled with terrors to most of us.

My introduction to him became possible at the middle of the term. He kept before him in the class-room a register of our names and addresses in which he apparently made notes of our class work. When a student was to be questioned, a name was selected and the possessor pinioned.

"Mr. Carlyle, Delhi," was read one day. My turn had come.

"Where are you, Mr. Carlyle? Oh! by the way, are you any relation to the Great Mogul?" For a moment the silence could be felt.

"Yes, sir; I believe I am his uncle."

After the cheering of the students subsided, "I beg your pardon, Mr. Carlyle!"

Of the genuineness of that apology, I was not quite sure, and felt it safer to take it with a grain of salt. Ever afterwards, we were friends.

His teachings in pedagogy could be summarized in one sentence: "Draw forth the good in a child, suppress the bad." As a teacher, he sought to reach the understanding and succeeded, his patience never failing him. Mere memoriter work—parrot exercises—he had no use for. He elucidated every subject he touched, Grammar and History especially. Those of us who took private tuition from him in Classics found him even stronger in these than in the subjects of the Normal School curriculum.

Of William Ormiston, possibly I am not an impartial critic. His influence over me was so complete that I scarcely maintained my individuality in his presence.

With rapidly uttered and tersest diction, flavored, to my taste with a strong element of Scotch, he fired his burning thought into my untutored mind, lodging his instructions there never to be obliterated.

To me he was teacher and text-book. His utterances, repeated one day, I could reproduce verbatim the next. He took full possession of me for the time. I was filled with his thought. My imagination kindled at the touch of his, and every fibre of my awakening intellect vibrated and thrilled under the spell of his eloquence, that swept me whither he willed. As a man he became my ideal. As a teacher he created within me a thirst for teaching that can never be quenched.

Two instances of his marvellous power over his pupils may be given.

He was at the blackboard dashing down some chemical notation. Behind him and certainly out of his sight were two inattentive, trifling but noiseless lady students. He talked as he wrote, eloquent even in Chemistry, and without any seeming interruption to his theme or change of voice he interjected, "Will those two ladies leave the room!" and down went the Chemistry, on went his talk and on went the ladies to the door of the room, in tears before reaching it

It was a privilege of the students to leave with him problems in Mathematics to be distributed in the class for solution. A quadratic fell to my lot, that proved a severe test. From seven in the evening until two in the morning and again from five till the ringing of the quarter-to-nine bell for lectures the same morning, I wrestled with it before I could verify my solution of it and have it ready for his inspection before the class. Such was my regard for the man, and such my high estimate of his good opinion of me, that rather than return to the class reporting a failure, although having earned the money, save what I had borrowed, to support me while at school, I should never have entered his class-room again.

Mr. S. P. Robins taught me how to teach. I had not, before meeting him, seen his equal as a teacher. I have never since. If Mr. Robertson laid bare to my comprehension what in academic work had before been dark or even a total blank, and elevated me towards the high, broad plane of his conception of education; if Mr. Ormiston gave me some appreciation of the majestic grandeur of educational work and inspired me with devotion to it, Mr. Robins taught me the science of teaching through means of the practice of the art. The masters of the Normal School operated upon me. They taught me the academic work as I might in turn teach it to others. Mr. Robins operated upon boys and demonstrated to me how to reach the understanding of children with instruction that at times escaped my own grasp in the higher institution. He taught me the lessons he taught the boys while teaching me to teach. In all my teaching since and inspection of the teaching of others, his teacher's technique has been my ideal and standard. At any moment I can recall him in those old gallery-rooms filled with boys. Short in stature and then also slim, he moved about nimble footed among the pupils, his nearer presence inciting them to greater effort. Nearsightedness causing him to peer into their exercises, adding earnestness of manner to an intensely earnest and sympathetic face, while upturned to his were the anxious faces of the pupils awaiting look of approval or hint of direction. No goody, goody talk. No coddling of the boys. He treated them as little men and they responded as men. That voice so pure, so flexible, that exact enunciation, and that clear flow of connected thought dealt out in easy steps of correct thinking that the pupils might keep step with him and arrive with him at the same conclusion, still hold me as with a charm. I have witnessed his work in the class-room, when his indescribable tact aroused his pupils to such continuous mental application that I could have begged him to slacken his hold of the class and relieve the tension of intellectual effort, worthy of grown men.

If a word of criticism may be permitted, allow me to say in those days, students of the Normal School received academic training in the Normal and Model Schools. Our masters were teachers and taught us as we were expected to teach our pupils. As a matter of course we taught the subjects as we had been taught them by masters in the art, so far as our aptitude permitted. The same influence is operating to-day. As inspector, I find teachers teaching academic work as they were taught it, not as they were directed to teach it in the training schools. In spite of the skill and patience bestowed upon teachers-in-training by the Model and Normal masters, during the brief period the latter have for operating upon their students, the students as teachers, teach as they were taught, in Public and High Schools.

The Toronto Normal School has been a light, set on a hill top. Her graduates throughout the country have diffused the light they received from her. The mass of youth, educated in our province by them, were for years indebted to her for their mental training and directly or indirectly for the intelligence that made them worthy citizens. Not only by renovating teaching has she been a blessing, she, by means of her students and their pupils, has thrown lustre into every line of industrial life, for, those educated within her walls have distinguished themselves on the farm, as tradesmen and manufacturers, in law and in the legislature, in literature and science, at the bedside and in the pulpit.

David Ormiston, B.A.
(A former teacher in the Boys' Model School).

It is needless to say that I have very great pleasure indeed in being present on this occasion to assist in celebrating the Jubilee of the Normal School, which has done so much for the advancement and education of our noble Province—a school from whose halls has gone forth a host of noble men and women who have carried the training obtained there to the utmost corners of the land, and almost every one of whom for a time at least became centres from which light and knowledge disseminated and not a few of whom have worked their way up into the professions and other walks in life, and are now found in places of trust and power in this our loved Province and fair Dominion.

And, Sir, it gives me special pleasure to see you presiding over this meeting, not merely because you are the Minister of Education, but because, Sir, before you attained to that position you were so long associated with the teaching profession. The teachers can and do all feel that you are one of themselves, and just because you were so long and successfully associated with the working of the system are you so well qualified for the honorable position you now so admirably fill.

Then, Sir, there is a pleasure of again meeting in these halls the friends and classmates of over forty years ago. Some of whom have passed away into the realm beyond, but many still remain, and I here would like to greet them all and wish them well.

In the fall of 1853 I came to Toronto from the northern part of the township of Darlington with the intention of preparing to enter the University, but as my brother was one of the masters in the Normal School I decided to take a course there first, which I have never regretted.

Very soon after coming to the city a young lady was spending the evening at the house and, of course, when she was ready to return home I, of course, was gallant enough to offer to bear her company, and I found the time pass very pleasantly, as the young lady was a good conversationalist, but after bidding her good night at the door and turning round to retrace my steps the aspect was very different, the several corners turned had not been carefully noted by me and I was much in doubt which to turn, and very soon concluded a country boy was in as much danger of losing himself in the city as a city boy would be in the woods in the country, and began to admire the wisdom of the men of the olden time who unwound the ball of yarn as they were led through the intricate labyrinths so that they, when left alone, might find their way out. However, by dint of perseverance, at last I found the corner lamp I had already marked as near our home.

And, Sir, what wonderful changes in the country and city during these years! No *Grand Trunk* or other railway traversed our country except the short Northern railway. The old fashioned stage the only means of travel, or else on foot as so graphically depicted by Dr. Dewart last night. And how changed the city, that section lying to the northeast of where we now stand was woods or open fields in which the wild flowers grew luxuriantly, and to the northwest, where Knox College and palatial residences now stand, were extensive fields where cattle pastured, and thrifty orchards bearing luscious fruits, which were a strong temptation to some of us students hungering for an apple such as we used to pick at home.

Men, too, have changed. We look around in vain for the venerable Chief Superintendent with his kindly greeting, the strong, striking countenance of the Head Master, with his bluff but withal cordial reception.

The very striking appearance and sympathetic hand-shake of the then assistant master, they, with others, have passed away, either by death or removed to other lands. One only I believe of those then in charge of the Education Department is still here, Dr. Hodgins, who was in the office from its very beginning, and who is now, I understand, writing a history of the Educational System of the Province. I personally am very sorry his fine gentlemanly presence does not grace the platform this afternoon.

The Normal School deserves the friendship and support of the women of our country. It was the first to throw open its doors to both sexes on equal terms. It was the first institution where women had a chance to meet with and be instructed by men of education and be prepared to take positions in which they could earn a livelihood outside of domestic employment. Now all our universities and schools are open to them, but it was different fifty years ago. And much of the success of the school was due to this circumstance, and great good has accrued to the country from the number of female teachers who have gone from this institution and after teaching as a profession for a while have still continued in a more limited circle the noble work they have undertaken.

And, Sir, as there seems to be some difficulty now in arranging for religious instruction in our schools, I will just mention how that matter was arranged in the Normal School away back in those primitive times forty years ago, for of course our moral and religious training had to be carefully cared for in those days, and as it was not convenient for a Presbyterian or Episcopalian minister to come each week, or for some other reason, I know that we students of those two denominations met together, and one week the Rural Dean Grassett, a man of scholarly tastes, a good teacher, and earnest Christian character, would give us a Bible lesson, instructive and cheering, and the next week Rev. Dr. Burns, a man of strong personality and a vigorous preacher and teacher, would for an hour in his peculiar way question, expound and enforce the truths of the lesson, rousing us all to think and not infrequently propose questions which shewed just an insinuation that we were not quite satisfied, which brought out the full power of the Doctor to explain and sustain his theory. And I can safely say I never enjoyed Bible teaching more than under these two men, and there was no jealousy or fear of proselytizing. It gave to those coming from distant parts of the country an exhibition of interdenominational courtesy that was of lasting benefit. Would that there were more of it to-day, and then there would be less difficulty in settling this somewhat troublesome question.

Another incident I should like to mention which took place not while I was a student but in the summer of 1857, when, owing to the sickness of Mr. Barron, who was appointed to take Dr. Ormiston's place, on his retiring to take charge of a congregation at Hamilton, I was asked by the Chief Superintendent to come from the Model School and teach the mathematical and natural philosophy classes in the Normal School. I remember how my knees seemed to give out under me when Dr. Ryerson took me to the desk and introduced me to the large class as their teacher for the session, but soon all fear was gone when we got to work and we spent a very pleasant summer.

It was during that session the school paper was started, or I should rather say papers, for, of course, under the regulations the male and female students could not associate sufficiently to publish one paper; so the female students read theirs one week and the male students theirs the next week. And there were some very spicy articles from time to time in reply to each other. It was the duty of the editor each Saturday afternoon to come to the platform and read the issue. I understand there has been a school paper in some form since that time.

And now, Sir, lest I trespass on your time, I will close by wishing that the Normal School may go on and prosper in the future as in the past, and that when, fifty years hence, the teachers and graduates meet to celebrate the centennial, the then Minister of Education and staff of teachers may be as able and efficient as those of the present day.

Rev. Mungo Fraser, D.D., of Hamilton opened his reminiscent address with pointing to the change in the arrangement and decorations of the amphitheatre He then dwelt on the splendid training which had been received by the students of the Normal. It was the best place he ever knew to take the conceit out of one and make a man essentially a man. Some very amusing incidents were related of the first two Principals, Mr. Robertson and Dr. Sangster. Rev. Dr. Ormiston, whom he spoke of as "that grand old man," also came in for some references full of respect and esteem. In closing he spoke of the delight which he had experienced at being present at this meeting.

It is to be regretted that a full report could not be obtained of Dr. Fraser's admirable address. He spoke extemporaneously and no reporter was present to reproduce his remarks in extenso.

Mrs. G. Riches.
(Principal of Sackville Street School, Toronto.)

After gazing on these grand mental pictures, unveiled here this afternoon, by so many brilliant artists, perhaps it will relieve and rest your mind's eye to look on a little bit of dark background for a time ; then you will be all the better prepared to appreciate the scintillations of wit and gems of humour that you will find farther down on the programme

There is not the slightest doubt that reminiscences depend upon individuality. A loving mother treasures up the cute little sayings and doings of her bright-eyed boy until her eye is dim and her face withered and drawn. The old general fights his battles o'er and o'er and "tells how fields were won." The millionaire recounts his clever speculation on the stock exchange; while the retired teacher points out with pride the prominent men and women who once as youths and maidens garnered up the gems of knowledge he so freely scattered on the fertile soil.

But in whatever field our reminiscences lie they are apt to reflect somewhat to our credit, be they educational, financial, military or family. And this is desirable. What miserable creatures should we be if we remembered all the contemptible meannesses of our past years. Time certainly is blind when he blots out the recollection of former disagreements and dislikes, so that when those whom we have not seen for years grasp our hand we think only of the pleasant associations connected with them, and our heart warms and a rush of welcome greeting is poured forth, the eye kindles as olden memories come tripping from the dead past and scenes of mirth and jollity are recalled until we feel as young as we did twenty, thirty or even forty years ago.

The majority of those here to-day came to this building first as rosy-cheeked lads and lassies, bringing suggestions of green fields and grand old forests in their wake. They had been the head boys and girls of their respective High or Grammar schools; the pride of their teachers and the envy and admiration of the pupils of the lower forms; and as they stood here, strangers in a great city, their hearts went back to the olden home, and they could hear the fervent "God bless you my child!" from the tremulous lips of their sire; and still feel the clinging of the fond mother's soft arms as the tearful kiss was pressed on their lips. Yes, it all comes back even now, and we "sigh for the touch of a vanished hand and the sound of a voice that is still."

But soon the stern realities of life in the shape of mathematical and scientific problems like the good Samaritan of old bound up the mental wounds, and in a few days the elasticity of youth sent the ball of mischief flying across forbidden boundaries.

The students were not allowed to speak or write to those of the opposite sex, but there was nothing said about *singing* to them, and many a "blush mantled o'er the cheek" and "two hearts beat as one" when the rich bass voice or mellifluous tenor trilled out the first emotions of love under the window of his student sweetheart; those who were not birds of gentle beak proclaimed their passion in luscious fruits surreptitiously placed in the desk. No note was needed, each felt the presence of the other and "Eyes looked love to eyes that spake again."

Then came Hallowe'en. Well do I remember a little group of five lonely girls, who on one bright Hallowe'en night sat poring over some dry deductions, every few minutes some one sighed and it was easily seen memory was recalling past Hallowe'ens. At last pencils and papers were laid aside and the handsome girl suggested we do something—but what? Then a little Scotch lassie remembered hearing her grandmother say that in Scotland the girls would go blindfolded into the kailyards to pull cabbages; the cabbage would determine the kind of good man each would get. If the head were solid and heavy he would be rich; if light, empty-headed and empty-handed; the stalk would determine his temperament, and the number of circles on it correspond to the number of years still to live single; then the cabbages were to be sent to the handsomest men in the town. At this recital we were filled with excitement and eager to peer into the future. Where could we get cabbages? Then we remembered some were growing behind where Mr. Doan lived, but the fence was high and we dare not trespass. Some one suggested a rope for a lasso. No sooner said than done. Up we sprang and in a few minutes the clothes line in our yard was *down* and we were *up* on the fence balancing ourselves on the scantling. With eager haste and persistent effort that rope was thrown in the direction of the cabbages. Some times it would catch on, then we like the disciples of Izaak Walton would try to land our fish or rather cabbage, but we had no landing net and if we succeeded in drawing it near the fence as soon as it began to ascend the heavy head would turn over and the root slip through the noose and down it would go. But we were not easily discouraged as the pile of cabbages drawn to the fence would prove. We succeeded in getting two very fine specimens over and they were carried to our room in triumph. We were so elated over our success that we could not leave well enough alone, the cabbages must be hung on somebody's door. Of course Mr. D. was the somebody and with his name attached the cabbbage was securely fastened to the door-knob of his domicile. The other one was carefully wrapped up in a Globe newspaper and quietly placed in a dark corner. Early next morning two tall girls wearing long cloaks were seen hurriedly walking along Gerrard Street carrying between them a suspicious looking parcel of great size; down Victoria Street they went, then a sudden start as they recognized Master Thomas J. Robertson, Jr., coming up the street. To conceal the load they were carrying they kept very close together, so close that just as they were passing him the paper burst and the root and stalk protruded some sixteen inches; the paper being made of straw seemed to split into a thousand fragments and at the same time sang its own dirge in piercing tones. Cloaks were quickly thrown over the cabbage and it soon found a resting place on the Head Master's door Then these conspirators ran home and demurely returned with their books at the proper time.

Some time during the noon recess a notice was tacked up in the waiting room to the effect "that the tall young ladies who wore long black cloaks were to report to the Head Master in his private room at four o'clock." Precisely at four, thirteen tall young ladies with black cloaks marched in, eleven of them very curious and two very sedate. With a "thank you ladies," they were dismissed.

During the week a kind invitation to take dinner with Mr. Robertson on Friday evening was sent to the five young ladies who had played such a conspicuous part on the fence top. Such a flutter of excitement followed. Best frocks were brought out, a little bow of ribbon placed here, a knot of lace there, our modest ornaments polished up, even a book on etiquette was consulted that we might be sure our native villages were not behind in the proper mode of procedure on such occasions. Expectation ran riot in our veins. How would Mrs. Robertson receive us? Would Thos. Jaffray, Jr., be there? If he were we knew Martha Zenobia would monopolize him. She was the clever as well as handsome girl, strange to say. All that week it seemed to us that when Mr. Robertson looked our way he had a peculiar expression in his eye but we were not sure, and we came to the conclusion that "Conscience makes cowards of us all" and hoped for the best. Friday night came at last. The small mirror placed at our disposal was in constant demand, hair was arranged and re-arranged, ribbons tied, untied and retied, and with a little pat here and a shake there we were ready at last. We had invested our little all in flowers for a corsage bouquet. These were carefully wrapped in tissue paper and carried in our hand to be pinned into position later on. Our regal girl, Martha Zenobia, was to go first and we were to follow her. Nothing like making a good impression we thought. Mrs. Robertson was exceedingly kind for which we were intensely grateful and our nervousness with its attendant awkwardness was gently on the wane when dinner was announced. We scarcely raised our eyes until the blessing had been invoked, then, just as we were devoutly thankful that all had gone so well, two immense plates of cabbage were brought in and placed directly in front of each of the two tall girls who wore long black cloaks. Best frocks, flowers, ribbons, lace, ornaments, manners were all merged for the time being into cabbage. The peals of laughter at our expense can be better imagined than described. Our punishment was certainly unique and as certainly effective.

J. H. Smith.
(Inspector, Public Schools, Wentworth).

It is my privilege this afternoon to congratulate you, Sir, upon the large gathering of educationalists who have assembled in this spacious building to commemorate the Jubilee of the Toronto Normal School. Fifty years ago it was opened under circumstances that pointed to it as an educational experiment. Many thought that our country was not far enough advanced to indulge in such luxuries as a special training school for teachers. They believed and doubtless were sincere in their belief, "That however well adapted such institutions might be to the wants of the old and densely populated countries of Europe, they are absolutely unsuited for a country like Upper Canada," and so far as providing properly trained teachers is concerned the people must resort as heretofore, "to securing the services of those whose physical disabilities from age render this mode of obtaining a livelihood, the only one suited to their decaying energies, or by employing such of the newly arrived emigrants as are qualified for common school teachers, year by year as came amongst us." Such were the exact words of the representatives of the people in one of the most progressive Districts of this Province. We are thankful, Sir, that,

"Old times have changed, old manners gone
A stranger fills the Stuarts throne."

Yes, a stranger to such thoughts, but not to the most advanced educational thought of the present day.

Fifty years ago this school was opened under the headmastership of the late T. J. Robertson, M.A., formerly Inspector of Schools in Ireland. The first few sessions were held in Government House, but owing to the destruction by fire of the Parliament Buildings in Montreal in 1849, the seat of Government was transferred to Toronto. This rendered its removal to other quarters a necessity and the old Temperance Hall was secured as a temporary home. In 1852 the present handsome and commodious building was completed, and the Normal School entered upon such a career of usefulness that its influence has been felt in every school in Ontario. In pursuance of the plan of having an educational museum and a School of Art and Design in connection with the Normal School, it became necessary to provide accommodation specially adapted for training purposes. A suitable building was erected in the rear of the Departmental Buildings, and the Normal School was transferred thereto in 1858, where it has since remained.

I have no doubt, Sir, that it is a source of personal pleasure to you to see so many of the veteran teachers of Ontario, assembled to do honor to their Alma Mater. I can assure you, furthermore, that I but voice the sentiment of this large assemblage of educationalists, when I say that we feel honored in having you—one of the most distinguished members of our profession—to preside on this our Jubilee Anniversary. Personally I feel highly honored in having the privilege of addressing such a representative audience on such an auspicious occasion. I am delighted to look into the faces, and to grasp the hands of so many of the graduates of former years, to recount the incidents of our college life, and to call up remembrances that have awakened feelings of mingled joy and sadness. Some have solved the problem that lies beyond the pale of this mortal existence, while others remain to do noble service in the cause of popular education. May the Toronto Normal School now as of old lead the van in educational thought and in educational progress.

But my purpose this afternoon is to deal with reminiscences. These of necessity must be largely of a personal nature. I know that in the kindness of your hearts you will not think me egotistical, if I refer to my personal experiences, for it is these, and I may say, these alone, that will give you a clear view of a student life. Some of these leave impressions that time may ameliorate but cannot destroy, for they have become a part of my life, and have had a large influence in shaping and developing my character. I shall however confine myself to two, lest I weary your patience. One of these I call " My Geography Lesson." What I learned about teaching geography has long since passed into oblivion, but what I learned about managing the more advanced pupils, when they had grown troublesome and vexatious has enabled me to overcome many difficulties both in discipline and in management. Nor has it been confined to the schoolroom alone. In my intercourse with men, while dealing with the many difficulties that naturally arise in the discharge of my duties as a Public School

Inspector, I have found the means I adopted to get control of these boys to be an invaluable aid in securing fair and generous treatment. Briefly told the incident is as follows:—

It fell to my lot one afternoon to take charge of some twenty-five or thirty boys in the senior division. These were pupils that had been in attendance at the Model School for some time, and were well acquainted with all the subjects in the course of study. It was therefore a difficult matter for me to present them with any new information or make the lesson attractive. When I began to teach, they gave me their undivided attention for a few minutes, then began a rattling of the desk lids and a variety of other noises that would soon have brought the Headmaster into the room to restore order, and I would have been given a low mark for practical teaching, if I had not been "plucked" out and out I appealed to them with but little effect, save to increase the disorder. The noise and confusion grew gradually worse, until, as a last resort, I frankly and openly stated my circumstances, told them what it meant to me, and illustrated my position by a reference to the fable of "The Boys and the Frogs." Be it said to the honor of these boys that they at once became quiet, paid the strictest attention to what I had to say, and I finished the lesson in such a manner that the Headmaster complimented me upon my success. I learned afterwards that this division had been a thorn in the flesh to many of the students. I felt then as I feel now that they possessed the elements of true manhood, and that they exercised a spirit of self-control that reflected credit upon their training in their homes and in the school. I shall ever remember them kindly for the heroism they showed that afternoon.

The other incident to which I have alluded has a humorous side to it, though not devoid of a practical and useful lesson. Pupils at school or young people at college rather enjoy anything in which the teacher or professors are over reached or out-witted. Such was the case in this instance. A young Scotchman presented himself for admission, and after the preliminary examination had been passed, took his place among the students. It will be well to remark here that one of the rules of this institution at this time was, that the students of opposite sexes were not allowed to communicate with one another without the special permission of the Headmaster or his assistant, under the penalty of a severe reprimand or suspension, according to the gravity of the offence. This young Scotchman, when he took the seat allotted to him very naturally glanced at the young ladies who occupied the opposite side of the room. His attention was arrested by the familiar appearance of the side view of a young lady's face. When she turned so that he could get a full view of her face he at once recognized her as a former schoolmate in far away Scotland. His first impulse was to defy the rule and speak to her, but his Scottish caution prevented him from doing anything so rash. When he returned to the waiting room he informed some of his fellow-students of the state of affairs, and they advised him to ask Mr. Robertson for permission to speak to her. Now Mr. Robertson enjoyed a joke, and had a keen relish for such scenes as are usually presented by two young persons of opposite sexes talking to one another in his presence about things that were not stictly pertinent to Normal School work. Indeed he sometimes used such incidents to brighten up his lectures and relieve the monotony of the recitation hour. This young man went directly to the private room of the Headmaster, stated his case fully and asked permission to have a friendly talk with the young lady. Mr. Robertson said that he could speak to the young woman on the condition that their conversation should take place in his presence. To this the young man after a moment's hesitation consented. Thereupon Mr. Robertson stepped to the door of the young ladies' waiting room, called her by name and asked her to step into his private room. As she entered the door the young man addressed her in Gaelic, and she replied in the same language. It is perhaps needless to say that Mr. Robertson never reported even the substance of the conversation much less the exact words.

Some persons, as you well know, have the gift of expressing their thoughts in poetic diction, while others have to be content with plain prose. One of the students of the twenty-fifth session had this gift and he gave vent to his feelings in the following poetical effusion, which was then known as :—

The Normal Student's Lament.

"Alas! my mind is not my own,
  My thoughts are bound in chains,
The muses far away have flown
  And fancy shuns my brains.

"In vain I long for pleasant rides
  Across the hills of snow,
Or o'er the glassy ice to glide
  'Neath which the streamlets flow.

"I have but Euclid's hilly mists
  Of circles, planes and lines,
The streams are formidable lists
  Of plus and minus signs.

"All classics I have put away,
  I dare not mind them here,
For Grammar and dull Algebra
  Instead of them appear.

"Mythology is quite erased
  By Henry's, Edward's, John's,
While rhyme and verse are now replaced
  By everlasting sums.

"I scarcely dare admire the day
  Or watch the twinkling stars,
For fear 'twill call my mind away
  From fractions, cubes and squares.

"My thoughts have left the azure sky,
  The smiles have left the moon,
While theorems their place supply
  And gladness yields to gloom.

"And if I think of sweet old home,
  Of friends lost to my view,
The briny tear perhaps may come,
  The lip may quiver, too.

> "But soon these tears I must erase,
> They interfere with books,
> They put the angles out of place
> And turn the lines to hooks.
>
> "The founts of joy, the youthful fires
> That struggled in my breast,
> That once with hope this heart inspired
> Are dwindling into rest.
>
> "My spirit flags within my frame,
> My heart is growing cool,
> It was not so before I came
> To this, the Normal School.
>
> "Because my mind is not my own
> My thoughts are bound in chains,
> The muses somewhere else have gone
> And fancy shuns my brains.
>
> "Then roar, ye winds, with all your might,
> In dreary dirges blow,
> Come howl, ye savage ghosts of night,
> And join my song of woe."
>
> Toronto, February, 1861. "OSCAR."

I cannot conclude this short address without referring somewhat briefly to the influence this school has exerted in advancing the educational interests of the common people. The number of pupils in attendance and the very great improvement in the matter of accommodation and equipment do not reveal the true sources whence this growth and development have arisen. Gratifying as these results are, and we are all proud of them, we have to look to other causes for the real source of this advance. It is deeper and is largely due to the lives and work of the graduates of this institution, whether they have remained in the profession or have sought and found other fields of labor. Their influence has been felt in every section of Ontario, and to-day we are reaping the fruits of their self-denying labors. They are workmen of whom we need not feel ashamed, for they were inspired by nobler motives than the mere acquisition of either wealth or fame. In honouring them we do honour to one of the noblest public institutions in this Province—the Toronto Normal School.

Ladies and gentlemen, I thank you for your courteous hearing.

A. S. Allan.
(Merchant, Clifford, Ontario).

I have pleasure in accepting the invitation of the committee to be present and in taking part in these gatherings to celebrate the Jubilee of the Toronto Normal School. It is a pleasure indeed to meet with those who were students with us in this institution many years ago. I thought I would be one of the oldest students, but I find some here who were in attendance the year in which the school was first opened. I can remember the year 1847. At that time my father was Superintendent of Schools for the District of Wellington, comprising the present Counties of Waterloo, Wellington and Grey, a great deal of which at that time was unbroken forest. Travelling was very difficult as roads were bad and settlements a long way apart. Teachers of those days laboured under great disadvantages, and there was great necessity of something being done to raise the standard of teachers. This institution was admirably adapted to the training of teachers for their profession, and it sent them out better prepared to enter on the duties of life, whether they followed the occupation of teaching or of some other calling.

It was my privilege to be a student here in the first session of 1862 and of 1864. It was indeed a privilege, for the training we received strengthened us in character and made us persevering and thorough. After leaving the Normal School in 1864 I was not engaged in teaching, but entered into mercantile pursuits, in which I have ever since been engaged. During the last twenty years a great deal of my time has been spent in municipal and political life.

The first thing I remember of my attendance at the Normal School was when we assembled in this very room to register. It was also in this place that those of the same denomination to which I belonged met to receive religious instruction from our teachers who were the venerable Dr. Jennings and Mr. King, now Dr. King, of Manitoba College. The ceremony of unveiling the portraits of the principals and teachers this afternoon was very interesting, and brought to mind many pleasant remembrances. The portrait of the first principal, T. J. Robertson, is, I think, a true likeness. He seemed to me always so stern, and I was afraid of him, although I cannot say that I disliked him. Grammar was one of his hobbies, and he was particularly severe on any one who dared to give any of the rules in Lennie's Grammar. I transgressed once and I received a whole lecture to myself. It was absolutely necessary that we should be able to read to his satisfaction " Paul's Defence Before Agrippa." However, he was a grand man, and it was a privilege to be a student under him.

The portrait of Dr. Sangster is very like the Doctor that we have with us to-day, but not like the John Herbert Sangster of my school days, for time has brought changes. Those who were fond of mathematics felt safe, but those who were not were in dread of being struck by his "lightning." I am sure all his scholars have retained pleasant recollections of his lectures. He gave us excellent advice that was of service to us in the several occupations in which we were afterwards engaged. He set us an example of application and perseverance. I am glad to see that he is present with us to-day. I have often said with pride that I had the privilege of studying under T. J. Robertson and Dr. Sangster.

In the Model School Mr. Carlyle was always very kind, but very firm.

To some of us the Model School was the terror of our lives. Most of the boys were experts in mischief. Mr. Disher was second master, but he died, leaving pleasant memories of his short stay. I cannot forget the genial old Drill Instructor, Major Goodwin.

As was said by Dr. Dewart last night, the Toronto Normal School in its day supplied a want to those who could not take advantage of other educational institutions, and as one of its students I shall always retain pleasant memories of this excellent institution.

IV.

THE CONVERSAZIONE.

A Conversazione was held, on Monday evening, in the Public Hall and Museum of the Education Department. It was one of the most marked features of the whole jubilee celebration, the attendance being very large and representative in its character. It was a most delightful reunion of the alumni of the school. Many who were unable to be present at the other meetings attended the conversazione. Hon. G. W. Ross, LL.D., Minister of Education, and Mrs. Ross received the visitors in the amphitheatre, and their task was no light one on account of the numbers. A short, excellent programme of music was rendered under the direction of Mr. S. H. Preston, Music Master of the Toronto Normal School. The artists who assisted were Miss Mary Wheeler, Miss Laura L. Phoenix, and Mr. Rachab Tandy. During the promenade which succeeded the concert, D'Alessandro's orchestra played a number of selections. At the close of the concert, Hon. Dr. Ross made a most felicitous speech which gave the key note for the promenade which followed. He invited the visitors to inspect the re-constructed Museum which had been recently re-opened after the enlargement of the building and the introduction of the department of Archæology.

V.

EDUCATIONAL ADDRESSES.

On the afternoon of Tuesday, November 2nd, commencing at two o'clock, four educational addresses were delivered in the Public Hall of the Education Department. The lecturers were selected by the committee and invited to deliver addresses from a distinctly representative standpoint. Mr. Kirkland, as being the present head of the Toronto Normal School; Mr. Hughes, as an Inspector and former Head Master of the Boys' Model School; Dr. Robins, as Principal of McGill Normal School, and a former Master in the Model School; and Dr. Sangster, as a former Principal of the Toronto Normal School, all represent phases in the progress of the professional training of teachers, which, it was thought fitting, should be presented at this Celebration.

A BRIEF SKETCH OF THE TORONTO NORMAL SCHOOL.

Thomas Kirkland, M.A.
(Principal, Toronto Normal School).

The decade that brought to a close the first half of the present century was characterized by the number of Normal Schools established in the different States in the northern part of this continent. The year 1839 saw three Normal Schools established in Massachusetts. In 1845 the Albany Normal School came into existence. In 1847 the Toronto Normal School was opened. The Philadelphia Normal School was founded in 1848, and in the same year a Normal School was established in St. John, New Brunswick. Connecticut followed with a Normal School the year after, and the decade was closed with the opening of the Michigan Normal School.

In 1846 Dr. Ryerson submitted to Parliament a report on a "System of Elementary Instruction for Upper Canada," in which he specially recommended that provision be made for the training of teachers. He rightly thought that the special education of teachers is an essential element in all systems of public instruction. The Government accepted his recommendation, and provided for the establishment of a Normal School in Toronto by appropriating for that purpose a portion of the legislative grant for public schools. The School was opened for the reception of students on the 1st of November, 1847, in the presence of a large number of visitors from different parts of the country. Parliament then met in Montreal, and in the vacant Government House in Toronto the new Normal School had its first abode.

Twenty students presented themselves at the opening, which number was soon increased to fifty-two, some of whom were sent by District Councils. Nearly all of them had been employed as teachers, and had improved the first opportunity of attending the Normal School in order to qualify themselves better for the duties of their profession.

The School was fortunate in securing for its first Head Master Thomas Jaffray Robertson, who had been a student of Trinity College, Dublin, and Head Inspector under the Irish National Board of Education. Mr. Robertson, therefore, brought from the Mother Country that scholarship and experience which admirably fitted him for the position. With Mr. Robertson was associated Henry Youle Hind, formerly scholar of Queen's College, Cambridge, and latterly a student at the Royal Commercial School at Leipsic, and who was familiar with the methods of teaching in France and Germany.

Fifty years ago no Darwin had enunciated the law of the "survival of the fittest." But, nevertheless, the fittest survived: for, fortunately, the operations of natural laws do not depend on our knowing them. Few of the fifty-two students who attended the first session of the Normal School have left "footprints on the sands of time." But two of them soon became well and widely known—the one as an eloquent preacher and the able editor of one of our most influential religious journals: the other became eminent as a teacher, and subsequently as the Headmaster of the Institution of which he was then a student. Edward Hartley Dewart and John Herbert Sangster still survive to attest the kind of education given in the Normal School fifty years ago.

The first session closed with a public examination which lasted two days. This examination recalls the names of many eminent men who have left their impress on Canadian history. Among those present were the Hon. Robert Baldwin, Bishop Strachan, Dr. Burns, the Revds. Messrs. Barclay, Jennings and Grassett. From the speeches delivered at the close of the examination we learn that it gave the highest satisfaction. both as to the amount of varied and useful knowledge imparted to the students, and the intellectual and thorough mode of imparting it; that the examination exceeded the most sanguine expectation of the warmest friends of the Institution. The proceedings were reported and commented upon by *The Patriot, The Herald, The Evangelist, The British Colonist, The Globe,* and *The Christian Guardian.* All are gone save the two last. Papers perish as well as men.

At the close of this examination, an address was presented to the masters, from which we learn that the course of instruction embraced a thorough analysis of the English language; geography, with all the aids that the best globes and maps could afford : history, ancient and modern ; logic ; the theory and practice of arithmetic and algebra ; a valuable course of agricultural chemistry ; a scientific knowledge of sacred music; instruction and experience in teaching in the Model School according to the system adopted in the best schools of the Mother Country.

The writer of the address from which I have quoted seems to have made the most of his materials, for the Model School was opened only in February of that same year, not quite three months before the close of the session. Its first Head Master was Charles Lowey, who survived his appointment only about nine months, and was succeeded by Archibald McCallum, who held the Headmastership for eight years. Like many eminent men, the Model School had a lowly origin. It was cradled in the Government House stables, and passed its babyhood in the basement of Temperance Hall, on Temperance street.

Only male students were admitted to the Normal School during the first session. A female department was opened at the beginning of the second session, when 118 students presented themselves, twenty-two of whom were females. The attendance increased during the session; but as the attendance increased the masters became more particular about the quality, for we are told that seven were dismissed for incapacity and two for improper conduct.

And here I may observe, that from the very beginning the system of instruction adopted in the Normal School was founded on Christian principles, and pervaded by a Christian spirit. An hour every Friday was devoted to religious instruction, when the clergy of the different denominations attended, and gave such instruction to the members of their respective denominations as they deemed suitable. This practice has been continued till the present time, and with the best results. Engraved on the corner stone of this building is the inscription, "Designed for the Instruction and Training of Teachers upon Christian Principles."

At the semi-annual examination in the Fall of 1849, His Excellency Lord Elgin, Governor-General, was present, and being desirous of encouraging the study of agriculture in Public Schools, established two prizes, one of £5 and the other of £3, to be awarded to the two students who should at the end of each half-year's session pass the best examination in that subject. These prizes formed an important feature in the Normal School examinations during Lord Elgin's tenure of office.

The year 1850 witnessed a new departure in the Normal School. Hitherto there had been two sessions in each year. But in order to dispense with attendance during the hot summer months, and to prolong the period of training, it was determined to have but one session of nine months. It was also arranged that in future candidates for admission should be examined by a committee of School Superintendents in the several counties. The long session did not fulfil the expectations of its friends, and it was soon abandoned. Its inauguration was followed by a falling off in the number of students; and, besides, the severe and long continued labor had a hurtful effect upon the health of those in attendance. In 1852 but eighty students entered, and only forty-one came through to the end. The session was closed with a five days' examination, four of which were devoted to written work. The arithmetic paper contained twenty-nine questions, ranging from vulgar fractions to annuities, and to be worked in one and one-half hours. Grammar, education and the art of teaching formed one paper of fifty-one questions, to be answered at one sitting of three hours.

The Normal and Model Schools had already acquired a name, but no local habitation of their own. Since the Government returned to Toronto, the classes had met in the Temperance Hall. But steps had previously been taken to secure a permanent abode. On the 2nd of July, 1851, the corner stone of the present building was laid by His Excellency, Lord Elgin, in the presence of a large number of spectators. It was stated that the plot of ground in which the buildings are situated contained eight acres; that two of them were to form a botanical garden, and three were to be set apart for agricultural experiments. At the time of purchase the ground gave little promise of what it afterwards became. It was "partly bog, and abounded in stumps." But in the fall of 1853 it produced thirty-seven specimens of grain, roots and vegetables, which were exhibited at the great annual show in Hamilton, and were highly commended by the judges. The building was designed to accommodate 200 students-in-training, and 600 pupils in the Model School. The space considered necessary for each pupil then must have been much less than what is considered necessary now. A second story has been added to the Model School which nearly doubles its seating capacity, and still it does not accommodate 600 pupils.

High hopes were entertained of the infant Institution. In his address His Excellency said: "I certainly think that no Government which is conscious of its own responsibility can possibly feel indifferent to an institution such as that of which we are now laying the foundation stone; an institution which promises, under God's blessing, to exercise so material an influence on the formation of the mind and character of the rising generation of this Province, and which cannot but exercise a powerful influence upon its future destinies."

The building was finished and opened with appropriate ceremonies on the 24th December, 1852. The chair was occupied by the Hon. S. B. Harrison, Chairman of the Council of Public Instruction, and around him were men whose names are familiar to all readers of Canadian history. Several of those present delivered addresses. The speech of the Hon. Chief Justice Robinson was most appropriate, judicious and comprehensive, and well adapted to promote the interests of the institution. Dr. McCaul, in a speech, the eloquence and elegance of which, we are told, drew thunders of applause from the audience, expressed a hope, which he happily lived to see practically realized, that the son of the poorest man in Canada might enter the common school, and, proceeding through the intermediate stages, take the highest honors at the University. The speech of the Hon. Francis Hincks showed a keen discrimination and a thorough appreciation of the nature, character and utility of the institution. Dr. Ryerson gave an admirable outline of the whole system of education. The *Globe*, in an appreciative article, says "that hitherto the chief difficulty of our common schools has been the lack of competent teachers. This lack is now in a fair way to be supplied; that this institution is, in fact, the heart of the educational body, the spring from which is destined to flow streams of pure water to moisten the dry educational field. It is to it that we must look for those who will go forth fully armed and equipped to fight our battles against ignorance and error, the darkness and superstition which would impede our national progress."

In the autumn of 1853 Mr. Hind accepted the chair of chemistry in Trinity College. His duties during the following year were discharged by Mr. Sangster. The Rev. William Ormiston was selected to fill the position lately occupied by Mr. Hind. Mr. Ormiston was a graduate of Victoria College, and had been professor of mental and moral philosophy in his Alma Mater, and had taught schools in the town and township of Whitby. He now accepted the second position in the Normal School, having formerly declined the first. Mr. Ormiston was a man of fervid imagination, full of enthusiasm, and had great command of language. Such men usually make superior teachers, if their students do not allow the flow of language to carry them on without proper attention to the matter. Few teachers were ever more beloved by their students. He is now living in California, and in a letter recently received from him he says: "I retain and ever will cherish a fond and grateful remembrance of my labors in the Toronto Normal School."

Mr. Barron, late Principal of Upper Canada College became successor to Mr. Ormiston. His previous training and experience were not such as were required to efficiently discharge the duties of the position to which he was now appointed. Mr. Walter A. Watts was imported to succeed Mr. Barron. He held office for about a year. Both were learned men, but it requires something more than mere learning to make a successful Normal School master.

Mr. Sangster was now appointed second master. Unlike his immediate predecessors, his past experience and intimate knowledge of both Normal and Model Schools rendered him particularly well fitted for the position.

In 1866, in consequence of the lamented illness of Mr. Robertson, Dr. Sangster became Head Master, and Dr. Davies, late Head Master of the Cornwall Grammar School, was appointed second master. In 1871 Dr. Sangster resigned the headmastership, and Dr. Davies succeeded to the position. Heretofore mathematics and science had been taught by the same master, but in order to give science a more prominent place in the curriculum, the Council of Public Instruction resolved to separate these subjects. Dr. Carlyle, who had been Head Master of the Model School for the past thirteen years, was appointed Mathematical Master, and the writer of this paper was selected to fill the position of Science Master.

On the platform, at the distribution of the prizes to the Model School pupils at the close of this year, sat two eminent men whose official labors were now drawing to a close, and who must have looked back with pleasure to the year 1844 when the one received the appointment of Chief Superintendent from the Government of which the other was Prime Minister. Dr. Ryerson had drawn the bill which

Chief Justice Draper had introduced and carried through Parliament by the authority of which the Public School System was founded.

From 1871 till 1883 the work of the Normal School was carried on under many disadvantages. One of these was the change in the matter of granting certificates. From 1847 till 1853 the students-in-training received their instruction in the Normal School and their certificates from the County Boards. The Chief Superintendent saw the evil of this and as soon as possible obtained power to grant certificates on the recommendation of the Normal School masters. In course of time Associate Examiners were appointed, and this method worked admirably till 1871. In that year the Council took the examination of the Normal School students altogether out of the hands of the Normal School Masters, and put it into the hands of a committee, which committee, strange to say, could examine candidates for first-class certificates, but had not the power to examine candidates for second-class certificates. This was owing to that awkward little word *only* getting into the wrong place. This anomaly was soon remedied, but the vicious principle was adhered to till the advent of the present Minister. The principle is not good in any case, but in a professional examination of teachers it has evils peculiar to itself, and one of them is that not infrequently good teachers fail to obtain certificates, while the less capable are successful.

Besides the evils arising from one class of persons acting as teachers and another class acting as examiners, there was another disadvantage under which the school labored. The period was one of transition. The Normal School was passing from a time when its work was largely academic to a time when its work became almost entirely professional, and many of the disadvantages of such a period are, perhaps, unavoidable.

But notwithstanding these disadvantages much good work was done, many excellent teachers were sent forth who are now faithfully discharging their duties in our Public, High and Model Schools, and not a few are among our most efficient Inspectors.

Shortly after the present Minister took office, the programme of studies was revised, enriched, and made more largely professional. The work done by the students during the Normal School session was allotted its proper share in determining their standing at its close. All that was good in the past history of the school was retained, and all that was best in modern educational methods was adopted.

In 1884 Dr. Davies resigned the principalship, and was succeeded by the writer of this paper, and in 1893 Dr. Carlyle retired after giving the Education Department thirty-six years of efficient service. Mr. Wm. Scott, B.A., formerly Head Master of the Model School, and for eleven years Mathematical Master in the Ottawa Normal School, succeeded Dr. Carlyle under the new title of Vice-Principal.

The time limit of twenty minutes allowed to these papers has made this sketch very imperfect. Much interesting matter has been omitted. The changes in educational methods which have taken place during the period have not even been touched upon. The names of many who largely contributed to the success of the School have had to be omitted. The Toronto Normal School deserves a much fuller recognition. Its impress is indelibly stamped upon Canadian History. It has given Ontario a Minister of Education and his Deputy. To our highest institution for the training of teachers in this Province it has given its Principal. It gave a Superintendent of Education to far away British Columbia in the West, and has given a Principal to McGill Normal School in the East. It has given the Provincial University one of her most eminent professors, and many of the most successful students of that institution received their first educational stimulus at the Toronto Normal School. The most rapid advance which this Province has ever made in education followed the appointment of County Inspectors in 1871, the great majority of whom had been trained in the Normal School. It has given professors to both the Medical Colleges in this city. It would be interesting, were it possible, to enumerate the Ministers, Doctors and Lawyers who received, when students at the Normal School, that impulse which bore them on to a high place in their profession. And not less important has been that matronly influence which has rendered many a home brighter and better because its mistress was once a student at the Normal School. Nor has its influence been confined to our own Dominion. In a letter recently received from the professor of mathematics in Cornell University, he says: "I first learned to work when a student at the Normal School."

But while we feel a pardonable pride in the good work done by the Normal School during the past half century, let us hope that it is only the beginning of its career of usefulness, that under the more favorable circumstances in which it is now placed it may from year to year send forth in increasing numbers teachers of the highest type, men and women, earnest, intelligent, enthusiastic, deeply impressed with their great responsibility and opportunity—the moulding of the characters of those who, under God, are to guide the destinies of this great Dominion.

THE SCHOOL OF THE TWENTIETH CENTURY.

James L. Hughes.
(Inspector, Public Schools, Toronto).

Evolution is the most vital and most hopeful principle yet revealed to human consciousness. Humanity climbs steadily towards clearer light, truer wisdom, and greater power. We marvel at the benighted condition of our grandfathers, but our own grandchildren will have still greater reason to pity us.

As the race accumulates wisdom and power, it sweeps onward and upward with accelerated speed. As generation succeeds generation, the record stones of progress are planted more widely apart.

The educational revelations of the nineteenth century have been more important than those of all preceding centuries. Pestalozzi and Froebel gave the world new educational aims, and revealed all the educational principles that are now regarded as vital and fundamental: Barnard and Mann gave America's greatest contribution to civilization by the organization of free public schools, supported and controlled by the state. Take away the results of the work of these four men, and there is little of value left in educational philosophy or practice.

The twentieth century will make a greater educational advance than has been made in the nineteenth century. This thought is not humiliating to us, it should increase our self-reverence as members of a progressively developing race. Our consciousness of the divinity in us is defined by the evolution of the race towards the Divine.

1. The schools of the twentieth century will be free. The nineteenth century schools are called free because attendance at them is free. The child will be free in the twentieth century school. Free growth is the only full growth. Subordination dwarfs the human soul at any stage of its development. There will be no truly free men till the children are made truly free. The coercive, mandatory, compulsory spirit will become but a shameful memory, when teachers aim to develop the divinity in the child instead of making their supreme purpose the restriction of its depravity. What weak, imitative, conventional, indefinite, unprogressive, dependent servile men and women most schools have made of the beings who were originally created in God's own image! How much worse they would have been if they had been subject to school discipline during all their waking hours' How original, self-reliant, self-directing and progressive they might have been! How much of independence, and helpfulness, and executive tendency they had when they first went to school compared with what they had on leaving school? The schools should not be catacombs in which are buried the self-hood, the originality, and the executive tendency of childhood. Schools should be gardens in which each child grows to be its grandest, most complete self. The child can never become its real self so long as adulthood blights it and dwarfs it by daring to stand between it and God.

Liberty is the only sure basis for reverent co-operative obedience. Anarchy is not born of freedom: it springs from coercion. It is a poisonous fungus that grows from the tree of blighted liberty. It grows rank and noisome from the sap that should have developed stately trunk, spreading branches, and rich foliage. Fungi come not on the tree of full, free growth, but where blight has brought decay and death. Conscious subordination secured by coercion blights and dwarfs individuality.

Divine law is often necessarily restrictive of wrong, but is lovingly restrictive. It is stimulating and growth-giving; never destructive. Coercion may repress evil; it never eradicates it. Coercion never made a child creative, and creative power is the central element of education. Coercion does more than restrict the power of the child; it corrupts its ideals. The common and unnatural dread of Divine authority arises from the degradation of human authority into unreasoning, unloving coercion.

The greatest improvement yet wrought by the new education is the altered attitude of adulthood towards childhood in disciplining it.

The reformation of the coercive ideals of adulthood has only well begun, however. The twentieth century will complete the reform. When adulthood recognizes divinity in each child and learns that the highest function of training is to develop this divinity, not merely to restrict depravity, then will the schools become what Froebel aimed to make them: "Free Republics of Childhood."

The dominating elements in a child's life are love of freedom and productive activity. The unity of these elements is the only basis for true discipline. Spontaneity in productive self-activity develops active instead of passive obedience, co-operation instead of obstinacy and stubbornness, activity instead of inertness of character, energy instead of indolence, positiveness instead of negativeness, cheerfulness instead of dullness, independence instead of subserviency, and true liberty instead of anarchy.

2. Teachers will not try to dominate the interest of the child in the twentieth century school The pupil's self-active interest is the only persistent propelling motive to intellectual effort. It alone makes man an independent agent capable of progressive, upward and outward growth on original lines It alone stimulates the mind to its most energetic activity for the accomplishment of definite purposes. Self-active interest is the natural desire for knowledge appropriate to the child's stage of evolution, acting with perfect freedom : it is the divinely implanted wonder power, unchecked by restriction and undiminished by the substitution of the interests of others.

The development of self-active interest is the highest ideal of intellectual education. School methods in the past have substituted the teacher's suggestion for the child's spontaneous interest, and have thus rendered it unnecessary, if not impossible, for the pupil's own self-active interest to develop. Interest is naturally self-active, and it retains this quality in increasing power unless parents or teachers interfere with its spontaneity. "Every child brings with him into the world the natural disposition to see correctly." The most unfortunate children are those whose untrained nurses, untrained mothers, or untrained teachers, foolishly do for them what they should do for themselves, and point out to them the things they should see for themselves, or worse still, things they should not see at all at their stage of development. Mother and child should not always see the same things in their environment. "See, darling," may prevent the development of the child's power to see independently. The child's own mind should decide its special interests.

Most parents and teachers make the mistake of assuming that they should not only present attractions to the child's mind, but also arouse and direct its attention. Whenever this is done by any agency except the child's own self-active interest its power of giving attention is weakened. No two children should be attracted by exactly the same things or combinations of things during a walk in the country, or in any other gallery of varied interests. The special selfhood of each child sees in the outer what corresponds to its developing inner life. The individual power to see in the outer that which is adapted to the development of the inner life, *at present most active*, is the arousing source of all true interest. When a teacher substitutes his own interests for those of the child, the child's interest is made responsive instead of self-active. Under such teaching the real life of interest dies, and teachers, after killing it, have in the past made energetic and often fruitless efforts to galvanize it into spasmodic responsive action. Allowing the motives of others to stimulate us to action is no more true interest than allowing other people's thoughts to run through our minds is true thinking. The responsive process in each case is prohibitory of the real self-active process which lies at the root of true growth.

The teacher of the twentieth century will multiply the conditions of interest. Whatever he can do to make the child's external environment correspond with its inner development, he will do carefully and actively. He will know that, if the conditions are appropriate, interest will always be self-active, and that only by its own activity can it develop power. Responsive interest never develops much intensity, energy, endurance or individuality.

When teachers complain that children are not interested in work, their statements are usually incorrect. It would be more accurate to say that children are not interested in the teacher's work. Adulthood should not interfere so much with childhood.

3. The child will be trained to find most of its own problems, in the twentieth century school. The child discovers its own problems before it goes to school. When it reaches the school its problems are showered upon it by the teacher. This difference in educative process is the chief reason for the rapid development of children before they go to school compared with their development afterwards. Before the twentieth century ends it will not be correct to define a school as a place in which self-active interest is checked, originality condemned, and brain development and co-ordination sacrificed to knowledge storing. If anyone claims that such a definition is unfair to the nineteenth century school, let him consider carefully what the condition and character of a man would be if he had been kept in school during the whole of his waking hours till he was twenty-one years of age. It will not always remain true that the race shall receive its brain development and co-ordination and its individual character force chiefly outside of school. The schools of the coming days will not weaken minds by the processes of storing them.

The power of problem discovery is much more useful than the power of problem solution, both to the individual and the race. Problem discovery is much more educative than problem solution.

The child now comes to school from its sphere of independence in problem finding, and is at once set to work at problem solving alone. In every subject the teacher brings the questions and assigns the lessons. The essential unity between insight and accomplishment, between discovery and achievement, between originating and operating, between self-active interest and executive power, between seeing and doing, between problem recognition and problem explanation, is destroyed. The teacher does the important part of the work. The vital and interest producing part of the process of learning is not performed by the child, and so its interest is inevitably weakened. Day by day it becomes less interested, less positive and more negative. Its nature adapts itself to its new conditions. Its function in school is to solve problems and answer questions, and it soon learns to wait for its problems and questions.

By such teaching the child is made dependent on the teacher in the most essential department of its intellectual power. Every man should be a discoverer within his own sphere. Every man would possess independent power of discovery if his natural wonder power had been developed properly.

The race creeps where it should soar, because the child's natural power to discover new problems is not developed. The wonder power of childhood which Mr. McChoakumchild proposed to destroy is the source of greatest intellectual and spiritual evolution. We fail to reach our best individual growth and our highest fitness for aiding our fellows in their upward progress on account of our intellectual and spiritual blindness. We are surrounded by material problems, intellectual problems and spiritual problems which are never revealed to us, but which we might see and solve if our discovery power had been developed in the schools as assiduously as our mind storing was carried on. Greater power of problem discovery will lead to increased power of problem solution and larger capacity and desire for mind storing.

4. Teachers will distinguish clearly between responsive activity and self-activity, between expression and self-expression in the twentieth century school. The neglect of selfhood and the warping of selfhood have been the greatest evils of school life in the past. Self-activity includes the motive as well as the activity. It must be originative as well as operative or selfhood is not developed. Even kindergartners often fail to see the full meaning of Froebel's fundamental process of human growth, self-activity. The highest ideal of executive development given by any other educator is co-operative, productive activity on the part of each individual. Froebel's ideal is co-operative, productive, *creative* activity.

Each individual has three elements of power—originative power, directive power and executive power: responsive activity does not demand the exercise of originative power at all, and develops directive power imperfectly. The central element of selfhood is originative power. A man's originative power constitutes his individuality. Originative power develops as all other powers develop, by full opportunity for free exercise. Froebel made self-activity the fundamental law of growth with the purpose of developing the complete selfhood of each individual. Unless the self of the individual is active, the development is partial and defective in its most important element. There are yet few school processes or methods that demand true self-activity. True self-activity includes the motive that impels to action as well as the resulting act. In every study, and especially in every operative study, the originative and directive powers should act with the operative powers. Education is defective in its most vital part if originative power is not developed.

One of the commonest fallacies in the list of educational theories is "expression leads to self-expression." Expression and self-expression are the results of two widely different intellectual operations. Self and expression should never be divorced. Expressive power has been trained, so far as it has been trained at all, independently. It has not been related to the selfhood of the child. The theory has been: train the power of expression and the selfhood will in due time develop and be able to use the power of expression we have so thoughtfully provided for it. The amazing stupidity of this course has begun to reveal itself. To some the revelation of the folly of training expressive power and neglecting the selfhood that is to use it came with such force that it led them to the other extreme, and they have propounded the maxim, "Develop the selfhood and expression will take care of itself." This theory is infinitely nearer the truth than the old one—the one still practised almost universally. It is true that clear strong thoughts never lack expression. Henry Irving was right when he said, "If you are true to your individuality, and have great original thoughts, they will find their way to the hearts of others as surely as the upland waters burst their way to the sea." But it is also true that the schools should cultivate the powers of expression, and add as many new powers as possible. Every form of expression should be developed to its best limit by the schools; expression in visible form by construction, modelling, painting, drawing and writing, and expression of speech and music should receive fullest culture in the schools. To add new power of expression opens wider avenues for the expression of selfhood, and thereby makes a greater selfhood possible. The supreme folly of teaching has been to attempt to cultivate the powers of expression and neglect the selfhood that has to use them. It is not wise in correcting this mistake to make another, by leaving developed selfhood without the best possible equipment of expressive power. Self and expression cannot be divorced without weakening both of them.

The revelation of the utter folly of training the powers of expression and neglecting to train the selfhood at the same time has been almost entirely confined, however, to the forms of visible expression. There are many good schools in which writing, drawing and other forms of visible expression are now used from the first as means of revealing selfhood, to enable the pupil to make his inner life outer, but in which the processes for developing the power of oral expression are still as completely unrelated to selfhood as they were in the darkest days of preceding ages. The processes of culture of the powers of oral expression have undoubtedly improved, but still the dominant principle is the fallacy "expression will lead to self-expression." The schools train in the interpretation and expression of the thoughts of others in the vain hope that to express the thoughts of others in the language of the authors will give power to express orally in good form the original thought of selfhood. There can be no greater fallacy. Actors have more power than any other class to interpret and express the deepest and highest thoughts of the greatest authors, but, although they are accustomed to appearing before large audiences, very few of them have well developed powers of self-expression. Responding to the motives of others does not cultivate our own motive power; allowing the thoughts of others to run through our minds does not make us original thinkers; expressing the thoughts of others does not develop the power of self-expression.

Self-expression is infinitely more productive than expression both in acquiring knowledge and in developing power. The effort of self-expression defines the emotions, sentiments or thoughts, and language forms an objective representation or body for them. The inner life is co-ordinated and classified, emotion and thought are related, and propulsive power is developed by the process of conscious self-expression in any form—language, music, drawing, modelling or construction. The aroused inner life is worse than wasted if it finds no means for expressing itself in outward form. It leaves in the mind a record for indistinctness and confusion and a habit of inertness, of conceiving without bringing forth, of planning without producing.

Expression in which there is no selfhood leads to enfeeblement of character. The more fully expression is self-revelation the more it develops selfhood, and the more it defines and classifies knowledge.

Self-activity arouses the only perfect interest and attention; it makes the mind aggressively active in regard to new knowledge, and therefore secures the most thorough apperception; it leads to the most complete correlation of the subjects of study; it develops selfhood, and reveals it to both teacher and pupil; it encourages self-faith and self-reverence by giving a consciousness of original creative power; it makes productive work an expression of joyous gratitude; it is the elemental law of human growth.

5. Teachers will aim to develop distinct individuality in the twentieth century school. The schools have definitely aimed to make the children as much alike as possible. They should really be made as unlike as possible, so far as the freeing of their individuality from constraint tends to make them unlike. All true harmony results from the unity of dissimilarity. No two trees or flowers are exactly alike. It would be a pity to have them so. The higher the organization the greater the capacity for variation. Men should see truth from different standpoints, and transform insight into attainment with widely varied powers. Each new view of truth, when revealed by an undwarfed individuality, gives new form or tone to revealed truth. The schools have made mixed characters, part child and part teacher. They have developed self-consciousness which is paralyzing, instead of selfhood which is strengthening and invigorating. Very few children are allowed to be their real selves and "live their souls straight out." Men have dreaded the depravity of the child so much that its divinity has not been allowed to grow. In attempting to restrict depravity the light of the divinity in the child has been shadowed, and lives of gloom and stagnation have resulted instead of lives of brightness and advancement.

The individuality of the child is the divinity in it, the element whose development should do most for the child and the world. The highest duty of the school is to develop the conscious personality of the child Real personality must be an element of strength. It should be the centre of a man's character. It should be his contribution to the general character of the race. Millions fail in life because they are never clearly conscious of their own personal power. Every individual failure retards the race. This is the true basis for the value of individuality. The revelation of the strength of self-hood as an element in the general strength of humanity leads to true self-reverence and self-faith. A man who has self-reverence and self-faith rarely fails. He uses the intellectual power he possesses. A man with moderate intellectual powers and well developed self-faith usually accomplishes more for himself and humanity than the man who has great intellectual power but little self-faith. It is not possible to give all children great intellectual power, but it is possible for the school to make each child as it grows to maturity conscious of its own highest power, and to give it faith in itself because of its consciousness of that power.

True self-reverence and self-faith are the opposites to vanity and conceit. Self-reverence and self-faith are strengthening and ennobling. They are the elements in character that lead men to do and dare and struggle hopefully. He who is sure he cannot succeed has already failed. He who has a reverent consciousness of power in his own personality, and has gained the faith that springs from this consciousness, succeeds always. He does not wait for opportunities, he creates them; he is not forced to act by circumstances, but moulds circumstances and conditions.

So long as a child or man lacks respect for the product of his own best effort, his power does not increase rapidly even by use. Self depreciation may neutralize the beneficent influence of activity or exercise of function. Faith in one's own power strong enough to lead to its use, and respect for the product of effort honestly made, give every conscious effort a widening and strengthening influence on character. Therefore the development of individuality should be one of the main purposes of every teacher.

The growth of individual inner life by originative and directive self activity is a vital law in education. Whatever there is of duty, of purity, of holy aspiration in the child's soul should be helped to grow. Soul-growth must be from within. Emerson was right in saying: "Though we travel the world over to find the beautiful, we must carry it with us or we find it not."

6. The schools of the twentieth century will give increased attention to physical culture, to arrest the physical deterioration of the race, and to strengthen it intellectually and physically. Play will become a definite element in human development throughout the entire course of school training, especially in cities and towns. It will some day be possible to find children of the fifth generation reared in a city.

One of the most necessary improvements in scholastic work is a recognition of the urgent need of bodily training. It is beginning to receive recognition in many schools and some universities, but the recognition so far given is more negative than positive. The body should receive definite, systematic training, because it is the executive agent of the mind; because energetic and sustained mental action depends on the support of healthy, well developed vital organs; because good health is essential to the highest success in the business of life; and because the bodily activities directly influence the development and organization of the brain and the rest of the neurological system. The body deserves recognition as a part of the inter-related, independent unity, man. A man cannot be considered properly educated so long as any part of his nature is undeveloped or untrained. No one department of human power can be educated at the expense of another department without injury to the organic whole. This is a fundamental principle which has so far received only partial recognition When it is fully understood, physical culture will be more universally adopted as an essential part of scholastic training, and physical development will be taken into consideration in awarding graduation diplomas and degrees. The word scholastic will yet have a wider meaning which will include the development of the physical nature as well as the storing of the mind. The schools and universities will soon break the bonds of mediævalism and extend the meaning of terms that have limited the range of the vision of educators for centuries. No definition of education now limits its meaning to mind storing, or to mind storing with power to reproduce at examinations what is in the mind: but the schools in giving diplomas, and the universities in granting degrees still act in conformity with this narrowest of all definitions of education. If, on the staff of a university there were one-fifth as many professors to train the bodies of students as there are to develop and store their minds, it would be easy to discover a system of ranking students physically on a basis as absolutely fair and just as that now adopted, in marking them for their intellectual acquirements. In some way every element that has a dominant influence in deciding a student's fitness for a successful and noble life should be considered by the faculty of his school or university in awarding him a diploma or a degree. The full comprehension of the law of unity will make clear the duty of all educators to train the body as the agent, and at the same time the developer, of the mind. Play will soon be recognized as one of the most essential departments of school work because it cultivates the motor brain and co-ordinates the sensor and motor systems better than any other school process; because it is the best school agency for developing energy, force of character, executive power and executive tendency, the habit of transforming insight into achievement, which makes character positive instead of negative; because it is the only complete means of self-expression; because it develops self-hood more thoroughly than any other educational work; because it reveals individual responsibility and the necessity for community of spirit and co-operative effort most effectively; and because it trains pupils to give reverent co-operative submission to law. Children joyously and actively submit to the laws governing the games they play, and in this way respect for law becomes an element in character.

7. The schools of the twentieth century will give manual training a prominent place on the programme of school work; not for economic reasons only, but chiefly for educational reasons: not to teach trades,

not merely to give greater hand skill, but chiefly to develop brain power, to promote brain co-ordination, and to aid in giving humanity a broad, solid, true basis for moral culture.

The educational advantages of manual training may be summarized as follows: It is an excellent kind of physical culture because it provides interesting occupation for the mind as well as the body. It is a great aid in discipline by providing a true centre of interest and a natural outlet for physical energy. It helps to develop the power of concentrating attention. Children soon lose interest in abstractions or in the acquisition of knowledge from books or from their teachers. Even real things lose their interest quickly if they are merely to be examined or studied. They never lose interest if the child is allowed to use them in the execution of its own original plans. It gives definite and applied training to the observant powers. It cultivates the judgment of size, form and relationship of parts to wholes, and thus forms a true basis for mathematical culture. It helps to form clear conceptions. We really know definitely only those things which we have wrought out as well as thought out. It applies knowledge as it is gained, and this is the only perfect way of gaining knowledge clearly and of fixing it in the mind as an available element in mental equipment. It makes pupils creatively constructive instead of destructive. It increases the opportunities for the discovery by the teacher of the special individual power of the pupil, and what is still more important, it helps to reveal the child to itself. It develops habits of accuracy, definiteness, exactness, and these are essential elements in truthfulness and fundamental constituents in character. It cultivates the power of self-expression. In early years the child's most perfect means of self-expression is construction with the sand, clay, stones, sticks, blocks, paper, cardboard, and other material things by which it is surrounded. It enlarges the brain, defines motor power, and co-ordinates the sensor and motor systems. Education is essentially defective at its centre of vital power if it fails to preserve the true harmony of effective development between the receptive and executive parts of the brain. It is a great moral agency. It increases respect for honest labor, and tends to make every man a producer.

8. The schools of the twentieth century will adopt the new ideal of *Nature* study. The old ideal trained children to study Nature in order that they might learn to love it: the *new* ideal will train them to love Nature in order that they may desire to study it. The old ideal destroyed life; the new ideal develops it. The old ideal was classification; the new ideal is *revelation* of life, evolution and God.

The term, "Nature Study," will not truly represent the Nature work of the future. The child's attitude should be reverent friendship, receptive contemplation, stimulating investigation, and sympathetic nurture. Nature is the sacred temple in which the child should have the life and power of God interpreted and revealed.

The prophet-souls of this century have seen the greater ideal, have learned the mystery of Nature's vital symbolism, and have prepared us for grander insights into the meaning of her forces and her processes. Wordsworth, Longfellow and Tennyson made us conscious of the active principle that subsists

> " In all things, in all natures, in the stars
> Of azure heaven, the unenduring clouds,
> In flower and tree, in every pebbly stone
> That paves the brooks, the stationary rocks,
> The moving waters, and the invisible air."

The fact that these advanced leaders of a developing race have had their minds filled with this vital thought indicates that the race itself is nearing the stage in its evolution when it will comprehend the thought, and make it an impelling force in its upward progress.

Froebel recognized the spiritual in the natural more clearly than any other man, and reduced the new ideal to a pedagogical practice by making nature contemplation and nature nurture the agency for fixing in the minds and spiritual natures of children apperceptive centres of life, evolution and God.

Even though the child may not be conscious of the fact, its life is enriched by an intimate acquaintance with Nature as it can be in no other way. Nature is a stimulating atmosphere in which the whole intellectual and spiritual being is invigorated, and through which God makes to the child manifold revelations.

The beauty, the symmetry, the harmony, the life, the freedom, the purity, the majesty, and the invisible forces of Nature fill the young mind with images that elevate and ennoble character. When these pure images are photographed on the sensitive nature of childhood, they can never be eradicated. When the pictures are developed by whatever experiences or circumstances, they are still pure, and help to counterbalance the evil that may come into our lives. "The holy forms of young imagination" help to keep us pure.

School gardening will be a recognized department of school work in cities and towns in the twentieth century. Every child will prepare its own soil in window-garden, roof-garden, or, best of all, in gardens in the school grounds, or in fields kept for school purposes. Germany began this work in Froebel's time. The English Education Department officially recognized it in 1896. All children should be trained to cultivate plants, partly in order to gratify their natural tendency to work in the earth, but mainly to use their interest in productive activity and the nurture of living things, especially plants or pets. Careful culture in the preparation of the soil and its proper enrichment, coupled with due attention to watering, weeding, hoeing, and, if necessary, to pruning, produces plants of grander proportions, greater beauty, and richer fruitfulness. By these results the child not only learns to recognize evolution, but it also sees that *it may become an active agent* in promoting evolution. It gains a conception—at first symbolic, afterward conscious,—of the greatest of all truths—*that it has power to help other life to grow to grander life.* By sowing the apparently dead seed, which afterward bursts into life and beauty, it learns that it has power to start life to grow that without its aid might have remained forever undeveloped. The teacher or parent does not require to point the lesson. The symbolism of the unconscious stage of childhood will naturally become transformed into conscious character in due time. It is impossible to over estimate the advantages of a training that, through the self-activity of a child, reveals to it the two vital truths—that it may aid all life—human life as well as plant life—to reach a higher condition of life, and that it may bring into existence new elements of living power, material power, intellectual power, or spiritual power, to aid in unifying and uplifting the race. The formation of these apperceptive centres in a child's mind qualifies it for the highest education it can ever receive. The life must remain comparatively barren in which these ideals have not been implanted. The time to implant them is the symbolic period of childhood, and the process is the nurture of life in Nature. The phenomena of Nature in their everyday manifestations provide most appropriate symbolism for children. They are thrice blessed whose early life is stimulated and enriched by free life in sympathy with Nature's life.

When a few generations have been trained in Nature love, Nature nurture, and Nature contemplation, humanity will more fully understand Wordsworth's inspired words:

"For I have learned
To look on Nature, not as in the hour
Of thoughtless youth.

"And I have felt
A presence that disturbs me with the joy
Of elevated thoughts ; a sense sublime
Of something far more deeply interfused,
Whose dwelling is the light of setting suns,
And the round ocean, and the living air,
And the blue sky, and in the mind of man :
A motion, and a spirit, that impels
All thinking things, all objects of all thought,
And rolls through all things. Therefore am I still
A lover of the meadows and the woods,
And mountains : and of all that we behold
From this green earth ;

well pleased to recognize
In Nature and the language of the sense
The anchor of my purest thoughts, the nurse,
The guide, the guardian of my heart, and soul
Of all my moral being."

9. The schools of the twentieth century will teach art as the highest form of expression to qualify for clearer interpretation of the artistic ideals of the leaders in human evolution, and to enlarge the expressive power of humanity.

We shall know in the twentieth century that in the culture of so definitely interdependent a unity as the human mind the attempt to train only certain powers and omit the training of others must inevitably result in the partial development even of those powers whose training is attempted ; that the progressive and harmonious evolution of the universal community of man depends on the complete development of the individuals of which it is composed : that the highest test of an educational system is its influence on the expansion and strengthening of the spiritual nature; and that the possibility of man's true unity with God increases as his training becomes more comprehensive and more definite.

The educational advantages of the study of art are many. The following are among the most important :

Art lays the foundation of true manual training, and it is itself the highest department of manual training.

Art endows man with additional power of *expression*. Every new power of expression increases the power of the mind itself. The possibility of mind growth is widened by increasing the powers of expression; first by the stimulation of the mind along new lines of feeling and thought, second by improving the processes by which feeling, thought, and knowledge are defined in the mind and wrought into character.

Art has a directly beneficial influence in the development of the mind by training the observant powers, the judgment and the imagination. It cultivates the powers of observation. Seeing is really an act of the mind.

Art develops *originality*, and qualifies men to aid in the increase of human wisdom and power, and the promotion of human happiness by the production of new thought, new appliances, new forms of beauty, and new conceptions of the æsthetic and spiritual evolution. Those are the highest school processes that do most to develop the child's originality and apply it to lines of utility and æsthetic culture. It is in this way that the sum of human power is increased, its happiness promoted, and the certainty of its progressive evolution established.

Art should be the highest form of *self-expression*, and the most perfect type of true *self-activity*. The teacher should improve the pupil's natural power of artistic representation, transformation and expression, and add as many new powers in each case as she possibly can, but her best work for her pupils is not the improvement of power nor the communication of power. Her work is not complete till she stimulates her pupils to *use* their powers in expressing their *own inner life.*

One of the most important educational advantages of art arises from its usefulness in revealing the child itself. It is an important epoch in the life of a child when it gains an inspiring consciousness of original power. Any form of *self*-expression may be made a means of self-revelation, but no other form exceeds art in the number and value of its opportunities for making clear to a child the transforming truth that it was intended to be *more than an imitator and follower*. The central element in strong character is self-reverence, based on a clear consciousness of power to be used in the interest of the community. Art should form part of the education of every man, that he may be qualified for the enjoyment of the best production of the human mind, and of the majesty, the beauty and the uplifting suggestiveness of Nature; that his life may be enriched with the graces of highest culture; that his sensual nature may be subordinated and his divinity stimulated by ennobling self-activity; that his spiritual nature may become the dominant element in his character: that his complete development may be reached; and that he may be able to recognize his Creator more definitely and enter into communion with Him more fully.

10. The everyday life of the school of the twentieth century will develop in the lives of the children the fundamental elements of true social and religious life, not by theories but by practical experience. The child will be allowed to be independently co-operative in order that it may learn man's greatest lesson, the interdependence of humanity, the basis of absolute harmony between individualism and socialism. The three essential ideals in the organization of a perfect character are love, life and unity. The apperceptive centres for these perfect ideals must be formed by experience, not by theory. In the loving home the child should gain its consciousness of love, from Nature its consciousness of life, and from the re-organized school its consciousness of unity. The supreme aim of education will be the unity of the race and its fullest ethical culture. Individuals will be made as perfect as possible in order that they may become elements in a grander community, and may thus reach their highest destiny, and secure their most complete evolution.

The ethical training of the future will rest on these broad principles: that humanity may develop progressively toward the Divine in conformity with the universal law of evolution; that every child has in its nature an element of divinity which should be fostered and brought into conscious unity with the Divine; that the natural tendency of childhood is toward the right if supplied with right conditions for the growth of its best; that the ideal side of the child's nature should be developed from the moment the baby receives its first impressions to prevent the growth of the sensual in its character; that training should begin at birth, but that it never should interfere with the child's spontaneity; that freedom is the only true condition of perfect growth; that coercion dwarfs and reward-giving as an inducement to good conduct degrades; that positivity or spiritual propulsion is an important element in character; that ethical culture must be given in each stage of development in order that the true growth of succeeding stages may be attained; that it is a grave error to attempt to give the child in any stage of its development ethical training or rules of conduct belonging rightfully to a later stage; that the first germs of religious growth are found in community, love, reverence, filial and fraternal relationships, and true living as revealed by the experiences of pure family life; that Nature is the child's symbolic revealer of God as life in the evolution of life to higher life; that the evil in a child's action results from suppressed or misdirected good; that religion should not be associated with terrors of any kind; that the child's religious experiences should be joyous and happy; that God should be revealed as a loving father; that the child should not be made conscious of evil in its own motives in its early life; that the child's life should be kept free from formalism and hypocrisy; that no dogmatic theology should be given in words until the child has experiences that can give life and meaning to the words; that the child's mind be not filled with meaningless maxims, mere ashes of dead virtues; that selfhood is the child's divinity and its development the great function of the home and the school; that selfhood should be made complete as a basis for the perfect unity with God and humanity; that self-activity is the process of growth morally as well as intellectually; that right-doing not only demonstrates faith but increases it; and that religion cannot be communicated to or taken into the life of man as a completed thing, or by the intellectual acceptance of opinions or doctrines, but that it must be a progressive growth in feeling and thought in which community, love, life, law, reverence, gratitude, joyousness, renunciation, unselfishness, freedom, and creative activity are essential elements.

PROTESTANT EDUCATION IN QUEBEC.

S. P. Robins, M.A., LL.D.
(Principal of McGill Normal School, Montreal).

I cannot adequately express my sense of the honor put upon me by being permitted to take a part in the exercises of this most impressive ceremonial. But any rising feeling of exultation in which I might under other circumstances be tempted to indulge, is effectually checked by many considerations. I am humbled by this audience. There are here so many my equals in age and opportunity who have accomplished so much more than it has been given me to do, that I cannot but wish that at this moment I filled a less conspicuous place. Again, there are many of you here who are just entering on careers of honorable usefulness that will overwhelm with oblivion the feeble results of the lives of the men of my age. I would not, if I could, push before you in your impetuous advance. The ruddy dawn of the twentieth century illuminates your faces, the eager force of youthful ardour is in your lives, not yet spent in conflict, not yet chilled by disappointment; and I, as one of a generation whose lives have lapsed, whose energies are exhausted, whose work is done, who sit close to the edge of the fast descending night, hesitate to obtrude on your notice lest you feel that I am delaying you, keeping you back from your conflicts, from your victories, and from your crowning.

Another thought sobers me; it is this, that I occupy the place assigned to me to-night because I am a survivor. Not all the bravest, not all the best share in the triumph that celebrates a battle won. While those who return from the fight, a shattered remnant, hear the acclaim of the populace, elsewhere the dead march wails and sobs above those who, rather than the living, were the victors. In the early days of this Normal School there were many of us gathered flushed with youth and hope. To-day we are but few worn by years and broken with toil. I address you to-day simply because I am a survivor.

I come to you to-day as one who after long separation returns to the home of his boyhood. My birth and my earliest childhood belong to another land, to the land of the primrose, the daisy and the wild rose; but my youth and my first manhood were formed in what we then called Upper Canada. I was a schoolboy in Peterborough when Peterborough was a small town hewed out of the all embracing forest, when the Peterborough Grammar School was housed in a log school house, nestling among the pines. A little later I was a young school master on the fourth line of Dummer. There I knew the struggles and shared in the privations of the first settlers, when yet in the keen January nights we could hear the long howl of the gathering wolves. Then after a term of teaching not far from Cobourg I drifted, still a mere lad, an insignificant lad, to this Normal School, meeting in the Temperance Hall on Temperance street, and here before my first session was done I was set to teach a part of the class with which I entered, and a little later on was employed in teaching mathematics to the elementary class in the Normal School, during its first session in these newly erected buildings. I have mentioned these things merely to reclaim my kinship with you now long unacknowledged and forgotten. So I leave in the oblivion of the dead past the rest of my career in this Province, which I regard, and shall ever regard, as my Province, my home, the land where all my kindred sleep their long last sleep, father, mother, brother, wife and child, waiting till I come not long hence to lay my weary form beside them.

I must hasten to say that in my earliest manhood, at the recommendation of our late chief, the Rev. Dr. Ryerson, ($\check{\alpha}\nu\alpha\xi\ \dot{\alpha}\nu\delta\rho\tilde{\omega}\nu$), and by the invitation of the widely known and as widely respected, Sir Wm. Dawson, I was called to Montreal to take part in the establishment of the Protestant Normal School of Lower Canada, and for more than forty years I have been intimately associated with the educational development of what is now the Province of Quebec.

Let me introduce you to that Province. You know your own Province well, the lakes which skirt your shore, the greater rivers which form in part your boundary, the green Niagara, the clear swift St. Lawrence, the brown Ottawa, and the smaller rivers which are your own, devastating torrents in the spring floods, brawling brooks losing themselves among the stones in the summer heats. Yours are the rolling farm lands, rising here and there to rounded hills shaped by the wear and tear of ages, out of the sands, the gravels, and the clays deposited upon the Silurian and Devonian rocks that are the ground floor of your Province. But Quebec has larger, bolder features, less fertile farming land, more of mountain and flood. I know not where you shall find a nobler landscape than that over which you look from the summit of Mount Royal, where the eye sweeps the vast plain watered by the Richelieu and the Yamaska and bounded by the more hilly countries from which the St Francis draws its waters, and over which peep the Adirondacks the Green Mountains and even the highest peaks of the Presidential Range in the White Mountains. Perhaps you would prefer the wilder outlook from the Terrace in Quebec where, over the quaint old city at your feet, you look far down the valley of the St. Lawrence, shut in between the heights of Levis and Cape Diamond, away beyond the Island of Orleans, the Valley of the St. Charles and the Falls of Montmorency, to the blue distance of the Laurentian Hills, intractable and sterile, oldest land on this continent. Rivers,—what glorious rivers, rolling cool and unfailing through the summer greenery, the broad Richelieu, the picturesque St. Francis, the lone St. Maurice, the wild Saguenay, the Cascapedia beloved by salmon. Mountains—some rising solitary like Mount Royal, Mt. Johnson, Belœil, some outliers of the great ranges south of us, some like the Shickshock Mountains and the Laurentian Range, defining for hundreds of miles the outlines of a continent. A land worthy to be loved, a land loved by those who sing "O Canada mon pays" with a fervour, so far as I know, unknown among the less enthusiastic dwellers in Ontario.

Let me introduce the people. There dwell in Quebec representatives of all races. There are U. E. Loyalists who, painfully toiling through the untrodden forests, settled in the hill country which we call the Eastern townships: disbanded soldiers, who, after the conquest, settled on the shores of the Bay of Chaleur and elsewhere; fur traders largely of Scotch origin who retired to Montreal after they had spent their strength in the service of the North West and the Hudson's Bay companies, immigrants from the British Isles, English, Scotch, Irish and Welsh, but the great mass of the population, a mass so great as to be almost unaffected by the characteristics of the strangers, are of French origin, "les habitants" as distinguished from "les intrus," the inhabitants as opposed to "the intruders." Of a population of almost 1,500,000 nearly 1,200,000 are French Canadians and all other nationalities are but little more than 300,000 in number; nearly 1,300,000 are Roman Catholics and scarcely 200,000 are Protestants. This people then, French in origin and language, Roman Catholic in religion, the most homogeneous population in the New World, the most devotedly Catholic people on earth, cannot be ignored by you. Questions of the most serious import rise as you look eastward. What is the manner of thought and of life of this member of the Confederation which contributes five persons out of every sixteen to the population of the Dominion : who, separated from others, but united among themselves, by the loving use of the beautiful French language, move in all educational, social, religious. and political questions with a united force that cannot be paralleled among our English speaking population; who are allied by their faith to 720,000 Roman Catholics of other Provinces : and who, being the first civilized inhabitants of this land, seized in the beginning and still firmly hold the outlet of the whole Dominion, striding across the Gulf of the St. Lawrence and possessing the wealthy and populous commercial metropolis of the Dominion?

This people live for the most part in a calm patriarchal simplicity that is unknown elsewhere on this restless continent. Frugal, thrifty, shrewd, gay, polite sons of the soil, they marry early, have very large families, are content with little, are cheerful in adversity, joyous in prosperity, live long and die resignedly. It will not be wise of you, because they now sit in quietness and obscurity under the easy rule of their priesthood, to underrate their strength or to undervalue their many excellent qualities. They have a capacity for being led, an unquestioning loyalty to competent leaders, to leaders who can reach their springs of action, which in many times of storm and stress have great advantages over the less easily organized individualism of men of the Germanic races.

I was asked to say a few words about the education of the people of Quebec. I did not think the time opportune nor my own abilities adequate for the discussion of a theme so large ; but I have consented to tell you something of the manner in which the education of one-seventh of the population is conducted, that part of the population which shows at some disadvantage beside the majority, less brilliant in social qualities, but solid, stern, tenacious, men of affairs, masters of business, Protestants in religion.

Two great educational problems are being solved in our Province ; and I do not think I overestimate the importance of the issues, when I say that they are worth the serious attention not merely of the provinces of the Dominion, but of the whole continent. One problem is this : " What will be the result of handing over a whole people, gifted with the highest qualities of the intellect, to the unquestioned educational control of a wealthy, powerful, perfectly organized and profoundly venerated priesthood"? The answer is not yet complete. But as far as it is wrought out, one result is that in our province we have 800,000 persons who can read and write, 100,000 persons who can read but not write, 600,000 persons who can neither read nor write, including under the last number 332 000 children under ten years of age. Another result is that over a large part, the larger part, of Quebec all disputation is hushed. No question of faith, morals or philosophy is ever raised. Doctrines are taught, they are not argued. The public mind is at rest. Some unappreciative persons say it is stagnant. Certain it is that over a vast extent of territory no one aims at, no one desires, change ; and religious belief and social practice have reached a uniformity, I think hitherto unexampled in the history of our times. The disturbing, unsettling influence of books and newspapers has been most successfully eliminated. As their fathers lived and died, so exactly live and die one million French Canadians.

The second problem, the one that more nearly concerns us at this time is, " With what degree of success can one-seventh of the people educate their children in separate, or as we call them in Quebec, dissentient schools ?" Will the struggle to maintain such schools in face of the overt or the covert hostility of an antagonistic majority be too severe ? Will the pecuniary sacrifices involved be continuously borne? Can the schools continue to be efficient ? In giving partial replies to these questions I must premise :

1st. That in the main the legal provisions under which dissentient schools are established are characterized by a fairness that merits approval. The spirit of the enactments may be thus summarized. Let Protestants be free to establish, with their own money, schools of their own, withdrawing entirely from Roman Catholic schools ; but let it be impossible for Roman Catholics to escape the cost of maintaining Roman Catholic schools and difficult to send their children to Protestant schools. You would not thank me to detail the provisions under which the thing is done ; but I may say that if the schools of a municipality be under Roman Catholic control any number of Protestants may unite to form a school, and club their school taxes for the purpose, or may similarly unite with other Protestant residents in a neighboring municipality, or may annex themselves to a neighboring Protestant municipality. So far is this liberty extended that an isolated Protestant may pay his taxes to support a Protestant school to which he sends his children, provided that the school be not more than three miles from his residence. You sometimes hear a great outcry on the part of Protestants, who accuse their Roman Catholic neighbors of grave injustices. The fault is usually not in the law, but in the neglect of those who complain, to maintain an attitude of sleepless vigilance, without which no liberties can be maintained. I deny that there is general intentional injustice. There may be, there doubtless are, cases in which the attempt is made to take advantage of the law by trickery, by concealment, and by misrepresentation, but such acts of bad faith are individual or local, and are not more frequent or conspicuous in school affairs than in other kinds of business, for honesty is not a universal virtue.

2nd. It is to be remarked that disputes over school matters between Roman Catholics and Protestants are in the nature of things possible only in a limited area. There are no longer, as thirty years ago there were, parts of the province distinctly Protestant. There are a few predominatingly Protestant. The counties of Argenteuil and Pontiac on the Ottawa River, and of Huntingdon, Brome and Stanstead along the line of 45°, have more Protestant than Roman Catholic pupils in elementary schools. But in nineteen counties there is not a single Protestant school; and in thirteen of these not a single Protestant pupil is reported attending school. In the remaining six counties there are in all nineteen Protestant pupils reported as attending Roman Catholic schools. Indeed, in the sixty-three counties of Quebec, there are only nineteen that have as many as 125 pupils enrolled in Protestant schools. The cleavage between the two systems of public schools is most distinct. To the east of the island of Montreal, north of the St. Lawrence, or abutting on the same river to the south, are twenty-seven counties, in fourteen of these there is not a single Protestant school; and only six Protestants are reported as attending Roman Catholic Schools. In the remaining thirteen counties, Quebec city is excluded, there are 1,559 pupils enrolled in Protestant elementary schools, and thirty-six Protestants in Roman Catholic elementary schools. How much of scattering of the Protestant population is implied, and how difficult it is to maintain schools, is illustrated by the statement that in seven other counties not included in the above list, in all forty-three elementary schools are maintained, in which the total daily attendance is 474 pupils, an average of eleven pupils in each school.

How hard it must be to maintain schools at all under such circumstances you can perhaps conceive. Yet how determined Protestants are to maintain schools, independent of ecclesiastical control is evidenced by the fact that while 33,500 Protestant children are enrolled in Protestant schools, less than 1,500, not quite one in twenty-three, are enrolled in Roman Catholic schools ; a number more than set off by the fact that nearly 2,900 Roman Catholic pupils are enrolled in Protestant schools.

The struggle to maintain schools for a small part of the population, scattered among a great majority, alien in faith and in language, is undoubtedly severe. Schools are small, are remote from each other, can pay but small salaries, too often cannot afford trained teachers, and are not seldom ill equipped, although the rate of taxation imposed is, in many instances, very heavy. Yet under circumstances so adverse, I am proud to report to you that your compatriots in the east have not lost their love of knowledge, nor abated a jot of their high courage. They are determined, cost what it may, that their children shall go out into life armed with every educational weapon that the utmost sacrifice can purchase.

Amid difficulties such as you can only dimly perceive, the Protestants of Quebec, 200,000 in number, less perhaps than the population of this enterprising city, last year maintained two universities, three affiliated colleges, one Normal School, 27 Academies and High Schools, 918 Elementary and Independent Schools. In the several faculties of McGill and Bishop's Universities, 1,239 undergraduates and partial students were enrolled. In the affiliated colleges there were 29 students in Arts ; and it is to be observed that the numbers I give do not include Theological students in the Diocesan College, the Presbyterian Theological College or the Congregational Theological College. In the McGill Normal School, 191 adults attended its several courses of study. Academies and High Schools gathered in 4,694 pupils : Model Schools, 3,679 : and Elementary Schools, 27,939. If deduction be made of Roman Catholic pupils and of the persons not resident in Quebec, there will still be a total of not less than 35,000 Protestants in Protestant educational institutions ; in other words $17\frac{1}{2}$ per cent. of the total Protestant population were enrolled in Protestant Schools in the year 1896. We are a struggling people ; we are not a degenerate people. We shall give a good account of ourselves.

What is to be the outcome ? A Protestant gentleman who has taken a very active part in public affairs, an M.P.P. of Quebec, said not a week ago, " In thirty years Protestant schools will be extinct in the Province of Quebec." I think he overrates the extent of the deluge, and understates the time necessary to bring it about. But, unless there be some great and as yet unheralded upheaval in French Canadian Society, the middle of the coming century will see the Protestant population of Quebec reduced to commercial colonies in Montreal and Sherbrooke, if, indeed, the latter colony shall then survive. For there is in daily, hourly operation an economic force unlike anything known in other Provinces of the Dominion, which closing with irresistible constriction upon Protestants in rural districts of Quebec extrudes them from the farming lands : fairly, honestly, slowly, but with the massive movement of omnipotent fate. This is the necessary consequence of the " dime." In Quebec all lands owned by Roman Catholic farmers must pay to the curé of the parish each twenty-sixth bushel of grain delivered in the incumbent's barn. Long ago the law decided that for this purpose potatoes are grain, and a recent pronouncement of the courts has declared hay to be in the same sense grain. Some lawyers hold that the lands of the Eastern townships sold in free and common socage are not liable to this impost; but our Canadian courts have decided that they are, and the issue has never been raised before the Privy Council.

The state of the case being as presented, you see the inevitable result. When lands held by Protestants are for sale, the church of Rome can always find money for a Roman Catholic purchaser, who is ready to pay, as you and I would do, a reasonable interest on the money advanced, but who, having purchased, must pay besides, the "dime," and become subject to legal taxation by the Fabrique, whenever it deems it desirable to add another to the magnificent temples of worship that stud the landscape. Roman Catholic farms are not for sale to Protestants, Protestant farms are being daily transferred to Roman Catholic ownership. Is it unaccountable that section after section has, within the last forty years that I have intimately known Quebec, changed its aspect; that Protestant schools have been closed and that Protestant churches are mouldering down amid their deserted graves and broken tombstones? Morituri vos salutamus.

The severity of the struggle has not been wholly harmful to us. He who fences continually with the bare point, if he survive at all, acquires a keenness of eye, an alertness of movement, a quickness of parry and return, that he who is opposed only to the button-guarded point will never learn: for the former fences with death, the latter only with amusing discomfiture. The consciousness that in every movement of the local political chess-board we put our all at hazard, has developed in us a wariness and strategy that have been of inestimable value in the conservation of our rights and privileges. And as blessings brighten as they take their flight, so our treasures are enhanced in value when they are endangered—I doubt that you who hold securely the priceless blessings of free schools, schools governed by the people for the people, cherish them with the passionate love and devotion that we, the Protestants of Quebec, entertain for our schools, maintained with difficulty, threatened with extinction. Pardon me if I say that we have one advantage over you that only the truly cultured educator can adequately value. We are, and we must be, a bilingual people. We must use two languages, and no man can adequately know a single language. He who studies a second language, by comparison and contrast knows the first better. And, when I speak of knowing a second language, I do not mean in the imperfect way in which some of us know Latin and Greek, having acquired the ability slowly and labouriously to spell out by the aid of lexicon and grammar the meaning of some passage in a classic author, but to know so that we can use to flash thought from mind to mind, and, what is still more difficult, to stir as we will the founts of pure, high, noble feeling—to know it as Sir Wilfrid Laurier and Sir Adolphe Chapleau know English. He that has so learned another language has added the excellencies of another national habit of intellect and emotion to that which he acquired in infancy with his mother tongue. Such advantages will thousands of your compatriots derive from their association with the gay, the keen, the brave descendants of sunny France, and from the mastery of their bright, clear, picturesque speech. One result of the complete severance between Protestant and Roman Catholic education, I confess I contemplate with misgiving, although some of my co-religionists are apt to be elated by it. Speaking in general terms, one-fourth of the inhabitants of the city of Montreal are Protestants ; they own one-half of the real estate of the city ; they pay one-half of the civic taxes. So they pay and receive one-half of the city school tax. For every Protestant child in the city of Montreal, three times as large an educational subsidy is available as for each Roman Catholic child. I do not think too much is spent on the education of Protestant children, but I fear too little is done for Roman Catholic children. Of course the whole island of Montreal was given to the St. Sulpicians in order, amongst other things, that they might provide for the education of the people ; and very much has been done by the teaching fraternities and sisterhoods of Rome to meet the educational needs of the children of her faith ; but if the result of insufficient public provision for the education of one part of the population of a great city shall be to separate the people into two classes of divergent faith, the one few in numbers, highly educated, wealthy, aristocratic in feeling, the other numerous, ignorant, poor, the prey of demagogues, continually chafing under a sense of disability, if not of wrong, I for one tremble for the result. Were I one of the unfortunate class, I should feel it to be of the instinct of self preservation, if not moved thereto by Christian charity, to see that the masses received an education commensurate to their needs. And, if this must be through the church of Rome, then through the church of Rome ; for to my mind it is infinitely better to teach a child the catechism, whether it have a Tridentine, or a Genevan, or an Anglican, or a Methodist flavour, if with it I teach him to read, to write and to cipher, than to leave him to grow up in barbarous ignorance. You may not agree with me ; but I think a bigot or a heretic better than a brute.

  I must close. I have already quoted the pathetic greeting of the Roman gladiators as they cast their last looks on sun and sky and crowding eager human faces. Methinks I had better quote it for myself. I see before me so many faces of the young, beaming with hope, kindled with aspiration. And I, I am not one of you ; I am one of these few old men, bent with years, broken with toil, baffled and beaten down. Moriturus vos saluto. About to perish, I hail you. To you, the happy days I shall not see; to you, the tasks I could not accomplish ; to you, the triumphs I shall not share ; moriturus vos saluto. Yet do I comfort myself by the reflection that with a fulness of meaning Horace never knew I can say " non omnis moriar." I shall not altogether perish. Friends and companions of my youth, our lives have not been lost. But for our efforts in the days of feeble beginnings these grand results in which the present generation so justly prides itself would not have been possible. No one of us was indispensable. If some of us had been utter failures, we should not have been missed in the final result. But altogether we accomplished that which prepared for what has followed. Had we not spent ourselves in laying foundations, buried out of sight, the men who are now building the fair superstructure would have had the work to do which we had neglected, and human progress would have been one generation late. Moriturus vos saluto. Non omnis moriar.

WHERE DO WE STAND EDUCATIONALLY, AS COMPARED WITH FIFTY YEARS AGO.

John Herbert Sangster, M.A., M.D.
(Second Principal of the Normal School).

Where do we stand, educationally, as compared with fifty years ago? This is altogether too large an order to be filled in the allotted time. Fortunately, the higher or university aspects of the question may be eliminated, as not directly bearing on the occasion we are here to celebrate. But, even restricting myself to a comparison of the elementary schools and teaching of the present with those of fifty years ago—the best view I can possibly offer you within the prescribed space of twenty minutes must, necessarily, be of a very cursory and incomplete character.

Fifty years ago the youth of our fair Province were not overburdened with educational privileges. Upper Canada College, and a few widely scattered Grammar Schools, afforded moderate educational opportunities to children of the favored class, but the Common Schools, even in cities and towns were, in most instances, so mean in appearance and so wretched in character and in appointments, and so barren of useful results, that private schools of a scarcely higher grade were patronized by all save the miserably poor. Methods of teaching resolved themselves into hap-hazard or the rule of thumb, and in school government moral suasion was, as yet, unknown. Robust or muscular pedagogy was then much in vogue, and children at school were accustomed to take their daily canings, almost as much as a matter of course, and, as regularly, as they took their daily meals. Nor were the teachers, as a rule, at all fastidious as to the instruments of punishment used. In western Toronto there still linger awful legends of a public school teacher of that period, who was much in the habit of employing his wooden arm, both as a switch for the unruly and as a pedagogic persuader, wherewith to hammer the three R's into unreceptive scholars —preferably addressing his striking appeals to the head, as being the shortest cut to the intelligence. And the legends in question, no doubt somewhat exaggerated, relate to breezes that occasionally arose, when the iron hook at the end of the artificial limb by misadventure, knocked out a few teeth, or broke a nose, or scraped off an ear, or put out an eye. In rural sections things were quite as bad or worse. The teachers were practically uncertificated, and almost universally incompetent. The schools were generally mere log shanties, uninclosed, and without appurtenances of any kind, destitute even of furniture save that of the rudest and most primitive description, while the whole text-book outfit of an entire school would, not frequently, consist of a few Testaments, a Gough or a Walkinghame's Arithmetic, and a Mavor's Spelling Book. Haply, if the school were above the ordinary run, or had any special claim of literary excellence, a chance copy of Fox's Book of Martyrs, or of the Spectator or of Baldwin's Pantheon, might be found in use in the highest reading class—the single book passing in succession to each reader, and the long words being skipped as equally unpronounceable by teacher and taught. This may sound like romance, but I am speaking from experience. True, that experience was limited to the only two country schools it was my good or evil hap to attend in my boyhood, but, as these were both in the even then well settled township of Whitchurch—a part of the now wealthy and enlightened Inspectorate of my friend Mr. Fotheringham, they may I presume, be accepted as fair samples of the schools at that time existing. Of these, one was taught or rather presided over, by a rollicking old sailor, whose strength lay in his frequent and picturesque use of nautical phrases, and whose weakness consisted in his too great devotion to whiskey, profanity and tobacco. The other was conducted by Tom Kelly—a large-hearted little cripple from "across the say," who was a cobbler by trade and a teacher by profession, and who carried on both occupations simultaneously in the school room. He would half-sole a pair of boots while hearing a class read, and would put a neat patch on a shoe while giving out a column of spelling. Poor Kelly was afflicted with some "throuble in his vitals," for which he had to freely take "doctor's stuff," which he procured from a little brown jug locked up in his desk. Every now and then when his "vitals" were unusually bad, he had to unlock the desk so frequently and take so much of the "doctor's stuff" that the little brown jug would give out, and then our teacher would become "spachless and all sthruck of a hape," and in that state we would have to carry him home and put him to bed. Such were not unfrequently the school experiences of fifty years ago. Teachers and schools of higher repute were to be found, but they were exceptions to the rule. Indeed, no words of mine can convey a more vivid portraiture of the literary and social status of the public school teachers of that day, than is incidentally and very unintentionally afforded by a single paragraph of the formal protest then made by the Gore District Council against the Chief Superintendent's project for establishing a Normal School for the training and better education of teachers. That important public body protested against the expenditure of public moneys for the support of a Normal School, on the ground that the scheme would prove inoperative, since (giving the words as nearly as I can recollect them) "For its supply of common school teachers, Upper Canada will have to depend in the future as it has done in the past, upon discharged soldiers, and those who, from physical or other disability, are unable to gain a livelihood by any other means."

It belongs not to me to dwell upon the revolution in educational affairs which followed the opening of the Normal School, or upon the admirable work done by its early as well as by its later graduates. Myself an ex-normalite of that period, and otherwise intimately related to our graduates as a body, I can scarcely hope to be accepted as an impartial witness in their behalf. That they did grand mission work is, however, conceded by all. They were the zealous and faithful apostles of the newer educational *régime*. Wherever they secured a footing in the land, they became the exemplars of higher educational aims, and of better educational results, and the unwearied advocates of a larger educational liberality. If, during the earlier years of the half century, success does not seem to have followed so closely on the heels of effort as at present, let us remember that teachers, then, had to contend with difficulties which, happily, no longer exist. Expansion of school curriculum and improvement in school technique were, naturally, then, of slow growth, since, among self-governed people, such as ours, all movement in that direction is, measurably, dependent on a developed public opinion for its support. Our early graduates builded as they were able, did the best it was possible to do with their materials and their opportunities. Perhaps their most arduous and most effective work was done quite outside the range of school routine. They had to preach and make possible the gospel of a free education to all. They had to succeed in the face of some active and of much passive opposition. They had to move the multitude, had to overcome the *vis inertiae* of the masses. They had to break down the prejudices of the people. They had to proselytize those with whom they came in contact. They had to energize the trustees and to relax their too tightly drawn corporate purse strings. They were met everywhere with the obstructionists' cry *cui bono*. They had to bear, with whatever of equanimity they could command, not only the malevolent criticisms of the ill-disposed, but with the fussy and ignorant interference of pretentious friends, and especially of those in authority. When, forty years ago, I ventured to devote an occasional hour to entomological and botanical excursions, with my classes, along the Hamilton mountain side, a kindly intentioned and influential member of the Board remonstrated with me against what he feared would be regarded as a very sinful waste of valuable time on pure frivolous pursuits—adding that, in his opinion, if such things had to be learned at all, it should be from proper text books. Then, and there, I was so strongly placed in my position that I could and I did persist in my methods of teaching these subjects, but, I was, in that respect, exceptionally fortunate. I am quite sure that, in most places, a teacher who then presumed to send or take his classes afield, on botanical rambles in search of plants and flowers, such rambles as are now prescribed by the regulations, and organized in every school, would have been looked upon as an educational crank, if not as an educational lunatic, and would, in all probability, have been summarily dismissed by his irate trustees as being too lazy himself to look up *garden sass* for his own dinner, or posies for his own button hole. Each succeeding year, however, witnessed an improvement in the sentiments of the community on matters relating to Public Schools, and, by degrees, the trials and annoyances of Normal School graduates became proportionately less grievous to bear. Let us, however, with kindling emotions, and with grateful appreciation, remember the pioneers of our brotherhood—the devoted men and women who, with unflagging zeal, and with conspicuous intelligence, cleared the way for the better things now within the teacher's reach. In an humble way they each and all left their impress for good on their day and generation. Many of them were sooner or later won to other, but, not to higher pursuits, and, whether they embraced law, medicine or divinity, or entered into mercantile or other departments of business life, or devoted themselves to literature or to art, to agriculture or to politics, I am proud to know that they, almost invariably, climbed high, and left the mark of good work and notable achievement on their chosen vocations. Some died in harness, teaching, to the end, still, alas! living not long enough to see, otherwise than by the eye of faith, the assured dawn of the brighter educational day, in the rosy glow of whose yet early morning hours, we are, here, now, assembled. But although the lowly log or frame school houses, sanctified by their hopes and fears, their joys and sorrows, their struggles and their triumphs, their patient labors and their ill-requited toil, may have now given place to costly brick or stone temples dedicated to learning; and, although the effacing finger of time—the weight of revolving years, may have already flattened the mounds over their unmarked graves, let us not, on this auspicious occasion, forget them, or refuse to recognize their claims, or neglect to pay tribute to their faithful well-doing, in the day of smaller possibilities in which their lots were cast.

Nor may we, even in this cursory glance at the work and influence of the Normal School in its earlier life, omit all reference to the revered father of the Public School system of Ontario. Dr. Ryerson laid and established the shapely and solid foundations on which the present Minister of Education is so wisely and so acceptably continuing to build—modelling and erecting and perfecting his particular storey of that noble superstructure, which must increasingly become the pride and the glory of the people. This institution was not only the first fruits and the most admirable outcome of Dr. Ryerson's enlightened policy—it was ever the cherished object of his solicitude and love. Here, therefore, within these rooms, wherein the unseen shade of his gracious presence, and the silent echoes of his much loved voice may be said yet to linger, let his memory be kept forever green. His life was an inspiration and a quickening spur to those who were privileged to associate with him, and to know him well, and to them, and to thousands upon thousands of his grateful fellow countrymen, his name will always remain the synonym of fervid patriotism, and of executive wisdom and power, and of large hearted humanity, and of Canadian manhood, and of Christian gifts and graces. Nationally, we are quite too close to him as yet to clearly perceive the grandeur and loftiness of his public personality. The future will esteem him much more highly than the present, will regard him as unquestionably the greatest Canadian of the century, and will accord him such lasting honors that, long after the bronze effigy of his person which ornaments these grounds, shall have crumbled into the dust of the ages, his name and the grand results of his life work shall still endure. Peace to his ashes! May our Canadian youth never cease to emulate his virtues, or to strive to attain to the measure of his glorious individuality.

To a brief statement of my impressions regarding some of the educational aspects of the present, I proceed with much diffidence. For twenty-five years past, my attention has been engrossed by my present pursuits —my energies have been devoted to the daily routine of medical reading and medical practice. During all those years I have found but little leisure in which to keep myself familiar with the trend of modern educational thought, or with the everchanging phases of modern educational development and technique. Hence, to-day, in the presence of an audience, composed largely or wholly of those hot from the educational work-shops or the educational directorate of the land, I am oppressed with feelings nearly akin to those which perplex a traveller, who, grown grey in foreign climes, has just returned to his own—his native land, and is there confronted with changes and evolutions and developments which almost amount to revolution. His once well-known land marks are set back or swept away. His trusted standards of comparison are superseded by newer ideals or by larger actualities. Even the modes of thought, and turns of expression, and fashions of speech, erst in use, have become so altered that his own vernacular now strangely halts upon his unaccustomed tongue. And thus, standing among once familiar surroundings, where, haply, in the past, he was wont to speak *ex cathedra*, he is now weighted with a strange and a mortifying consciousness of inaptitude and uncertainty, which prompt him to be wisely silent. And yet, Sir, on this occasion, and, in this presence, I feel that silence on my part might be misconstrued. I bow to the inevitable, and am quite content to be regarded as an old young man, or, if you so prefer it, as a young old man; but I am not content to be regarded as having yet arrived at that stage of senility, when a man becomes all retrospect, and is no longer anything better than what Horace terms "laudator temporis acti." Nor am I disposed to lay myself open to the imputation of being, either so ungenerous as to withhold my poor meed of praise from, or too generous to frankly express my disapproval of, whatever, in the newer educational dispensation, may, to my judgment, appear to merit the one or the other.

It appears to me that no particular, pertaining to the departmental evolution of the past twenty-five years, more obtrusively challenges comment, from one who has been out of harness for that length of time, than the fluent character of both the legal enactments and the departmental regulations that now conjointly determine the educational "modus agendi" of the Province. The more or less rigid conservatism of former years seems to have given place, not only to a more prompt adoption of obvious improvements and needed reforms, but even to what may, perhaps, in some instances, be termed a tentative groping after better things. At first view I was inclined to look upon this want of fixity in enactment and administration, as a defect in the system. More careful consideration, however, leads me to regard it as an evidence of vitality and progress, rather than of weakness or vacillation. It may, I think, be accepted as showing how quickly amenable the Department is to public opinion when conveyed to it through legitimate channels. The community influences the educational executive in many ways, but chiefly, through the Press, the Legislature and the Inspectorate. It is gratifying to know that, upon the whole, the Press has given the Department a generous support. Except at recurring periods of political excitement, it rises superior to party proclivities, and during the past fifty years, and especially during the past twenty-five years, it has done noble work for the furtherance of the educational interests of the Province. The leading newspapers of the day may be only self-appointed educational assessors, but they are none the less valuable or influential on that account, and, as a rule, they have not abused their power, or been heedless of their responsibilities, or deaf to the calls of duty. Their appraisements of school laws and regulations and methods and results are, except when obviously warped by party bias, or written with party intent, of great service, in keeping the administration in close touch with the people. Their suggestions, often acted on, are frequently of much practical value. Not always so, however, and the fact that inspiration derived from this source, is not uniformly plenary in kind may, perhaps, explain why, in some instances, enactment has been followed by repeal. Even the adverse criticisms of the party press—sometimes rather free and always quite pointed—may not be an unmixed evil, if, indeed, they be an evil at all. In my opinion they are, not an evil, but a necessary and a valuable feature of the system as it now exists. If newspapers in this way, dispense more strychnine than sugar, they administer it only in small doses, and, though bitter in taste, it exerts an excellent tonic effect. When the strictures thus made touch real evils or suggest real improvements, reform or adoption, sooner or later, inevitably follows; and when they are "*vox et praeterea nihil*" they probably still serve the minister as an unfailing antidote against the malady called "Swelled head", which occasionally attacks those who live on the mountain tops and who are too exclusively fed on party pap and party soothing syrup and party exhilarants. By the joint efforts of the two sections of the press, the Minister of Education certainly enjoys the unique privilege of being the best painted man in the Dominion. He is painted from every conceivable and from nearly every inconceivable standpoint, and in every known and nearly every unknown shade of color. If the artists of one political camp dip their brushes only in rose-pink and sky-blue, those of the other camp use only plain black and white and especially black. He is not likely to ever pine and grow thin from stress of repeating Burns' ardent aspiration :—

> "Oh ! wad some power the giftie gie us
> To see oursels as ithers see us.
> It wad frae mony a blunder free us."

He has probably long ago lost his own identity and forgotten how he ever looked to himself through his own eyes. The very freedom with which such adverse criticisms are hurled at him may, possibly, serve to keep the Departmental atmosphere strongly charged with the tensional electricity of patriotic thinking, and high resolve, and heroic doing, since it constantly reminds him and his subordinates

> " If there's a hole in a' your coats
> I rede you tent it ;
> A chiel's amang you takin' notes,
> And, faith ! he'll prent it."

But, although the Minister comes in touch with the community at many points—the Public and High School Inspectors are the official tentacula by which he grasps and apprehends—are the especial agents through and by whom he perceives and acts. He is the brain, the executive, the central intelligence of the system, they are its afferent and efferent, its sensory and motor nerves, not only carrying the instructions and behests of the Department to teachers and trustees, but also gathering up from these, and from other peripheral sources, intimations of public and professional approval or the reverse, and impressions concerning the existing condition and tendency of things, and the present and prospective requirements of the public service, and, either by formal reports, or by personal conference, promptly conveying these to the Minister, for his information and guidance. When the efficient and thorough system of inspection which now prevails was first established by the late Chief Superintendent, I was satisfied that it would prove to be the key-stone and connecting bond of the whole—that the success and integrity of the entire educational chain would very largely depend upon the zeal and faithfulness with which the Inspectors did their work. Time has but confirmed the correctness of my views in that respect, and now, we are all agreed, that it would be difficult to over estimate the value of the educational services of these public officers, or to adequately express the obligations of the Province to them in that behalf. It is, I take it, an important part of their unspecified function to serve, as they were designed to serve, as a pledge of the intrinsic democratism of our Public School system. Appointed by the people through their elected representatives in County Council assembled, they are paid by the people, they are responsible to the people alone, they hold office only during the pleasure of the people, and yet, as I have explained, they are at the same time so related to the Department, that, conjointly with their High School confreres, they inspire all or much of the school laws and regulations that are from time to time enacted. Thus it may be truly said that the very genius of our Public School system is democratism pure and simple. It may indeed be fairly questioned whether, even in any State of the American Union, the people have as potent and as controlling a voice in educational concerns as have the citizens of Ontario. In such a system mobility of regulation and enactment is inevitable, is the exponent of its progressiveness, is a proof of its vitality, is the measure of its adaptability to the public service. To taboo all educational essay or trial would amount to educational stagnation if not to retrogression. All that can be required to preserve the integrity and continuity of the system, as a whole, is that, while the central authorities show, as they must show, a reasonable readiness to " prove all things" that seem to make for the betterment of educational concerns, they shall equally manifest a fixed resolve to only " hold fast that which is good."

I note, with much pleasure, the increased care taken to make the teaching, both in Public and High Schools, progressively more and yet more real and common-sense in its character. The course of instruction is more extended, the technique is improved and proportionately higher results are obtained. Of this, in my opinion, there can be no possible doubt. In this connection, both the Department and the Province are to be congratulated on the greatly improved school equipment now provided by trustees. I can remember when it required all the insistence of the Educational office to induce or to compel a Board to supply its school with a paltry set of four or five maps and a few pictures of objects. I am credibly informed that, now, schools are almost universally well equipped; that each High School in the Province has not only a well furnished laboratory where every student has to learn whatever he acquires of chemistry practically, by self-conducted experiment and simple qualitative analysis, but also an ample set of philosophical apparatus, including a working telegraph, a working telephone, a working electro-motor, and other appliances for the practical teaching of science. I further learn, with much satisfaction, that, except as works of reference, text-books, in the teaching of science, are practically discarded. The student of botany is referred to the dead or living plant, is required to identify the specimen by name, to dissect and demonstrate its parts, to discuss its root, stem, leaves, flower, fruit and seed; its relations, properties and uses; and to correctly place it in the natural system of classification. The youthful zoologist goes quite as deeply and as practically into the investigation of animal forms, and whether he is working on a mammal, bird, fish or reptile, or on one of the lower animal creations, he is required with scalpel and microscope, to separate and examine the histological elements of each. Nor is it only in the natural sciences that real, as distinguished from perfunctory, teaching appears to be insisted upon. I observe with much approval that your regulations require your examiners in the languages, ancient and modern to test each pupil's knowledge by his ability to translate, and to grammatically analyse and discuss sight passages not included in the prescribed texts. In English literature, the intelligent and appreciative study of assigned English classics, by the aid of a living teacher, and the liberal memorization of their finest passages—invaluable as even this alone would be —is by no means all that is demanded. To test his knowledge and the quality of the teaching he has received, the examiners are here again required to prove him by sight passages not included in the assigned work, so as to gauge his ability to interpret and appreciate literature for himself. The course of bookkeeping, I notice, is either general or special. The former aims at giving an ordinary knowledge of the subject such as is required by everyone—while the latter is so full and is taught so practically that a pupil who takes it and secures the Departmental Commercial Diploma is, I should say, fully competent to take his place forthwith at the accountant's desk. In stenography he is required to practice until he attains a rate of at least fifty words a minute. And although approved typewriters are not yet supplied to each school, they, and other good things, will no doubt, eventually, get there.

My remarks in this connection may seem to apply more especially to High Schools, but I wish to say that, in my opinion, Public Schools are not a whit less worthy of praise than their more advanced sister institutions. An educational chain can be no stronger than its weakest link. That the Public Schools, in their limited sphere, do not form a weak link in our educational chain must, I think, be patent to all who take the trouble to look beneath the surface. Many of the best and most experienced teachers in the Province are engaged in Public School work and the realness and excellence of the teaching done there is freely attested by appreciative inspectors and trustees. Even the youngest third-class teacher employed in a public school, must have passed the departmental tests as to knowledge, must have spent the prescribed time in a training or Model School, for instruction in the science and practice in the art of teaching, and must have obtained a certificate of qualification in these respects from a County Board of Examiners—while those with higher pretentions and more advanced certificates, must have passed the higher Departmental tests as to scholarship, must have spent one year at least in actual teaching, and, subsequently thereto, must have graduated from a Normal School. Both the literary and the professional competence of Public School teachers is thus assured, and the vigor and the value of the work done by the inspectors, I have already alluded to. That the results are eminently creditable to all concerned, is altogether beyond any peradventure, is, in fact, shown by the remarkable success with which Public School pupils pass the successive tests for promotion from grade to grade, and for entrance into the High Schools. Considering the average age of the candidates, the High School Entrance Examination is quite a severe test, and it is rigorously applied. It appears to be a much more advanced test than it was twenty years ago. Yet the Public Schools now send up more than twice as many candidates for this examination as they did then, and, of those sent up, sixty-one per cent. now pass, while twenty years ago only fifty-two per cent. were successful. If these facts mean anything they mean that the Public Schools do more work and do better work now than they did twenty years ago.

One of the most distinctive, and, in my opinion, one of the most admirable features of the educational present is the comprehensive and thorough system of examinations now controlled by the Department. I can recollect their comparatively humble origin. Forty-two years ago, the Hamilton School Board commissioned me to spend a few weeks looking into the city Public School systems of New York, Pennsylvania and the New England States. Of the different educational centres I then visited, the school system of Boston was reputedly, and, I think, actually the best. On my return home I graded the Central School, and introduced grade limit tables and promotion tests similar to those used in Boston, but more thoroughly applied. These were subsequently adopted in the Provincial Model School, and were officially prescribed for use in all graded Public Schools. In due time they were extended and made to apply to Grammar or High Schools and Collegiate Institutes. Ultimately they became expanded to their present phenomenal proportions by the absorption of County Board and Normal School academic tests for the teachers' certificates, and the matriculation tests of the different universities, technical colleges and schools, and learned professions. The latter functions were, doubtless, largely imposed upon the Department by outside pressure. Of this, my own profession furnishes a notable instance. The Medical Council, of which I have the honor to be an elected member, formerly held its own examinations for matriculation in medicine, through two appointed examiners, one at Kingston and the other at Toronto. The examination cost the candidate $10 in place of the $5 now paid, or, taking into consideration the travelling expenses often from remote parts of the province to these centres, it involved, in many cases, four or five times as great an outlay as at present. The examinations were otherwise unsatisfactory, and the Council decided to accept, in lieu of them, one or other of the Departmental tests, then in force. It has never seen cause to regret its decision to that effect, and, to-day, such is our confidence in the realness and absolute value of the Departmental examinations, that the representative members of the Council would not willingly set aside the Departmental Certificate, in favor of any unlimited university qualification even up to, and inclusive of, a degree in Arts. Practical educationists know very well that the dependence to be placed on the certificate or diploma or degree in Arts of any institution, is determined, not chiefly by the face value of its requirements, or by the extent or parade of its curriculum, but by the thoroughness and stringency with which its examination tests are applied. Our objection, in the Medical Council, to accept university standing as qualifying for matriculation means, not that we have no confidence in any university, but that when eight or ten universities become competing bodies, so far as medical matriculation is concerned, there is no surety that their tests are equally applied, we know that in the past the tests of some were applied with discreditable laxity and, consequently, as we dare not discriminate, university standing, in this connection, represents to us an unknown or a variable quantity. We know also that the drift of candidates is always towards the least exacting examining body. Hence our fixed resolve to stand by the Departmental tests; and it is no secret that other technical colleges and other professions take the same stand, as the Medical Council, in this matter. I have only to add, that, in my opinion, the Departmental examinations are the touchstone, as the Inspectorate is the keystone, of the entire educational system of the province, and that neither can be tampered with without gravely marring the integrity and efficiency and equipoise of the whole. The decentralization of teachers' examinations and of those of university and profession matriculation, due to the present plan of making each High School a centre at which candidates may write, has undoubtedly been a boon to all. I may, perhaps, be permitted to add, in this connection, that it would be a concession generally appreciated by the public to increase, by at least one-half, the time assigned to each paper at these examinations. There are many reasons which readily suggest themselves to practical teachers, why, if the Department errs, here, at all, it should be on the side of over-liberality. It is unquestionably a fact, that, with more time, hundreds of candidates would make a better showing than they now do, and, thus, in many cases, unintentionally unjust rating would be avoided.

There are other features of the educational system at present in force, which seem, to me, to merit unqualified approval but I have no time now to discuss them. I particularly regret that I am thus precluded from saying some of the good things, I have in my heart to say, about the kindergartening which has, since my day, been incorporated into the system. I remember, however, with great pleasure that the very last lectures on education, I had the honor to deliver in this Institution twenty-six years ago, were devoted to a description of the kindergarten, and to the advocacy of its early introduction into our cities and towns.

Are we to conclude then that our school system is faultless? Happily No! Not that, by any means. Imperfection is the hallmark of all mundane affairs. Progressive institutions, like progressive individuals, live and grow strong by effort, by constantly struggling to attain to higher phases of existence. If, by any chance, an institution ever reaches perfection, there is, for it, no more struggle, decadence sets in, and death by cardiac failure, or by senile gangrene, or by general paresis closes the scene. I trust, therefore, that our school system is not yet within 1000 years of perfection. If time served, I would like to point out several particulars in which it is more or less faulty, I can only now shortly indicate two or three of these. For instance. I am not altogether in accord with the complete divorcement of the academic and pedagogic functions in our Normal Schools. That, formerly, the energies of the school were far too largely devoted to academic work, I readily admit. Nevertheless the other extreme may be found to be equally a mistake. There are, I take it, sound pedagogic reasons why these institutions should still do a limited amount of academic work. I think those reasons are so imperative that they must, eventually, force their own recognition, and I venture to predict that a longer experience of the present system will lead to a partial restoration of the feature now so rigorously excluded.

I strongly approve of the recent change made in the constitution of County Boards of Examiners; yet I am not quite satisfied with the constitution of these Boards. The certificate of the Board is a legal authorization to teach and the examination leading thereto, should, undoubtedly, be in the hands of teachers and Inspectors. Doctors, lawyers and clergymen are possessed of varied and multiplied excellencies among which, however, are not any special qualifications to serve on County Boards. And seeing how sensitively jealous these professions are of any outside interference with their own guild rights and immunities, I am only surprised that they did not long ago, themselves protest against being placed in a position, where they were compelled to do unto others as they would not that others should do unto them. It would, in my opinion, be a still further improvement to throw, for examination purposes, two or three adjacent counties into one, so as to make the joint Board a larger body. And to make it still more independent of local influences, which tend to relax, which, in this case, strongly tend to relax vigor and stringency of function, it may be found necessary to give one or more appointees of the Department seats in each of these joint County Boards, as a guarantee to both the public, and the central authorities, that these examinations, which are certainly not the least important in the whole series, are real, and not merely perfunctory.

I have no sympathy with the cry that the Department encourages cramming in the High Schools. As far as I can interpret the spirit and intent of the Departmental regulations, and instructions to examiners, every possible preventative measure, that can be adopted, is explicitly enjoined ; and, moreover, the eminently real and practical teaching done in the High Schools would seem, of itself, to render cramming, in most subjects impossible. And, further, in the few subjects such as History and Geography in which cramming might be resorted to, the peculiar forms of the questions given on the examination papers would seem designed to preclude anyone, who had merely crammed for the test, from passing it at all. But, while there is not, and cannot be, much cramming, in the only sense in which careful people use that term, there can be, and, I fear, there is a very lamentable amount of over-study in connection with High School work. I regard this as the worst feature of the entire system, but I am not very clear as to where the responsibility rests, or what, if any, remedy can be applied to prevent or to lessen the evil. Your system, Sir, is an eminently successful system. I doubt whether more work or better work is accomplished in Public and High Schools anywhere else in the world. I will go further, and say I doubt whether as much good work is done anywhere else in schools of a similar grade. But to accomplish these desirable results your schools are run at high pressure. Your system is designed to take out of both teachers and taught all there is in them. The educational dilettanteism, which so largely prevails to the south of us, finds no place here. Our American neighbors run what may be termed a decorated educational accommodation train, where we run an every day through express. Our educational conductors and engine drivers are earnest, keen-eyed, hardfisted men, in work-a-day clothes, who mean business, and are bound to run their trains on time. I have the pleasure of knowing many of our High School Masters, personally or by repute. In scholarly attainments and knowledge of their profession—in zeal and in the faithful discharge of duty, they are, I know, easily the peers of the best men of their class elsewhere in the world. We have much reason to be proud of them. I know that some—I believe that many deplore this tendency to over-study, and do their best to prevent it, but the remedy lies not with them. The evil is perhaps, inherent to any advanced school curriculum, vigorously pursued. Your course of study is necessarily arranged so as to meet the requirements of students of fair or average ability. Unfortunately, there are, in every school, some pupils of less than average ability, who can only keep up with the class by extra work. If their inferiority is marked, the extra work may become excessive. It is true that pupils can vegetate in the High School for years without writing for any examination whatever, but neither they nor their parents want that. The former are self-impelled to over-exertion by a not unnatural anxiety to do as well as others. The great factor, however, in promoting over-study on the part of High School pupils, is, I fear, a sort of *vis a tergo*—the pressure brought to bear on them by ambitious or injudicious parents, who are loath to believe that their family half-pint pots are not just as capacious as neighboring family pint or quart pots. The Head Masters, as I have said, discourage overstudy. They do it to their great honor, because somewhat to their own detriment; for, unhappily, their own efficiency and success are largely measured by the results they reach at these examinations. Parents and trustees watch for the annually published lists, and eagerly scan them, in order to compare their schools and their teachers with those of other districts, and, if any marked falling off appears, unpleasantness of various kinds and degrees is sure to follow. It would appear then that, as the responsibility for over-study rests chiefly or wholly with the people themselves, its remedy or prevention also lies chiefly in their hands. Experience and a keener appreciation of parental responsibility may, in time, teach the lesson that it is often a father's duty, here, to put down the brakes, in place of turning on more steam, and the family physician frequently has it in his power to offer wise counsels in this respect. And I am glad to be able to record my conviction that my professional confreres seldom or never neglect to point out the dangers of over mental application. The Department can apparently do little more than has been done to prevent its necessity. The separation of the Matriculation and Junior Leaving examinations into parts I and II, which may be passed separately, and in different years, is evidently, a concession to students of less than average capacity, but further relief in that direction is clearly barred by the risk of running into the burlesque of "education-with-examinations-on-the-instalment-plan." One can see several possible ways out of the difficulty, but, none without hazard of grave injury to the integrity and value of the whole system. For instance, if the annual lists were published, as a whole, in strict alphabetical order, and not by districts or schools, over-study or much of it would at once cease, but in that case, I fear that our fast educational express would be apt to degenerate into a mere decorated accommodation train. He who may be able to devise a scheme which shall prevent all over-study, without, at the same time, hobbling the progress of those with average or with superior abilities, will richly deserve the thanks of every one.

Of our Public School system I have only to add that, as far as rural sections are concerned, it has, probably, in its present shape, reached the limit of its usefulness, and that unless it be materially altered, it will not likely prove equal to the requirements of the future. To be prepared to compete in the keen commercial and industrial struggle of the twentieth century, farmers sons and daughters will, unquestionably, need an educational equipment, which in kind, and in extent, the present system cannot supply, and was never intended to supply. This difficulty has cropped up in other lands, and, so far, only two solutions have been tentatively put forward. One is the creation of special schools; the other is the amplification of existing schools. Not the least important objections to the creation of special schools are: first, the deterioration or degradation of ordinary Public Schools which would inevitably result; and, second, the improbability that they could be established in sufficient number to better reach the requirements of the rural population than they are now served by the High Schools. The amplification of all rural Public Schools would involve the obliteration of school sections as they now exist, and the subdivision of a township into only three or four districts in place of the sixteen or twenty now obtaining. This plan would secure to townships all the benefits of graded schools, would obviate the present waste of teaching energy, and would admit of a very material extension of the school course of study. Its adoption would probably involve, as it does in some of the New England States, the carrying of distant pupils to and from school at the public expense, but that outlay would be trifling compared with the saving effected by having to equip and maintain only three or four schools in place of sixteen or twenty. The problem of making the Public Schools equal to the new demands made upon them, may be regarded as the most important now before the Education Department; and he who solves it satisfactorily and secures therewith the indispensable concurrence of the people, will do a grand work, and will deserve honor, second only to that conferred upon Dr. Ryerson himself.

V.

THE JUBILEE BANQUET.

The Jubilee celebration was brought to a conclusion by a banquet at the Rossin House, on Tuesday evening, November 3rd, at which about one hundred gentlemen were present. If the evening had been fine, and, if the ladies had been invited, it is quite certain that a very much larger number would have attended. The chair was occupied by the Hon. Geo. W. Ross, LL.D., Minister of Education, and the vice-chairs, by Principal A. MacMurchy, M.A., of Jarvis St. Collegiate Institute (representing the students who attended before 1876), and Prof. J. G. Hume, M.A., Ph. D. of Toronto University (representing the students who attended since 1875). To the right of the chairman, sat President James Loudon, M.A., LL.D. of Toronto University ; the Rev. E. A. Welsh, M.A., D.C.L., Provost of Trinity College, Toronto ; Rev. A. H. Reynar, M.A., LL.D., of Victoria University ; Rev. E. H. Dewart, D.D.; Rev. G. M. Milligan, M.A., D.D.; and Prof. John Macoun of Ottawa ; and, to the left, sat J. Herbert Sangster, M.A., M.D.; S. P. Robins, M.A., LL.D., Principal of McGill Normal School, Montreal ; J. A. MacCabe, M.A., LL.D., Principal of Ottawa Normal School ; G. R. Parkin, M.A., LL.D., Principal of Upper Canada College ; and G. S. Ryerson, M.D., M.P.P. The following gentlemen were also present :— Messrs. Wm. Scott, B.A., Dr. Fotheringham, Robert W. Doan, Robert W. Murray, Dr. J. H. McFaul, Rev. R. P. Mackay, M.A., Toronto ; Dr. W. L. Herriman, Lindsay ; James Maxwell, Melville Cross; G. H. Armstrong, B.A., B. Pæd., A. McMillan, E. R. Dewart, D. J. Flynn, John Millar, B.A., Toronto ; W. Carlyle, Woodstock ; Prof. H. W. Hart, London, England ; S. McAllister, W. F. Chapman, Toronto ; C. B. Linton, Galt ; G. K. Powell, Arch. MacMurchy, M.A., Toronto; Dr. Stalker, Ridgetown; Jas. A. Youmans, Bear's Hill, Alta. ; Henry R. Alley, W. Pakenham, B.A., A.C. Casselman, J. F. White, W. Prendergast, B.A., Toronto ; John Dearness, Chas. Clark, London ; Dr. John S. King, Wm. Houston, M.A., Toronto ; J. H. Smith, F. C. Blaicher, B. E. Charlton, Dr. James Russell, Hamilton ; W. A. Douglas, Toronto ; Chas. A. Barnes, B.A., London ; J. E. Hodgson, M.A., A. McIntosh, Toronto ; Thos. Pearce, Berlin ; Rev. Dr. Mungo Fraser, Hamilton ; John C. Copp, T. M. Porter, W. E. Groves, Toronto ; C. Ferrier, Mimico; W. J. Hendry, Toronto ; Dr. J. M. Platt, Picton ; Principal Kirkland, M.A., Normal School, Toronto ; Dr. A. McPhedran, Toronto ; Dr. Aaron J. Campbell, Gravenhurst ; Geo. M. Ritchie, J. W. Rogers, E. W. Bruce, B.A., J. Bennett, I. J. Birchard, M.A., Ph. D

Toronto : W. E. Tilley, M.A., Ph. D., Bowmanville: Joseph Richardson, Tavistock ; Abram Bretz, Toronto : J. S. Deacon, Milton ; G. D. Platt, B.A., Picton ; Dr. S. P. May, Dr. E. J. Barrick, R. W. Hicks, Toronto ; Rev. J. A. Morrison, Col. Sam. Hughes, M.P., Lindsay.

Vice-Principal Scott read a letter of regret from Chancellor Burwash, stating that his enforced absence was owing to sickness. In it reference was made to the happy relations which had always existed between Victoria University and the Normal School, and to the fact that Victoria was the first University in Ontario to accept Normal School certificates as equivalent to matriculation.

The Toast List.

The Chairman, in introducing the toasts agreed upon by the Committee, spoke as follows :—I regret that the Alumni of the Toronto Normal School have not during the past half century cultivated greater loyalty to their *alma mater* and a more fraternal spirit among themselves. The Toronto Normal School has rendered invaluable service to the Province as one of its greatest educational forces. From the very first, it established a high standard of fitness for the teaching profession, and during its whole career, it has clearly shown that the intelligent study of correct methods of teaching is of the utmost importance to every one who would wish to excel as a teacher. The Normal School has also given a great stimulus even to teachers who were unable to avail themselves of its advantages. Oft-times, the holder of a Normal School certificate had opportunities of showing the superiority of the methods of study and instruction which he had acquired within its halls and many were ready to profit by his example and his success. In fact, every profession has been enriched because of the existence of this Normal School. To the young man whose ambition carried him beyond the ranks of the teaching profession, the Normal School was indeed an inspiration, and to-day not a few doctors and lawyers and clergymen had their ambition to improve their position in life, aroused by attendance at the Normal School.

When the Toronto Normal School was established fifty years ago, our School System was in its infancy ; Dr. Ryerson had just a year or two previously been appointed Chief Superintendent. The whole system of education was in a transition state. Who can tell to what extent the attention given at the Normal School to pedagogical principles, influenced the legislation with regard to Public and High Schools, the preparation of text books, the courses of study, and everything that has contributed so greatly to the efficiency of our School System ?

Let us not forget the part Dr. Ryerson played in the establishment of a school whose Jubilee we are now celebrating. Let us not forget the efficient work done by Dr. Robertson, the first Principal of the Normal School, and by Dr. Sangster, his successor, nor let us forget the spirit which animated these men while endeavoring to lead their students to form higher ideals of the profession in which they were then engaged, and of the influence which the school room should exert upon the country to which they belonged. Modern civilization would be greatly handicapped were it not for the trained teacher. We may, therefore, as the Alumni of this institution whose record is so closely connected with the educational evolution of the country, rejoice to-night that its influence, though not perhaps so fully recognized as it should be, has been felt in every corner of Ontario and possibly of the Dominion, and as loyalty to the country was always an essential part of our instruction, I now propose that we begin the proceedings of this evening by drinking to the health of Her Gracious Majesty, Queen Victoria. I give, "The Queen, God bless Her." This toast was honored with becoming enthusiasm, the whole audience joining in singing the National Anthem.

The "Dominion Parliament" was responded to in happy terms by Dr. Platt, ex-M.P., who expressed the opinion that the more graduates of the Normal School there were in the Dominion Parliament the better it would be for the Parliament and for the country.

"The Ontario Legislature," which was proposed in a happy speech by the Chairman, was responded to by Dr. Ryerson, M.P.P., who had been very much impressed with the Jubilee and the celebration which had been held. During the past fifty years the educational institutions of the Province had left a decided mark upon the national life. There was the deepest interest taken in educational matters by every member of the House, no matter on which side of the Speaker he sat, and, although there might be some difference of opinion as regards some of the details in the matter of administration and education, they are all agreed that the educational system is one of which, as Ontarians and Canadians, they were justly proud.

Col. Hughes, M. P., who responded to the toast of the "Army, Navy and Volunteers," was introduced by the Chairman as one who had reflected credit upon the Normal School from which he graduated. The Colonel justified the introduction of military drill into the Public and High Schools of the Province as necessary and advantageous, in order that a spirit of patriotism may be inculcated and habits of discipline formed.

The toast list was then handed over to the first Vice Chairman, Principal MacMurchy who proposed the toast of "Higher Education."

President Loudon, who was the first to respond, as representing the University of Toronto, congratulated the Normal School upon the very great success which had attended the celebration. There should be, he opined, the closest possible connection and kindliest feelings between the Normal School and the Colleges and Universities, all of which are links in our splendid system of education.

Provost Welch, as one of a very small minority of those present who had not been connected with the Toronto Normal School, responded on behalf of Trinity University. He paid a tribute to the importance of the teaching profession, which was second only, if indeed second at all, to that of the sacred calling of the ministry.

Rev. Dr. Reynar, after apologizing for the absence of Chancellor Burwash, said he felt at home in an assembly of the alumni of the Normal School, whose founder (Dr. Ryerson) was a Victoria man. It had also been his pleasure years ago to advocate the acceptance of

Normal School certificates by Victoria, and he had enjoyed the satisfaction of ultimately seeing them accepted.

Dr. Parkin, who replied on behalf of Upper Canada College, referred to the great influence which the Normal Schools exercised upon the public life of the lower Provinces by furnishing men who had won their way to seats in the Cabinet.

In proposing the toast of "Sister Institutions," Professor Hume referred to Sir Wilfrid Laurier as a representative Canadian who had graduated from a sister educational institution in the Province of Quebec.

Dr. Robins, of McGill Normal School, Montreal, in responding to this toast, expressed his regret that the conduct of public education is Provincial, rather than National, and appealed to the Hon. Geo. W. Ross to use his great influence in the direction of an enlargement of our educational horizon.

Dr. MacCabe, of the Ottawa Normal School, also responded to this toast, and expressed his high appreciation of the successful work done by the Toronto Normal School during the last fifty years, and he hoped that success would continue to follow its efforts.

Dr. Sangster, in proposing the toast of the ex-students of the Toronto Normal School, said :—

To most of us this is an occasion fraught with very mingled feelings of joy and sadness. It is a matter of regret that we could not all be here—that some of our graduates have been riven from us by the hand of death, and that others are almost equally separated from us by sickness, or by intervening space, or by any other insuperable obstacle. Especially do we grieve that many whom we knew and loved as fellow students, and others whom we knew and loved as preceptors, or pupils, or associates are beyond the reach of our felicitations, peacefully resting from their labors, where they banquet not. And touching these, we sorrow that, in our varied spheres, we were not, it may be, while they were yet present with us, always as careful as we might have been to cheer and help them on their way—that, perhaps, we did not always withhold the angry word that smites like a knife and rankles in the wound. In a peculiar degree is this sorrow mine to-night, in that, while to me were given special opportunities to encourage and to cheer, to me also were assigned especially strong temptations to vex by sharp reproof, and I greatly fear that I only too frequently neglected my opportunities and succumbed to my temptations in that respect.

But it is a matter of rejoicing that we can here to-night still grasp the living fingers, and gaze into the kindling eyes of so many of our fellow graduates—that here to-night we once more thrill at the touch of long vanished hands and harken to the music of long silent voices, and trace the lineaments of once familiar faces, and the contour of once familiar forms. We are especially glad that, though we may hail from many lands, may have wandered into many diverging paths of life, may have different faiths and belong to opposing political camps, we are here to night in our homogeneous capacity—a brotherhood—claiming a common educational origin and acknowledging the same *alma mater*. To-night we remember no past differences, no estrangements, no causes of strife, no grounds of offence. We entertain none but kindly memories of one another, and harbour only loyal good wishes for each other's future well-being and success.

The graduates of the Normal School, down to 1875, number I am told over 3,000. After teaching acceptably for longer or shorter periods of time many of these left the profession and climbed worthily, elsewhere, into positions of great responsibility and power. Today some of these fill the chief pulpits of our own and other lands, or are among the luminaries of the Bench and the Bar, or are the ornaments of the Medical and other Professions, or are among the most successful Men of Business here and among kindred people, or fill the seats of honour in Senate Chambers or Legislative Halls, and we are proud to convey to these, our distinguished brothers, our hearty congratulations on the proud pre-eminence they have so nobly achieved. But assuredly no less proud are we of those of our ex-students who have not suffered themselves to be seduced from their first love, but are educators still. Of these some are now among the most valued Public School Inspectors in the Province, some fill, and most efficiently fill, professorial chairs in native and foreign universities, some worthily and acceptably fill preceptors chairs in our own *alma mater* and in other Normal Schools, some are successful masters in High Schools and Collegiate Institutes and some are still engaged in the perhaps humbler but certainly no less useful and honourable work of teaching in Public Schools. Of those still in harness a few have taught continuously for fifty years, others for forty, thirty or twenty years We rejoice that so many have not turned back after putting their hand to the educational plow. They have been and many of them still are engaged in a work of grandest potentialities. Their labours may be truly said to have touched the chiefest life springs of the nation. Who shall attempt to estimate the aggregate of all the good they have accomplished during the past fifty years ? What tapeline has inches enough, what cyclometer has miles enough, to measure the length and breadth of the elevating and refining formative influence they have brought to bear on the young ? What plummet is long enough to sound the depths in the ocean of Canadian humanity, which they may have first irradiated with the light of Divine Love or with the ardent fire of high resolve or with the steady glow of heroic doing ?

A teacher is much or is nothing according to the spirit in which he works. I know of no thing that is smaller or more contemptible than a teacher who is a mere day-laborer, working for hire, as though he were commissioned simply to kill six hours a day for five days in the week. On the other hand I know of nothing that more completely fills my whole soul with kindling appreciation, and a satisfying sense of privileged power, than the spectacle of a true teacher in action —a large-hearted, whole-souled, keen-eyed man or woman with energy and will power oozing from every pore of his corporeal being—with gaze resolutely fixed beyond the drudgery and daily routine of his office, on the formative, moulding, mind-making functions that are his, and working with intelligence and determination towards the realization of his ideal, on each mass of plastic humanity in his art studio.

Such teachers we know have been some, such teachers we hope have been many, of the ex-students of the Normal School. Well may such men and women magnify their office, for it is indeed a noble office. It may be debatable whether it were better to be a great cobbler or a little king, but, personally, I would rather be a really great teacher than anything else beneath the sun. And yet, even a truly great teacher makes little or no noise in the world. His power, like many of the most potent forces of nature, works silently and is felt rather than seen. His influence in the world is exerted indirectly through the patriots, the statesmen, the heroes, the large-hearted, clear-headed, right-principled, conscientious men and women whom he has fashioned and formed. He does not himself aspire to be a Bismarck or a Gladstone, a Chamberlain or a Herschell, a Newton or a Darwin a Macdonald, a Laurier, a Meredith or a Mowat, but he may help to mould and to develop those who may prove to be the peers of any or all of these. It is not his to make laws, or to regulate commerce, or to lead armies, or to control senates, or to rule empires, but it is his to nurture and to qualify and to train and to influence those by whom laws are made, and commerce regulated, and armies led, and senates controlled, and empires ruled. To take the child just entering the Kindergarten and to mould its character, and to unfold its powers, and to elevate its affections, and to ennoble its aims, and to fix its principles, and to stamp it with the seal of full, glorious, heroic manhood. To soften firmness into mercy, to chasten honour into Christian fidelity, to exalt generosity into virtue, and charity into beneficence, and self negation into heroism—this is the teacher's highest vocation, this is his grandest mission, this is the field in which his noblest and best work is done. God bless our teachers and put it continually into their hearts to do the highest work within their reach!

It affords me much pleasure to propose a toast, which I am sure will, on this occasion, find a response in every heart here.

"The Ex-students of the Toronto Normal School."

A number of ex-students, including Prof. Macoun of the Geological Survey, Ottawa; Dr. James Russell, of Hamilton; Dr. Herriman, of Lindsay; Mr. B. E. Charlton, of Hamilton; Dr. Barrick, Inspectors Dearness and Pearce, and others, responded on behalf of the Alumni in speeches which rang with enthusiasm for the institution which had done so much for them.

"The Learned Professions" was proposed by Dr. McPhedran, who called attention to the great progress which has been made in all the professions and especially in Medicine during the last fifty years.

The last toast on the list was to the Press. A fitting response was made by Mr. W. J. Green.

VII.

BIOGRAPHICAL SKETCHES.

Biographical sketches are here given of the official heads of the Education Department from the time of its establishment to the present time, and of their deputies; also of the members of the present staffs of the Toronto Normal and Model Schools.

Rev. Egerton Ryerson, D.D., LL.D.

Rev. Egerton Ryerson, D.D., LL.D., late Chief Superintendent of Education for Ontario, was born in the Township of Charlotteville, near Lake Erie, in 1803. He was educated in his native county and at Hamilton. He taught school for a short time. On his twenty-second birthday he was ordained a deacon in the M.E. Church by Bishop Hedding. On the establishment of the *Christian Guardian*, in 1829, he was appointed its joint editor. In 1835 he visited England to obtain a Royal Charter for Upper Canada Academy, now Victoria University. In 1844 he was appointed Superintendent of Education for Upper Canada, "with the understanding that he would re-lay the entire foundation of the system, and establish it on a wider and more enduring basis." In 1846 the Legislature passed a new School Act, and again in 1850 it passed a law admirably adapted to the excellent municipal system of Canada, so popular in its character and comprehensive in its provisions and details that it is still, in a consolidated form, the statute under which the Public Schools of Ontario are maintained. In 1863 Separate Schools were established. At various times the Grammar Schools were improved and Meteorological Stations were established in connection with some of these schools.

Dr. Ryerson visited the schools of Europe and the United States at various times. In 1857 he made his third educational tour, and at Antwerp, Brussels, Florence, Rome, Paris and London he procured an admirable collection of copies of paintings by the old masters, statues, busts, etc., besides various other articles for an educational museum in connection with his department.

In consideration of his able services to his country, the University of Victoria College conferred upon him the degree of LL.D. in 1861. In 1867 he made a fourth educational tour in England and the United States, and on his return submitted to the Government two very valuable reports: one "on the systems and state of popular education in the several countries of Europe and the United States of America, with practical suggestions for the improvement of public instruction in Upper Canada"; the other "on institutions for deaf and dumb and blind in various countries."

For many years, Dr. Ryerson had felt that our new political conditions necessitated a change in the management of the Education Department. He, therefore, in 1869 and 1872, urged upon the Government the desirability of relieving him of his arduous duties, and of appointing a Minister of Education in his place. Early in 1876, his recommendations were acted upon and he retired from the responsible post which he had so worthily and honorably filled for thirty-two years. He died at Toronto on the 19th February, 1882. He is the author of The Loyalists of America and their Times.

Hon. Adam Crooks, M.A., LL.B.

The Hon. Adam Crooks, LL.B., late Minister of Education for the Province of Ontario, was born in the Township of West Flamboro', Wentworth, in 1827. He was educated at the Public Schools in his own neighborhood till his twelfth year, when he entered Upper Canada College, and in his eighteenth year he matriculated at King's College—now the University of Toronto. He greatly distinguished himself by the stand he took in Classics and Metaphysics On graduating he entered upon the study of law and was called to the bar of Upper Canada in 1851. He soon established a lucrative practice. In 1852, the degree of M.A. was conferred upon him and in 1863 that of LL.B. He was elected Vice-chancellor of the University of Toronto in 1864. He resigned this position in 1872. In 1863 he was created a Queen's Counsel. In 1871 Mr. Crooks was elected a member of the Provincial Legislature for West Toronto, and became Attorney-General in the Blake administration. When Mr. Mowat reconstructed his Cabinet in October, 1872, Mr. Crooks became Provincial Treasurer and to his department was added, in 1876, that of Minister of Education. He resigned the Provincial Treasurership in 1877 and continued his administration of the Education Department until failing health compelled him to retire in October, 1883. He died in 1885.

Hon. Geo. W. Ross, LL.D., M.P.P.

The Hon Geo. W. Ross, LL.D., Minister of Education for the Province of Ontario, was born near Nairn, Township of East Williams, Middlesex County, 18th September, 1841. His parents, James and Ellen (McKinnon) Ross were both natives of Ross-shire, Scotland. At the early age of sixteen, he commenced his career as a public school teacher, continuing as such until 1869, when he entered the Normal School, Toronto. In 1871 he was appointed Inspector of Public Schools for the County of Lambton, and subsequently to the same position for Petrolia and Strathroy. He took a leading part in the establishment of County Model Schools for the Province, prepared a syllabus of lectures for their direction, and for a time acted as their Inspector. From 1876 to 1880 he was a member of the Central Board of Examiners. He matriculated in law at Albert

University in 1879, where he graduated (LL.B.) in 1883, and in 1886 he received the degree of LL.D. from St. Andrew's University, Scotland. In 1887 he was called to the bar, but, owing to his public duties, never entered actively on the profession of law. He is the author of certain works that have been extensively read, viz :—" The Life and Times of the Hon. Alex. Mackenzie," (which was written in conjunction with Mr. Buckingham, Mr. Mackenzie's private secretary), and a report on the schools of England and Germany, also " Patriotic Recitations " for Ontario Schools, and a " History of the School System of Ontario."

In politics he has always been a Liberal, and in 1872 was elected as such to represent West Middlesex in the House of Commons ; was elected by acclamation in 1874, again re-elected in 1878 and 1882 but the following year (1883) relinquished the seat to accept the portfolio of Minister of Education in the Ontario Ministry—being elected as M. P. P. for his old constituency the same year, which he has continuously represented ever since.

As Minister of Education, he has had passed many bills conducive to the perfection of the educational system, among which are the consolidated Public Schools Acts, High Schools Act, Separate Schools Act, and an Act respecting Mechanics' Institutes, etc.

He was for some time editor of the *Strathroy Age*, and the *Huron Expositor*, of which he was part owner ; and later, in conjunction with Mr. McColl, edited the *Ontario Teacher*, a journal that has been of great service to the profession. In 1886, he attended (as Hon. Commissioner) the Colonial and Indian Exhibition, held in London, Eng.

For many years he has been identified with the temperance cause, and for two years (1879 and 1880) held the high office of Most Worthy Partriarch, Sons of Temperance Division for British North America. In religion he is a Presbyterian, and an elder of Old St. Andrew's Church, Toronto. He is a member of the A.F. and A. M ,G.R.C., and the I.O.O.F. He is also LL.D., of Toronto University and Victoria University.

John George Hodgins, M.A., LL.D., F.R.G.S.

John George Hodgins, M.A., LL.D., F.R.G.S., was born in Dublin Ireland, in 1821. He came to Canada in 1833, and received his education at Upper Canada Academy and at Victoria College, Cobourg. He was graduated an M.A. in 1856 by Victoria University. Subsequently, he took the law course at Toronto University and was graduated LL.B. in 1860, and LL.D. in 1870. He was called to the bar of Ontario in 1870.

In 1844, he entered the Education Department as Chief Clerk and in 1846 became secretary of the Provincial Board of Education, better known as the Council of Public Instruction. In 1855, he was appointed Deputy Superintendent of Education, and in 1876 became Deputy Minister of Education. This office he retained until 1889, when he became Librarian and Historiographer of the Education Department.

Dr. Hodgins was for many years the editor of the Upper Canada Journal of Education. He was one of the pioneers in school book literature in Canada. His published works include "Lovell's General Geography," "First Steps in General Geography," "School History of Canada and of the other British North American Provinces," "The Canadian Speaker and Reciter," "School Manual," "Lectures on School Law," "Sketches and Anecdotes of the Queen," "The School House and its Architecture," "Dr. Ryerson—His Life and Work," "The Documentary History of Education in Upper Canada," and "The Legislation and History of Separate Schools in Upper Canada."

Alexander Marling, LL.B.

Alexander Marling, LL.B., late Deputy Minister of Education, was born at Ebley, Gloucestershire, in 1832. The family came to Canada in 1842. Alexander was educated at Upper Canada College, and in 1854 he entered the Education Department under Dr. Ryerson. In 1858 he became Chief Clerk, and on the appointment of the Hon. Adam Crooks as first Minister of Education, he was appointed Secretary of the Department.

In January, 1890, he became Deputy Minister. He died in April, 1890.

He was entered, after examination, as a law student and member of the Law Society, but his official duties did not allow his advance to the bar. He, however, proceeded to the degree of LL.B. in the University of Toronto, and was graduated in that degree in 1862. He edited the Canada Educational Year Book—a neat and skilful compilation of information respecting the educational system and *personnel* in each Province of the Dominion.

John Millar, B.A.

John Millar, B.A., Deputy Minister of Education, was appointed in May, 1890 Mr. Millar's early life was spent in the Township of Brock, County of Ontario, where he received his elementary education, and began in a rural school the profession of teaching. Afterwards he attended, during the 27th and 28th sessions, the Toronto Normal School, and was awarded a First Class Grade A Certificate. He taught two years in the Township of Barton, County of Wentworth, and five years in one of the graded Public Schools in the City of London. Mr. Millar was graduated B.A. in 1872 at the University of Toronto, having pursued most of the required four years' course while engaged as a teacher. In High School work his experience was gained in St. Thomas, first as an Assistant, and, subsequently by promotion, as Principal. Under his management, the High School was in a few years raised to the standing of a Collegiate Institute. Mr. Millar was Principal of the Public Schools of St. Thomas while Principal of the Collegiate Institute. He was for two years Chairman of the High School Section of the Ontario Teachers' Association, and for four years was a member of the Senate of the University of Toronto, having been twice elected as one of the representatives of the High School Teachers, to that body. Mr. Millar annotated several editions of the English Classics, which were extensively used in the High Schools. He is also the author of the "School Management," authorized for the use of teachers; "Books: A Guide to Good Reading"; "The Educational System of the Province of Ontario," which was prepared for the World's Fair at Chicago; and "The School System of the State of New York." In religion Mr. Millar is a Methodist, and has held several important positions in that body, including that of Representative to the General Conference.

Thomas Kirkland, M.A.

Thomas Kirkland, M.A., Principal of the Toronto Normal School, is a native of County Armagh, Ireland. He is a graduate of the Dublin Normal School, of the Albert College of Agriculture, and an M.A. of Toronto University. Coming to Canada in 1854, he was appointed assistant master in the Oshawa Central School, and Head Master in the following year. In 1856-7 he was Head Master of the Henry Street School in the town of Whitby, and in 1858 he became Mathematical Master in the Barrie Grammar School, then a large boarding school under the Rev. William Checkley. In 1863 he was appointed Head Master of the Whitby Grammar School, which position he held till 1871, when he was selected by Dr. Ryerson for the new position of Science Master in the Normal School. This position he held till 1884, when, on the resignation of Dr. Davies, he was appointed to the principalship of the Normal School by the present Minister of Education.

Principal Kirkland is the author of a work on Elementary Statics, of a work on Elementary Chemistry, and joint author of works on Arithmetic which have been used as text-books in all the Provinces of the Dominion.

Wm. Scott, B.A.

Wm. Scott, B.A., Vice-Principal of the Toronto Normal School, was born in the parish of Ashkirk, Roxburghshire, Scotland in 1846. He came with his parents to America in 1853. He received his elementary education in Bowmanville under the late Mr. Rollo and Dr. Kelly, now Inspector for Brant County. He began to teach in 1862 in the County of Durham. He attended the Toronto Normal School during the thirty-ninth and fortieth sessions in 1868 and was awarded a first-class grade A certificate. He was private tutor in the late Sir David Macpherson's family for eleven months. He was appointed second assistant in the Boys' Model School in October, 1869; became first assistant in August, 1871, and Head Master in May, 1874. Mr. Scott was graduated B.A. in 1876 in the University of Toronto and was appointed Mathematical Master of the Ottawa Normal School in September, 1882, and in 1889, he became Mathematical and Science Master of that institution. In January, 1894, he was transferred to the Toronto Normal School. He is the joint author of the Canadian edition of H. Smith's Arithmetic and of Kirkland and Scott's Elementary Arithmetic.

Angus McIntosh.

Angus McIntosh, Head Master of the Boys' Model School, received his early education at the village school at Branchton and at Galt Grammar School, then under Dr. Tassie. He attended the Toronto Normal School, during the forty-second session, 1869, and afterwards in 1876-7, in all about two years, taking the professional and non-professional work concurrently. He obtained a second class B certificate in 1869; a second A, in 1874; a first B, in 1877; and a first A, a High School Specialist's (in English) and an Inspector's certificate, in 1886. He taught three years in a country school, Waterloo County, one year in the village school at Branchton, two and a half years in Galt Central School, seven years in Brantford Collegiate Institute and thirteen years in the Provincial Model School, Toronto; during ten and a half years of this latter period, he has been Head Master of the Boys' department. He has been a member of the Brant County Board of Examiners for the last sixteen years, and for two years he was a member of the Revising Board of Examiners for the School of Pedagogy. His work, during the last thirteen years, has been intimately connected with the practice-teaching of students, attending the Toronto Normal School.

Margaret T. Scott.

Miss Margaret T. Scott, Head Mistress of the Girls' Model School, was educated at the Public and High Schools of Dundas, Ont. She taught in the Township of Pickering: then she removed to Strathroy to teach the third form of the Public School. Subsequently she was appointed to teach the English subjects in the Institute for the Blind at Brantford. She resigned this position for one in the Presbyterian Ladies' College, Ottawa; this position she resigned to accept her present one in 1884.

Robert W. Murray.

R. W. Murray, first assistant master in the Boys' Model School, Toronto, was born in the County of Huron. His Public School training was obtained in S.S. No. 1, Tuckersmith. In 1873 he entered the Toronto Normal School and obtained a third class certificate in July and a second A in December. For the next five years he taught in the Public Schools of Huron and Perth. He attended the Brantford Collegiate Institute and obtained a first class certificate in 1880, and, during the latter half of this year, he was on the staff of the Galt Collegiate Institute. He was Principal of the Picton Model School from 1881 to 1885, and of the Public Schools of Brockville in 1886. In 1884, he obtained a first B; in 1885, an Art School certificate; and, in 1886, first A, High School Specialist's (in English), and Public School Inspector's certificates. In 1887 he was appointed to his present position on the staff of the Model School.

May K. Caulfeild.

Miss May K. Caulfeild, first assistant in the Girls' Model School, is of Irish parentage. Her education was received at home under the direction of her mother, at Vienna High School and at St. Thomas Collegiate Institute. She attended the Toronto Normal School in 1885 and obtained a first-class certificate in 1886. She was appointed to the Model School Staff in 1887.

Thomas M. Porter.

Thomas M. Porter, second assistant master in the Boys' Model School, is a native of Peterborough County, Ont. He received his non-professional training at the Bailieboro' Public School, the Bowmanville High School, and the Galt Collegiate Institute; and his professional training at the Port Hope Model School and the Toronto Normal School. He was Principal of the Bensfort Public School for two years; of the Simcoe Model School for one term; and of the Athens Model School for three years and a half. In September, 1888, he was appointed to his present position on the staff.

Mary Matilda Aloysius Meehan.

Miss Mary Matilda Aloysius Meehan, second assistant in the Girls' Model School, received her non-professional education in Loretto Convent, in the Provincial Model School and in the Toronto Normal School, and her professional training in the Toronto Normal School, while the professional and non-professional courses were taken concurrently. She was appointed to her present position in January, 1883.

Jeannie Wood.

Miss Jeannie Wood, third assistant in the Boys' Model School, received her non-professional education in the Hamilton Collegiate Institute, and her professional training in the Hamilton Model School and in the Toronto Normal School. For some years after graduating from the latter she was teacher of Mathematics and English in the Ontario Ladies' College, Whitby, and since October, 1889, she has been third assistant in the Boys' Model School.

Alice Stuart.

Miss Alice Stuart, third assistant in the Girls' Model School, received her non-professional education in the Public Schools and Collegiate Institute of Woodstock and her professional training in the Woodstock Model School and in the Toronto Normal School. She was appointed to her present position on the Provincial Model School staff at Toronto, in September, 1890.

Hattie B. Mills, B.A.

Miss Hattie B. Mills, B.A., fourth assistant in the Boys' Model School, received her collegiate education at Hamilton Collegiate Institute, under the principalship of the late Charles Robertson, M.A. Obtaining a first-class non-professional certificate in 1891, she passed to the Wentworth County Model School, where she spent a year in training for primary work under the direction of S. B. Sinclair, M.A. She taught for two years in the Public Schools of Hamilton, and obtained during that time a Specialist's standing in French and German, and third year standing in Modern Languages and Philosophy in Toronto University. In the fall of 1894, she attended the Toronto Normal School (winning the gold medal for general proficiency) and taking the examination of the School of Pedagogy at Christmas, 1894, obtained a High School Specialist's certificate in French and German and first class professional certificate as Public School teacher. After teaching for a year in the Public Schools of Toronto and Hamilton, she completed her third year in May, 1896, at Toronto University. In September, 1896, she was appointed to her present position in the Provincial Model School, completing her Arts course in May, 1897, and obtaining the degree of B.A. in the departments of Modern Languages and Philosophy. In December, 1897, she passed the professional examination for Specialists in English and History at the Ontario Normal College.

Sara Ross.

Miss Sara Ross, fourth assistant in the Girls' Model School, received her non-professional education in the Public Schools of St. Mary's and Petrolia, and in the Collegiate Institutes of St. Mary's and Strathroy. Her professional training was received in the Sarnia Model School, the Toronto Normal School and the School of Pedagogy. She taught in the Public Schools of Lambton, Middlesex and York. She was appointed to the Toronto Model School staff in 1892.

Eugene Albert Masson.

Monsieur Eugene Albert Masson, teacher of French in the Model Schools, was born at Paris, France, educated in a Jesuit College, and then served in the French army for one year. After engaging in his father's business for several years, he went to New York in 1889, where he entered the Berlitz School of Languages (Madison Square). In 1891, he came to Canada and entered the Ingres and Coutellier School of Languages as teacher of French. In 1895, he was appointed instructor in French at Victoria University, at the Model Schools and at Miss Veal's School for Young Ladies.

Alexander Clark Casselman.

Alexander Clark Casselman, Drawing and Writing Master of Toronto Normal School, was born in Stormont County on June 26th 1860. He obtained a second A certificate in 1880, a first C in 1885, Science Specialist's and Public School Inspector's certificates in 1897. His education was received at the Public School in Finch Township; and at Williamstown High School, one year; Morrisburg High School, nine months; St. Catharines Collegiate Institute, six months; Toronto University, two years; and at Stormont County Model School and Ottawa Normal School. He taught a Public School for six years and was Science Master of Iroquois High School for six years. In 1892 he was appointed to his present position.

Sydney H. Preston.

Sydney H. Preston was appointed Music Master of the Normal and Model Schools in 1882. He was born at Ottawa, and he began the practice of his profession in Perth, Ontario. He has held responsible positions in Toronto as organist and conductor, and as teacher of vocal and instrumental music; but of late years has relinquished outside work in order to devote himself exclusively to the duties of his present position.

Thomas Parr.

Staff-Sergeant Thomas Parr, instructor in drill and calisthenics at the Normal and Model Schools, was born in London, England, in 1841, and enlisted in the Seventh Hussars, in 1858. He served in Bengal, India, from 1859 until 1870, and received a medal for long service and good conduct. He was one of the promoters of the famous "Musical Ride," under H. R. H. Prince Arthur, in Norwich, England, 1875-6. He came to Canada in 1879 and was engaged as drill master in Upper

Canada College until 1884, when he was transferred to his present position. At one time, Sergeant Parr was Fencing Master and Drill Instructor for the Seventh Queen's Own Hussars, and during a considerable portion of the time the School of Pedagogy was located at Toronto, he gave instruction to the students in Drill.

Wilhelmina MacKenzie.

Miss Wilhelmina MacKenzie, teacher of Physical Culture in the Normal and Model Schools, was born in Kincardine, and educated at the Model and High Schools there. She came to Toronto in 1892 to attend the Conservatory School of Elocution and Physical Culture. She was graduated from this institution in 1894, and taught at Havergal Ladies' College for two years. She then went to New York to attend the "New York School of Expression." She took the full course there in physical culture and elocution and graduated in 1896. She was appointed to her present position in 1897.

Louisa H. Montizambert.

Miss Lousia H. Montizambert, teacher of Scientific Sewing in the Normal and Model Schools and only daughter of Edward L. Montizambert, late law officer of the Senate, Ottawa, was born in Quebec. She received her education at Private Schools in that city. She studied scientific sewing at the Pratt Institute, Brooklyn. She was appointed to her present position in August 1897, being the first to teach this subject in the Toronto Normal and Model Schools.

Kate H. Mitchell.

Mrs. Kate H. Mitchell (nee Miss Kate Long), teacher of Domestic Science in the Normal School, was born at Brantford in 1859. She was educated in the Public Schools and Collegiate Institute of that city. She obtained a third and a second class certificate, and after teaching for a number of years in Brant County and in Brantford, she took the course in "Domestic Science" at Philadelphia in 1895-6. She obtained a first-class certificate and she has been engaged in giving instruction in this department in the following institutions: "The Fred. Victor Mission," the Y. W. C. A., St. Margaret's College, Mrs. Neville's and Miss Veal's Ladies' Schools, Grace Hospital and the Provincial Normal School.

Mary E. Macintyre.

Miss Mary E. Macintyre, Directress of the Kindergarten department, received her non-professional education at the Strathroy Collegiate Institute and her professional training at the West Middlesex County

Model School and the Toronto Normal School. After spending one year as assistant in the Kindergarten department of the above school, she took charge of that department in the State Normal School at Winona, Minnesota, and returned at the end of the year to occupy her present position.

Ellen Cody.

Miss Ellen Cody, assistant in the Toronto Normal Kindergarten, was educated at Newmarket High School and at the Toronto School of Art. She received her professional training at the Newmarket Model School and at the Toronto Normal School, after which she was made permanent assistant in the Kindergarten department.

VIII.

NAMES OF STUDENTS.

The names of all successful students of the Toronto Normal School, who attended between November, 1847 and December, 1875, together with biographical notes on all of those about whom it was possible to receive information, are given below. The committee found very great difficulty in obtaining exact information, regarding many of the persons here named in the lists for the different sessions, partly on account of the lapse of time and partly owing to the fact that many of them have removed to distant parts of the continent and could not be traced. However, the greatest care has been taken in examining the official registers and in verifying all accounts sent in by inspectors and others who interested themselves in the matter; it is therefore hoped that the notes and name lists will be found correct as far as they go.

FIRST SESSION.

(November, 1847—April, 1848.)

Ardiel, Isaac : Taught school for one year in the Gore of London ; studied Law in London ; died at Racine, Wis., U.S.A., in 1854.

Bell, Robert, Whitby : Taught for a short time in the Model School.

Burr, James, Toronto ; Burr, Rufus, Hamilton.

Carruthers, James : Taught subsequently in Toronto ; died about 1853.

Chapman, Isaac : Died at Thornhill.

Clark, Alexander, Toronto ; Cook, Gilbert W., Crowland ; Cooper, Thomas, Crowland.

Crane, Isaac : Taught seven years ; entered the Wesleyan Methodist ministry and remained in it till 1888 ; resides at Drayton.

Dewart, Edward Hartley, D. D. : Taught several years; entered the Methodist ministry in 1851 ; was ordained in 1855 ; was editor of the *Christian Guardian* from 1869 to 1895 ; has filled many prominent positions in the Methodist Church ; is a distinguished author ; resides in Toronto.

Foster, E., Oakland, Brant.

George, David : Taught for some time in Toronto, where he afterwards kept a store ; now deceased.

SECOND SESSION.
(May, 1848—November, 1848.)

Anderson, Mary Anne, Toronto.

Bigham, Robert, Reach ; Blush, Rodolphus, Rainham.

Brown, Rachel Catherine, Stamford, Welland : Long deceased.

Byam, Jesse F.: Taught six or seven years in Welland, Lincoln and Hastings ; spent some time in Australia ; took part in the American Civil War ; engaged in business in Peel County from 1866 to 1881 ; is still living in Toronto.

Byams, John H., Crowland.

Cairnduff, Henry W.: Marysburgh.

Cameron, John : Taught for a time in Peterboro' County between Douro and Asphodel.

Campbell John, Puslinch ; Cawthorne, John B., Oxford ; Clark, Jannet, Welland ; Clyde, David, Addington.

Copp, Elizabeth : Taught till 1851 a private school in Toronto ; married in 1862 Mr. Gilbert of Ottawa ; died in 1866.

Corbett, Jane (Mrs.), Toronto.

Corwin, Elizabeth : Taught for a time ; married Mr. Wilson ; long since dead.

Dingman, Garrit : Taught five years, entered the Methodist ministry, and remained in it for forty-four years ; is now superannuated.

Evans, George W., North Gwillimbury : Deceased.

Ferguson, Thomas A., Vespra.

Foster, Daniel R.: Taught at Oakland, Boston and Waterford ; became a merchant ; now a private banker in Waterford.

Grace, James : Taught for some time, went into agriculture and horticulture near Brantford ; has filled many municipal and other local offices ; lives in Brantford, where he acts as insurance agent ; is a Justice of the Peace.

Grant, John, M.D.: Now a prominent physician in Napanee.

Haigh, Mary E.: Taught in the Central School, London ; died within a few months after she began work there.

Hawkins, James : Taught in Pickering before attending the Normal School, and afterwards at different places in York County for fourteen years ; farmed near Markham till 1885 ; died in Scarboro' in 1893.

Hawkins, Mary Anne, Toronto.

Hoit, Daniel Young: Taught in London East until 1881 ; went to the United States.

Hughes, Mary, Toronto ; Hunter, William, Ontario.

Kingsmill, Elizabeth, Peel.

McCaffry, John, Toronto ; McClelland, Alexander, Toronto ; McClelland, James T., York.

McDiarmid, Peter : Taught for two years in Prescott County ; emigrated to Minnesota, U.S.A., where he filled for many years different public offices, including membership in the State Legislature ; now lives in Washington State.

McElroy, Anne J.: Taught one year in Smithville and one in London ; married in 1851 Robert Reid who has been for twenty years Collector of Customs in that city ; still lives there.

McGuin, John B.: Taught the Newburgh Academy ; became Clerk of the County Court of Lennox and Addington ; died in 1886.

McKinnon, Alexander : Subsequently on the editorial staff of the *Hamilton Times*.

McLean, Anna, Toronto.

Malcolm, Sherman : Taught four years, and then took up the work of land surveying, which he has practised almost ever since ; lives at Blenheim.

Milne, Thomas : Became a veterinary surgeon, and practised at Ingersoll.

Moore, Hiram A., Woodhouse.

Morrison, Anne M. : Married Mr. James Cummings ; resides in Hamilton.
Mosley, Robert, Whitchurch, York : Deceased.
Moss, M. Minerva, Stormont.
Niven, Isabella, Lincoln.
O'Halloran, Michael, Toronto ; Orr, Elizabeth, Toronto.
Pennington, Richard, Scarboro', York : Deceased.
Plant, William, Prescott.
Robinson, Robert : Taught in Stamford ; now deceased.
Rogerson, John, Bowmanville.
Rose, George : Taught four years in Dundas County, and the remainder of his period of thirty-seven years of work in the County of York, part of the time as Mathematical Master in the Newmarket High School ; still resides in Newmarket.
Ruby, Adam J. : Taught for some years in New Hamburg, Berlin, and Zurich ; abandoned teaching for farming ; now engaged in the business of insurance in Berlin.
Simpson, William, Hillier, Prince Edward : Deceased.
Sinclair, Archibald C. : Taught till 1855 in Glengarry ; studied Medicine in McGill University, and practised nearly thirty years at Port Elgin, in the County of Bruce, filling most of the time the office of Coroner ; is now practising at Rossland, British Columbia.
Somerville, Robert, Simcoe ; Stewart, Alexander, Hamilton ; Stewart, John, Hamilton.
Taaffe, John : Taught in the London Central School from 1853 till his death in 1861.
Tait, Francis A., Middlesex; Taylor, John, Uxbridge ; Thiese, Andrew, Waterloo ; Townsend, William, Hamilton ; Triller, Arthur L., London.
Turner, Alfred : Died a few years ago in Toronto.
Wickson, Samuel : Spent some years in the service of Hugh Scobie, a well known pioneer publisher in Toronto ; entered the legal profession, and is still in active practice in Toronto.

THIRD SESSION.
(November, 1848–May, 1849.)

Armstrong, Anne, Ontario ; Armstrong, Mary Anne, Peel.
Beaty, William : Taught at Boyne, and afterwards went to farm in Muskoka District.
Boaslaugh, Hervey M., Lincoln ; Buckland, Samuel P., Tecumseh.
Burgar, Catharine : Married Mr. Wright ; since deceased.
Campbell, Archibald, Elgin ; Campbell, William, Elgin ; Carson, James, Toronto.
Dean, Harriet : Now Mrs. George Gooderham, Toronto.
Diamond, Abraham : Taught in the Belleville Grammar School ; practised Law and served as Police Magistrate in Belleville ; died there ten years ago.
Diamond, Irvine : Taught several years ; has been a member and chairman of the Belleville School Board ; is now an insurance agent in that city.
Donnelly, Elizabeth, Kingston.
Elliott, John, Peel.
Fletcher, William : Entered the ministry, died in Nebraska, U.S.A., some years ago.
Foster, Jane : Taught fourteen years ; now Mrs. Jane Williams, a widow residing near Hewitt P. O.
Futhy, Robert : Taught until superannuated ; died about nine years ago ; resided near Feversham, in Grey County.
Haley, Amy M.: Taught some years ; married Mr. James Bradburn of Markham ; resided more recently near Tilsonburg, where she died a few years ago.
Hamilton, Robert W., Whitby ; Hellems, Martha E., Crowland.

Henry, George : Became a wealthy lumberman ; endowed schools in the Township of King ; deceased.

Hinchy, John, Toronto ; Humphreys, James, Manvers ; Huttan, William L., Toronto.

Kennedy, Mary Anne, Whitchurch ; Kimball, James M., Nelson, Halton.

Lakeman, Margaret, Blandford, Oxford ; Lewis, James, Hamilton ; Lynch, Francis, Peel.

McCausland, John, Toronto.

McClelland, Robert : Taught in St. Catharines until the time of his death, which occurred about sixteen years ago.

Macdonell, Donald, Lochiel ; McDougall, Joseph, Toronto ; McFarlane, Duncan, Ontario ; McIntosh, Mary, E. Zorra.

McNab, Finlay : Became a Baptist minister, and afterwards taught High School in Picton, Carleton Place and Arnprior ; is now insurance agent at Arnprior.

Maguire, Sarah A., Blandford.

Miller, George : Taught till 1855 ; entered the Methodist ministry ; resumed teaching from 1860 to 1867 ; continued in the active work of the ministry from that time until superannuation in 1895 ; still living in Woodstock.

Miller, Henry, Markham ; Milne, Elizabeth G., Oxford ; Moffat, Alexander M., Elizabethtown.

Murray, John : Went to a Commercial College in Buffalo, U.S.A. ; spent some years in railroad work at Thorold ; subsequently taught in Commercial Colleges in Terrebonne and Montreal till his death a number of years ago in the latter city

Nash, Alfred, Hallowell, Prince Edward ; Nixon, Robert, Hamilton, Northumberland.

Orfuno, Samuel, Toronto.

Pinnock, James T., Augusta.

Powlass, Isaac : An Indian from the Grand River Reserve ; now deceased.

Price, James, Chinguacousy.

Reid, John N. : Became a successful medical practitioner at Thornhill ; was appointed a member of the teaching faculty of Rolph's Medical School, Toronto, in 1857, and continued teaching in it till its dissolution in 1870 ; died not long afterward.

Robinson, Thomas, Smith.

Salt, Allen : An Ojibway Indian ; received his early education at Grape Island in Rice Lake and at Old Credit ; taught at the Alderville Mission School both before and after attending the Normal School ; while teaching the Indian Mission School at St. Clair he entered the ministry of the Methodist Church in 1853 ; has served as a missionary among the Indians of Rainy Lake, Garden River, Christian Island, St. Clair, Muncey, and Parry Island ; at the latter place he has resided for the past fifteen years.

Smith, John, Toronto ; Smyth, Thomas H., Halton ; Sovereign, Jeremiah W., S. Dumfries ; Steele, Mary, Humberstone.

Thompson, Elizabeth : Erin, deceased

Thornber, Alice, Georgina ; Towler, M. A., Toronto.

Watson, Thomas : Taught at Allanburgh, Lundy's Lane, Stamford, and Port Hope, till 1881, in the last named place for thirty years ; he still resides there.

Weldon, Alexander : Taught many years in Elgin County until his health failed ; long deceased.

Willcock, Abel, Peel ; Williams, Maria Louisa, Toronto.

Wilson, Nicholas : Has taught for fifty years in the City of London, nineteen years in the Public Schools and thirty-one in the High School, of which he is still one of the assistant masters. In January, 1897, the jubilee of his entrance on his work in London was appropriately celebrated.

Winters, Judson : Taught several years; is now living at Lacroix, Wisconsin, U.S.A.

Winters, William C. : Died in Australia about 1850.

FOURTH SESSION.

(May, 1849—November, 1849.)

Armstrong, Andrew : Became a clergyman ; now deceased.
Barber, Sarah, Yonge, Leeds ; Baxter, Thomas, Toronto ; Beatty, Edmund, Cobourg.
Bigger, Marsina : Has spent most of his life in business at Niagara Falls South, where he has been very successful.
Bogue, Henry, Toronto ; Bristol, Bernice, York ; Brooke, C. R., Toronto.
Butchart, John, Wellington : Deceased.
Callinan, James, Toronto.
Clarry, William : Taught for some time and then turned to farming ; died in Markham.
Coulter, Thomas : Taught two or three years ; went to British Columbia in 1862 ; on his return went into business, and spent the latter part of his life as an officer of the municipality of Almonte ; died in 1883.
Cox, Mary Anne E., Montreal ; Cox, Caroline, Montreal.
Coyne, Samuel, Toronto : Deceased.
Davis, Harvey J., York.
Davy, Nelson M., Richmond, Lennox : Deceased.
Dawson, Rebecca, York.
Day, James E. : Became secretary of the Hamilton Water Works Board ; moved to Toronto to become a partner with Bryant & Stratton in one of their commercial colleges ; afterwards established one of his own, and conducted it for many years till his death in 1890.
Drury, Mary S., Simcoe.
Ferguson, Thomas A., Rama, Ontario.
Finch, Jeremiah : A physician at Hastings, Minn., U. S. A.
Freeman, George, Cramahe, Northumberland.
Graham, Robert, London.
Haley, Augusta Anne : Now Mrs. Jeffrey, of London.
Haley, Phebe C. : Went to San Francisco, California, over thirty-five years ago.
Holt, Samuel N. : Practised Law ; retired to a farm near Port Rowan, on which he resides.
Jones, John, Prince Edward.
Kelly, Bridget : Entered St. Joseph's convent in 1858, died in 1865.
Kent, Douglas G., Brantford.
Keown, Mary J. : Began to teach in the Public Schools of Toronto in 1852, and continues to do so to the present time.
Keys, Thomas : Taught for many years in Grantham Township ; turned to farming, and was appointed Treasurer of the County of Lincoln ; died three years ago in St. Catharines, where he resided.
Lacey, Walter P., Peel ; Laing, Adam, Flamboro', Wentworth.
Loscombe, R. R. : A distinguished barrister residing in Bowmanville ; has been Mayor several years.
McBeath, John, Simcoe ; McEwen, William, Bathurst, Lanark ; McFadden, Moses M., South Gower, Carleton ; McLean, John, Vaughan.
McLellan, James A. : Taught public school for some time in St. Mary's, Ontario, and afterwards the Yarmouth Academy in Nova Scotia ; graduated M.A. in 1863 and LL.D. in 1873 in the University of Toronto ; filled for some years the position of High School Inspector ; has been since January, 1891, Principal of the Ontario Normal College ; has written several psychological and pedagogical works.

McMullan, William, Ernestown.
Merigold, Robert : Taught for some time ; turned to farming ; now deceased.
Martin, Elizabeth, Toronto.
Moore, William : Engaged in milling business in Meaford.
Nash, Thomas W.: Has been for many years a resident of Kingston, where he is Secretary-treasurer and chief engineer of the Kingston and Pembroke Railway.
Nixon, Thomas : Taught the Newmarket School until appointed Superintendent of North York : resigned this office to go into mercantile and manufacturing business in Newmarket, Clarksburg and Toronto; was from 1874 to 1878 an officer of the Dominion Government in Manitoba and the North West Territory ; has been since 1881 right-of-way agent on the Western Division of the Canadian Pacific Railway; resides in Winnipeg.
Patterson, Patrick, Grantham, Lincoln.
Peters, Nicholas : Taught for a few years and then turned to farming.
Ross, Andrew : Was a Township Superintendent before that office was abolished in 1871; went into the oil business in London, East; died there about 1880.
Ross, John, Oxford.
Scarlett, Edward : Taught for some time ; was Inspector of Schools in Northumberland for forty-one years; died in 1895.
Scully, Thomas, Ottawa.
Thompson, James, Hillier, Prince Edward.
Wharin, Mary : Taught in London till her death, which took place within a few months after she began work there.
Wilson, Esther, Hamilton ; Winters, A. J., Grimsby, Lincoln ; Woods, Jas., Cramahe, Northumberland.
Young, David, Woolwich, Waterloo.

FIFTH SESSION,

(November, 1849—May, 1850.)

Baikie, James, Trafalgar ; Ballard, Margaret, Whitby ; Bavis, Mrs. Eliza, Darlington ; Bell, Elizabeth, Amherstburgh ; Black, Alexander, Hamilton ; Blanchard, M. D., Elizabethtown.
Brown, James Coyle : Taught in public schools in rural districts, and in centres of population from village up to city ; was appointed in 1871 to the inspectorate of Peterboro', which he still holds.
Brown, Henry W.: Taught a number of years; now deceased.
Cameron, Jessie, London.
Campbell, Clarissa Emily : Now a widow, residing with her son near Denver, Col., U.S.A.
Campbell, Reuben, Montague ; Chadwick, Jane S., Woodhouse.
Clark, Mrs. Dorcas: Was appointed the first Head Mistress of the Girls' department of the Provincial Model School, resigned that position in 1865 and went to California ; in 1867 became associate principal of the Baptist College at Petaluma; became in 1868 teacher of History and Mathematics in the State Normal School at San José; was Vice-principal of the San Francisco Girl's High School from 1874 to 1888, when she retired from professional work after fifty-five years of almost continuous service; still resides in San Francisco.
Coleman, Anne W., Blanshard, Perth ; Collins, Mary Ann, Markham, York.
Curry, Reuben C.: Taught nearly five years in Prince Edward ; entered the medical profession, and has practised since 1857 in Picton, Port Hope, Guelph and Toronto ; in the last named place he has resided for twelve years.
Davison, Eleanor, Ontario ; Dean, Andrew, Brock, Ontario.
Dickson, Robert: Taught nearly seventeen years, and was superannuated on account of infirmity; still resides at Hubrey, Middlesex County.

Dundas, Anne Jane: Married Mr. Flint; died twenty-four years ago.
Endecott, Nancy, Whitchurch, York.
Farquharson, Robert. Reach, Ontario ; Fisher, Andrew, Nelson, Halton.
Freed, Selina H.: Taught in Binbrook, Grimsby and Copetown ; married Mr. Elliott ; deceased.
Gamble, Ann, Ontario.
Gray, J. B.: Taught two years in Port Dalhousie, sixteen as first assistant in the Hamilton Central School, two as Principal of the Galt Central School, and six as Principal of the St. Catharines Central School; after six years of supervisory work in that city he was appointed Inspector for Lincoln, which office he has held for twelve years.
Hall, Thomas, B.A : First Principal of the Port Rowan High School ; now teaching in California.
Herriman, W.L.: Taught for a few years and then entered the medical profession, practising at Orono, Port Hope and Lindsay; in the last named town he has lived for sixteen years, giving, however, a good deal of his time and attention to agriculture, especially in connection with a settlement which he has founded at Honora Bay, on Manitoulin Island ; is an enthusiast on the subject of agricultural education.
Hewlett, John: Drowned about thirty years ago in Georgian Bay near Meaford.
Hoover, Eleanor, Grantham, Lincoln ; Hull, Richard, Ontario.
Jamieson, Thomas, Vaughan, York, deceased.
Kee, David, Vaughan, York.
Kilborne, Ira B. : Entered the ministry: Deceased.
Lester, Alexander : Entered the Methodist ministry ; died some years ago.
Livingston, Mary A., London ; Livingston, Sarah Jane, London ; Lynch, Philip, Toronto.
McCausland, Robert : Taught many years in Toronto ; superannuated in 1884.
McDonald, Alexander, Toronto.
McIntyre, D.: Practised Medicine ; died at Strathroy in 1865.
McKay, George, West Zorra. Oxford ; McRay, James, West Zorra, Oxford ; McLennan, John, Charlotteville, Norfolk ; McNab, Michael, Toronto ; McQuade, Michael, Goderich.
Meredith, William, Bathurst, Lanark.
Meredith, William H.: Taught for twenty-five years, for the most part in the County of York, afterwards filled positions as book-keeper in Toronto ; died in 1894.
Mowatt, George : Became Superintendent of schools in North Hastings ; died many years ago.
Oakley, Francis : Entered the medical profession ; practised in Oakville and afterwards in Toronto, where he still resides.
O'Grady, John F., Toronto.
O'Donnell, Margaret : Taught fourteen years in Norfolk County ; married Mr. John McMahon of Elora in 1872 ; died in 1891.
Pastill, N., Wentworth.
Pease, Hannah : Married ; resides at Thornbury.
Pew, Robert, Welland.
Richmond, Sarah : Did not teach ; married Mr. Benjamin Willmott in 1851.
Rogers, W. D., Ontario.
Sinclair, Duncan : Taught four years in Kent ; engaged in business till 1864 ; resumed teaching in Chatham, and continued it till his death in 1878.
Smith, David : Taught in the Township of Moulton.
Spong, George, Etobicoke, York.

Stewart, Duncan : Taught for some time ; went into railroad business ; now lives in St. Paul, Minn., U.S.A.
Stoddard, Lucy : Died at Spencerville in 1857.
Thompson, Martha : Married Mr. Levi Goodwillie ; deceased.
Thompson, Jane, Niagara, Lincoln.
Tobias, Fanny R.: Taught at Drummondville.
Trenholm, William, Augusta, Grenville : Deceased.
Walker, John, Waterloo.
Walker, John G.: Never taught; died in England many years ago.
Warwick, Frederick : Still living at St. Paul, Minn., U.S.A.
Weed, Amelia A., Toronto ; Wells, George, Beauharnois, Quebec.
Williams, Walter S.: Taught a short time ; studied Law ; lived formerly in Napanee, but resides now in California.
Willson, Henry, N. Gwillimbury, York.
Wilson, John H.: Taught five years, graduated in Medicine in Victoria University and in the University of New York ; was a member of Victoria teaching faculty for two years ; has since practised Medicine in St. Thomas where he still resides ; he was for eight years a member of the Ontario Legislative Assembly and eight years a member of the Canadian House of Commons.
Wright, Eliza, Ontario.

SIXTH SESSION.

(September, 1850—May, 1851.)

Bailey, Elizabeth Jane, Wentworth.
Bethell, Fanny : Taught in London ; married Mr. David T. Ware.
Bond, William, Toronto.
Campbell, Catherine, Halton ; Carey, William, Toronto.
Caulton, William : Taught a few years, then entered the medical profession ; died in 1894.
Conger, Peter D., Prince Edward.
Corbin, Tamar Jane : Taught a few years ; married ; died in 1894.
Cowan, John : Studied for the ministry of the Methodist Church.
Crewson, William, Waterloo.
Gamble, Aaron, York.
Gillies, Daniel : Taught school for eleven years ; became a farmer, and was for some years Reeve of East Williams, Middlesex Co.; died in 1893.
Hammond, James, Lanark.
Harrison, Edmund B. : Taught till 1864 in and near Ridgetown, Kent ; became local Superintendent of Schools for the county in 1871 ; was continued in the same office for East Kent when the county was divided in 1877 ; retired in 1885 to his farm near Ridgetown where he now resides ; was offered the headmastership of the Provincial Model School in 1858, but declined it.
Hayward, Edward, Northumberland ; Hiams, D. McD., York ; Heffernan, Elizabeth, Toronto.
Herman, Royal : Became a Provincial Land Surveyor and Civil Engineer ; is still practising his calling at Rednersville.
Hicks, Andrew, Russell.
Jamieson, John, York.
Kelly, Sarah, Toronto.
Kennedy, Marianne : Taught in the Toronto Public Schools from 1853 to 1897 ; deceased.

McCammon, Samuel : Principal of the Gananoque Public School for six years ; has ever since resided in Gananoque and given continuous attention to educational matters ; has been Secretary-Treasurer of the School Board since 1854 ; was formerly an Inspector of the town schools and a member of the County Board of Examiners ; has been engaged in business ever since he gave up teaching.

Marsh, John S., Middlesex ; Martin, Robert, Simcoe ; Meighan, John, York ; Morden, John M., Middlesex.

Morrow, John : Taught a few years, and went into other occupations for a time ; resumed teaching and continued till 1866, in that year was appointed to the Inland Revenue service of which he is still a member in Toronto.

Robertson, Duncan : Taught in Ottawa for several years ; removed with his family to British Columbia, where he still resides.

Scouten, Michael S., Addington : Deceased.

Smith, Dennis, Kent.

Starr, Francis : Taught about seven years ; turned to farming, and still follows that occupation near Newmarket.

Stone, H. W., Prescott.

Van Every, Jane : Taught in York for three years ; married Mr. Joshua Lochie, and resides in California.

Welch, Almira, Welland.

Yeomans, John H., Hastings.

SEVENTH SESSION.
(August, 1851—April, 1852.)

Adams, Maria J.: Married Mr. A. McCallum while he was Principal of the Provincial Model School ; died not long afterward.

Arthurton, Samuel L., Welland.

Barr, James, Oxford.

Connell, Thomas : Taught in New York State, died more than twenty years ago.

Demill, Adelaide, Prince Edward.

Eckert, William D.: Taught two years in Prince Edward, and has taught forty-five years continuously in Middlesex, twenty-six of them in London, where he is still Principal of a large public school.

Emslie, Peter, Wellington : Deceased.

Fitch, Benjamin Franklin : Graduated in the Department of Modern Languages in the University of Toronto ; practised Law in Brantford, where he died a few years ago.

Gage, Edward F., Durham.

Garland, Thomas : Taught for many years in Carleton, Bruce and Lincoln ; died about ten years ago.

German, George G.: Taught in Hastings County ; was Principal of the Mount Elgin Industrial School for Indians ; engaged in commercial business in Belleville, removed in 1866 to Strathroy, where he still resides and takes an active interest in education.

Girvin, Margaret : Married ; resides on Sandwich Island.

Guthrie, John : Died about forty years ago.

Halliday, David : Died lately near Renfrew.

Harding, Samuel W.: Taught a number of years ; became book-keeper in the Methodist Book Room ; died several years ago.

Henderson, Apphia S., Middlesex ; Henderson, Susan, Prince Edward.

Jennings, Emily H. : Taught in Chippawa, in Brantford High School, and in Mount Pleasant Public School ; married Mr. John Stowe ; studied Medicine in New York, and began practising in 1867 in Toronto, which is still her home ; registered in the Ontario College of Physicians and Surgeons after taking a course of lectures in the Toronto School of Medicine ; has been, and still is, actively devoted to the work of social reform.

Johnson, Catharine : Taught from 1852 to 1855 in the Girls' Department of the Provincial Model School, and six years in Willowdale in York County ; married in 1860 the Rev. Charles Fish, Methodist Minister, now superannuated and living in Toronto.

Johnson, John E., Leeds.

Johnston, John : Taught in Simcoe County, became a farmer in Flos Township ; died in 1894.

Kessack, Christina : Taught in St. Thomas ; married Rev. J. Hugill in 1854 ; died at Galt in 1856.

Lapraik, Archibald, Halton ; Loree, Darius, Welland.

McNally John E.: Taught three years in a private school, and three in a Public School near Aurora ; has lived ever since in Aurora, engaged in business ; has held a number of public offices.

McNaughton, Thomas: Practised Law in Cobourg.

Martin, Alexander: Spent nine years in teaching and inspecting, and thirty-six in the Methodist ministry ; now living in Toronto.

Morden, E. R.: Taught for a few years ; studied Medicine but did not practise ; turned to horticulture and the nursery business, which he still follows at Niagara Falls South ; has taken an active interest in agricultural education.

Peacock, George : Taught eight years at Port Burwell ; is now farming, living at Mount Salem.

Phillips, John R.: Now Rev. John R. Phillips, of St. Thomas.

Powell, Julia Ann, Northumberland ; Procunier, Elijah, Norfolk.

Robins, Sampson Paul : Taught from 1852 to 1854 as third master in the Boys' Department of the Provincial Model School, and for two years as Principal of the Brantford Central School ; in 1857 took part, under Dr. Dawson, in the organization of the McGill Normal School, Montreal ; after thirteen years' service became, for other thirteen, Superintendent of Protestant Schools in that city ; has ever since been Principal of the McGill Normal School.

Ross, Samuel, Simcoe.

Shaw, Joseph W., Brockville.

Slaven, Annie Eliza, Prince Edward: Went to California.

Tilley, William: Was Science Master for several years in Napanee High School ; died in 1886.

Walsh, Catharine, York : Deceased.

Webb, Henry F.: Became a manufacturer in Trenton ; now deceased.

Young, Matura, Prince Edward.

EIGHTH SESSION.

(May, 1852—November, 1852.)

Allen, Lewis, Addington : Deceased.

Beattie, Mary, London.

Bedford, Alice : Married Mr. William Coates ; died twenty years ago.

Bell, Elizabeth N.: Married Mr. John Baxter ; lives as a widow in Chatham.

Bell, Alexander, Peel ; Bio, William, Middlesex ; Bingham, Charles, Elgin.

Brookfield, E. W.: Taught fifteen years in rural schools ; spent sometime farming ; became Collector of Customs at Fort Erie in 1885, and retired in 1896 ; resides now on his farm in Crowland Township.

Cameron, Alexander, Victoria.

Campbell, John : Taught for many years as Head Master of one of the Toronto Public Schools ; still resides in that city.

Campbell, R. O.. Taught in rural schools in Grenville, Dundas and Carleton, and also in Madoc, Burritt's Rapids and Kemptville ; rendered military service during the Fenian Raid, rose to the rank of Colonel of the 56th Battalion ; retired in March 1897, retaining his rank ; retired at the same time from teaching ; resides in Kemptville.

Charlton, Benjamin E. : Taught a year and a half in Hamilton Central School, and then went into business as a manufacturer ; has filled several prominent positions including that of Mayor of Hamilton, President of the Board of Trade, and President of the Street Railway Company ; still carries on business in that city ; is one of the Commissioners of Queen Victoria Park, Niagara Falls.

Chisholm, Daniel, Lanark : Went to British Columbia.

Christy, George B., Prince Edward ; Clark, Emily M., Toronto ; Collins, Thomas, Carleton ; Connor, Isaac, Wentworth.

Daniell, Ellen, Peel.

Davidson, Alexander : Surveyor ; lives at Arkona.

Dowling James, Leeds.

Edmonds, Joseph, Peel.

Fleming, Anna, Toronto ; Fleming, John H., York ; Foley, Thomas, Peel.

Freeman, William : Taught in Milton, studied Medicine, and has practised for many years in Georgetown.

Gothard, Joseph : Went into railroading and telegraph operating.

Hagar, Azubah, Welland ; Hagar, Lydia L., Welland.

Herrington, Walter S., Prince Edward : Died young.

Higgins, Fanny, Northumberland.

Hoig, Martha R. : Taught several years ; married Mr. James Gibson of Oshawa, where she still lives.

Huckins, James M. : Taught in Ontario County.

Hunt, Ambrose : Now a clergyman in the United States.

Huntsman, William V. : Taught many years in Oxford County ; is now farming in Muskoka.

Irwin, William Henry : Taught for twelve years ; retired from the profession, and is now a publisher in Hamilton.

Kelly, Michael Joseph, M. D., LL.B. : Taught Grammar School in Bowmanville and Waterdown ; was engaged in literary work for several years ; when the office of County Inspector was created by the School Act of 1871, he was appointed to that position in Brant County and he still discharges its duties ; was a member of the Central Committee of Examiners.

Kilmer, Edward, Hastings : Went into railroading.

Liddy, George P., York.

McBrien, James : Taught fifteen years ; when the office of Public School Inspector was created by the School Act of 1871, he was appointed to it in Ontario County and still continues to discharge the duties assigned to it ; lives at Prince Albert.

McCarkill, Peter, Ontario.

McLean, John, Brant : Taught many years until 1883, ; now deceased.

McPherson, John : Retired from teaching in 1867 ; resides in Ottawa.

McQuarrie, Duncan : Taught some time ; retired from active work ; now deceased.

Magan, Elizabeth : Taught successfully in Hamilton, Toronto, Bel'eville, and Joliet, Ill., U.S.A. ; is now Superior of the Loretto Convent at Niagara Falls.

Magan, Grace : Taught under Dr. Sangster in the Central School Hamilton, and in Loretto Convent, Lindsay ; is now Sr. M. Delphina of Loretto Abbey, Toronto.

Martin, Henry, Toronto ; Mishaw, Spencer Daniel, Toronto ; Moorby, Samuel, Toronto ; Morrison, Peter, Lanark.

Newman, Timothy, Prince Edward.

Oliver, John S., Leeds.

Poole, John Wesley : Taught seventeen years in the counties of Lincoln and Perth, and in the town of St. Mary's ; has filled many public offices in St. Mary's, where he has resided for the past forty years.

Ralph, William, Middlesex.

Rothwell, John, Lanark.

Rothwell, Samuel : Taught several years ; became a clerk in the Department of Agriculture at Ottawa ; was superannuated in 1891 ; still resides in Ottawa.

Reazin, Henry : Taught Grammar School for some years ; was appointed Public School Inspector for West Victoria under the School Act of 1871, and still holds the position.

Reilly, Daniel John, Toronto ; Rice, Emily, Durham.

Robertson Minnie : Taught a private school in London till 1857, when she married Mr. Wm. Saunders, now Director of the Dominion Government's Experimental Farm near Ottawa, where she resides.

Robinson, Elizabeth, Toronto.

Scudamore, Henry Thomas Bernard de Lambton ; Siggins, Ann, Toronto.

Slaven, Thomas : Taught for some time in Ontario ; went to California, U. S. A., where he is now a Superintendent of Schools and is also engaged in business.

Sliter, Alonzo, Leeds : Was Principal of Pakenham Public School for several years ; superannuated ; now deceased.

Smyth, Charlotte S. : Taught in one of the Toronto Public Schools as Principal till 1862 ; married Mr. Thomas Scott, and now resides at Glenmorris.

Storrie, Sophia J., London.

Strachan, Alexander R. : Studied Medicine and practises in New York, U.S.A.

Toof, Maria E. : Took a course of study in Oberlin, Ohio, U.S.A. ; has devoted most of her life to literature and travel ; married Mr. A. W. Lauder who attended during the tenth session of the Normal School and was afterwards a member of the Ontario Legislative Assembly ; still resides in Toronto.

Trull, William Warren : Taught eight years ; then went into business of various kinds in Orono, where he still lives.

Van Camp, Lewis : Practised Dentistry in Berlin for over thirty years ; died this year.

Watson, William : Taught in the Port Hope High School.

Whitcomb, Huldah S., Prescott.

Williams, Marilla : Taught for a time ; married a clergyman ; is now living in the United States.

Williams, Matilda : After teaching for some time married a clergyman, and now resides in the United States.

Willson, Elvira, Welland.

NINTH SESSION.

(Nov., 1852—May, 1853.)

Appleton, Lydia Ann, York.

Bales, Elizabeth, York ; Barber, Eliza, Middlesex ; Bell, Thomas, York ; Boyd, W. T., Peel ; Brethoer, Samuel, Ontario ; Buyers, Margaret, Welland.

Caldwell, Mrs. Anne, Toronto ; Callaghan, Elizabeth J., Welland ; Carter, Tryphena S., Middlesex ; Carr, Sarah, Wentworth.

Campbell, Helen : Married Mr. J. Moore ; now residing in Winnipeg.

Campbell, Robert A., Lincoln ; Campbell, Ellen, Toronto ; Clarke, John, Brant.

Coote, Elizabeth : Taught a year and a half in Hamilton Central School, and one year in a private school at Oakville ; in 1857 married Mr. William McCraney who was afterwards a member of the House of Commons ; now resides in Vancouver, B. C.

Currey, Edward, Lincoln.
D'Evelyn, John : Became a physician ; died about twenty years ago.
Dougherty, Samuel, Toronto ; Douglass, Elizabeth, Halton.
Ede, Joseph, Durham.
Elson, John : At one time a merchant in Komoka.
Farland, Eliza J., Lambton.
Fellker, Frederick : Taught for a number of years ; entered mercantile life ; moved to the Western States where he now lives.
Fitzpatrick, W. D., York, : Now deceased.
Foster, Jennette Gray : Taught for six years in Haldimand and Welland Counties ; married Mr. Andrew Kinnard ; died in 1894.
Haycock, Charles W., Brant.
Hendry, Christina : Married Mr. D. White ; now deceased.
Hill, Richard, Elgin ; Hoig, Ellen L., Toronto ; Houghton, Mary, Oxford : Howard, Jane Amelia, Lambton ; Howard, Lydia E., Lambton ; Howe, Charles, Prince Edward.
Huffman, James C. : Taught for some years ; became a farmer ; died in 1895.
Hume, Annie C : Died at Wingham, Ontario.
Jones, Richard : Practised Medicine in New York.
Kay, Jane : Taught rural schools till 1855 ; married in 1856 Mr. John Darch, who died ten years afterward ; kept on her husband's business in London, which is still flourishing.
Kennedy, John T , Lincoln.
Kennedy, Lachlan, Halton : Became an engineer and land surveyor.
Kerby, May Elizabeth, Welland.
King, William Henry : Studied Medicine ; practised for some years ; now deceased.
Lanon, Griffin Patrick, Toronto ; Lemon, Caroline, York.
Lucas, Sarah Ann : Married Mr. T. Atkinson ; now deceased.
McDiarmid, Angus : Taught for a short time ; engaged in farming for several years ; entered the Civil Service, Ottawa, in 1874, and retired from it in 1895 ; still lives in Ottawa.
McDonell, Augustine, Glengarry.
McKenzie, Alexander, Middlesex : Deceased.
McLeay, Murdo : Lives in Watford, County of Lambton.
McTaggart, Neil : Taught school till 1857 and then became a farmer ; died in 1895.
Malcolm, John G., Oxford ; Markham, Patrick, Toronto ; Martin, Alexander, York.
Minchin, Charles : Died at Brantford in 1883.
Misener, David : Became a farmer ; deceased.
Mulholland, Hiram : Taught many years in Halton County ; was Local Superintendent of Schools.
Murray, George, Peel.
Nesbitt, James, Peel.
O'Brien, Patrick, Toronto.
Parnell, Mary Jane : Taught for several years ; married Mr. George Merrick of Merrickville ; now resides in Ottawa.
Patterson, H. H., York ; Pettit, Hiram, Durham.
Pew, E. A. C. : Now a well known promoter of railways and other works of public utility.
Price, Edwin : Taught for a number of years ; studied Medicine, and now has a lucrative practice.
Pritchard, Frederick W. S. : Became a physician ; now deceased.
Procunier, Daniel, Norfolk.

8

Quinn, Ann Jane : Taught in Yorkville, now part of Toronto ; married Mr. Robert McCausland ; died in 1894.

Quinn, Sarah B. : Taught in Toronto ; married Mr. Edward Perry of that city ; died about 1890.

Rae, Francis : Taught at Prince Albert in Ontario County ; practised Medicine in Oshawa ; appointed Registrar of the county ; died in 1896.

Richardson, Sarah J., Kent ; Riddell, Andrew, Toronto ; Roberts, John, Ontario.

Robinson, Eliza R. : Taught in Toronto ; married Mr. Taylor ; now deceased.

Rock, Warren : Taught in the Model School, Toronto ; entered the legal profession ; became an eminent practitioner in London ; died some eight years ago.

Rogers, Thomas A., Toronto ; Ryan, Elizabeth, Halton.

Sanders, Rosina A. : Taught in Hamilton Central School ; married Mr. Cranfield, a teacher in that city.

Sharp, Phoebe Louise : After teaching for some time in Welland County married Dr. R. A. Haney, formerly of Fonthill but now of Caistorville.

Simmons, Daniel L., Northumberland : Deceased.

Simmons, John, Toronto ; Simmons, Mary, Northumberland ; Smith, Henry F., Lincoln ; Smith, Jane, Wellington ; Smith, Jane, Peel.

Smith, Melissa : Taught a short time ; married ; now deceased.

Smith, William, Peel ; Stevenson, Samuel, Oxford.

Stewart, William : Taught for some years ; spent some time in the office of the North American, then edited by the Hon. William Macdougall ; studied Architecture and is now one of the leading architects in Hamilton ; designed the new Collegiate Institute in that city, and the Central School in Brantford.

Stuart, Mary : Retired from teaching ; lives at the family homestead, near Belton, in Middlesex.

Tobias, Mary : Taught in Niagara, then in the Buxton Mission, Chatham ; married Rev. Mr. McSweeney ; resides in New York.

Tocher, Isabella, Ontario ; Todd, Mary Ann, Toronto ; Trousdale, James D., Frontenac.

Vanalstine, Charity A., Welland ; Vanalstine, Elizanath, Welland.

Van Every, Elizabeth : Taught eight years in York County ; married Mr. Josiah Purkiss, then a merchant in Thornhill ; now resides in Toronto.

Vardon, William : Entered the medical profession ; practised in Ontario and the United States ; died at Berlin a few years ago.

Walker, Amand E., Lincoln ; Willson, Crowell, Welland ; Willson, Hester, Welland ; Willson, Pamelia, Welland ; Wilson, Mary, Brantford ; Wilson, Mary Ann, Toronto ; Wilson, Robert, Hastings ; Wood, Sarah, Norfolk.

TENTH SESSION.

(May, 1853—November, 1853.)

Abercrombie, William, Prince Edward : Died about 1855.

Adams, Wilbur Fisk, Halton.

Bearss, Mary M., Welland.

Bly, William Henry : Taught in Prince Edward ; engaged in business in Trenton.

Bowerman, Ichabod S., Prince Edward.

Bowerman, Thomas M.: Still living on a farm near Wellington in Prince Edward County.

Bowes, Sarah : Taught for twenty-five years in Public, Private and High Schools ; became an active organizer and platform speaker for the Women's Christian Temperance Union ; went to British Columbia in 1886 ; has charge of the "Chinese Girls' Rescue House" in Victoria.

Carlyle, William : Taught for some years in Norfolk and Brant Counties ; entered on a course of study with a view to the Congregational Ministry, and took contemporaneously a partial Arts course in the University of Toronto ; abandoned the ministerial course on account of throat disease ; taught in Hamilton Central school, and was afterwards Principal of Galt Central School for seven years, till his appointment in 1871 to the Inspectorship of Oxford County.

Clark, Charles, Haldimand ; Coe, Richard, Durham ; Costello, Edmund P., Brant.

Curry, William : Taught for several years ; was superannuated ; lived at Hillier, Prince Edward, until very recently.

Danard, Asa B.: Taught for some time ; is now farming near Owen Sound.

Dixon, John, Welland ; Draper, James, York.

Edmonds, Joseph, Oxford ; Evans, John, Halton.

Falloon, Charles Edward, Halton.

Foster, Jane : Taught for four years in Haldimand and Welland ; married Mr. James Williams.

Gibbs, Robert : Taught at Salem and Elora : still resides at the latter place.

Hankinson, Charles : Taught for some time in the Baptist College, Woodstock ; now deceased.

Hay, Robert, Brant.

Hellyer, Robert : Taught many years at Port Dover ; became a physician : now deceased.

Hume, Thomas : Taught in the Township of Pittsburgh.

Jessop, John : Taught in this Province till 1859 ; went to British Columbia, crossing the plains and mountains on foot ; maintained a private school in Victoria for three years ; started a successful agitation for free non-sectarian schools on Vancouver Island, and became Principal of the first school under the new system ; was Superintendent of Education for the united Province of British Columbia from 1872 till the abolition of the office in 1878 ; has been immigration agent for British Columbia since 1883 ; still resides in Victoria.

Kelly, David, Prince Edward.

Lauder, Abraham W. : After teaching for some time entered the legal profession and practised in Toronto ; represented South Grey in the Legislative Assembly of Ontario till his death in 1884.

Logan, Robert, Middlesex ; Lyon, Lydia L., Brant.

McCracken, Mary : Taught under Dr. Sangster in the Central School, Hamilton ; afterwards in Brantford Central School ; went to McGill College Model School, Montreal, as first Head Mistress.

McDonald, Angus, Victoria ; McDougall, Hugh, Russell ; McGee, Robert, Grenville ; McKay, William, Ontario.

Maguire, Jacob Choate, Durham ; Marlatt, Mary, Oxford ; Martin, James, Haldimand ; Masters, Caroline A., Toronto ; Masters, Delia A., Toronto ; Mills, Sophronie A., Northumberland ; Montgomery, William,[1] Wentworth ; Moriarty, James, Renfrew.

Phillips, Martin, Brant.

Robins, Samuel : Taught in the Public and High Schools of Bowmanville until 1856, when he died suddenly. He is a younger brother of S. P. Robins, the Principal of McGill Normal School.

Robinson, Julia A.: Taught in Toronto ; married Mr. Conlon ; resides in that city.

Stafford, Alexander, Toronto ; Stewart, William, Toronto.

Stone, Adeline : Taught two years ; married Mr. J. W. Fowke ; resides at Oshawa.

Sweeney, Margaret : Now Rev. Mother Sebastian, St. Joseph's Convent, Hamilton.

Turner, Alfred, Ontario : Left the profession.

Turner, Isaac : Went immediately into mercantile business ; moved to Manitoulin Island in 1879 ; retired from business in 1889 ; now resides at Little Current.

Warren, Joseph, : Taught until 1876 in Perth, in the County of Lanark, and in Pembroke and Eganville in the county of Renfrew ; was appointed a Customs officer ; still resides in Pembroke in that capacity.

Will, Phineas, Oxford : Left the profession.

Williams, David L.: Taught some years ; is now a farmer in Northumberland County.

ELEVENTH SESSION.

(November, 1853—May, 1854.)

Adams, Mary: Taught in Hamilton till 1863 ; then in the Girls' Model School, Toronto ; succeeded Mrs. Clark as Head mistress in 1865 ; retained that position till Dec., 1866 ; married Mr. Grinton.

Anderson, Jane, Toronto.

Bales, Sarah : Married Mr. A. R. Christie ; now a widow ; resides in Toronto.

Bannister, Charles : Taught a number of years in St. Catharines ; became a journalist there; died twenty years ago.

Bird, Francis Wesley : Entered the medical profession after teaching in the Central School, Oshawa ; removed to the United States.

Blaicher, Peter C: Became a druggist in Hamilton ; has been Mayor of that city, and still resides there.

Bowes, Harriett: Married Mr. James Field, Hamilton ; now deceased.

Bristol, Coleman, Lennox: Now deceased.

Brower, John Ransome : Taught some years ; became a farmer, and is now a buyer and exporter of cheese; resides in Belleville.

Burgess, Margaret, Haldimand.

Cattanach, Catharine : Taught in the Cornwall Public School for three years ; married the Rev. Hugh Campbell, M.A., of that town; since his death has lived in Toronto.

Clarke, Esther, Halton.

Coady, Mary: Not now teaching ; resides in California ; wife of Prof. Wright.

Coyne, John : Taught many years in Toronto; superannuated in 1884.

Decow, Mary Anne : Married Rev. George Cuthbertson ; resides in Toronto,

Decow, Rebecca : Taught some years in Norfolk County and Oakville ; is still teaching in Hamilton.

Ecroyd, Alfred Ernest: Taught some years ; died a few years ago.

Goldsmith, Gilbert: Taught for some time ; entered the Methodist Ministry , died several years ago in the United States.

Higgins, Kate, Toronto.

Hollingshead, Silas: Taught at different places in York County ; entered the medical profession, and practised till 1879, retired to his former home near Newmarket, and died there in 1881.

Holmes, Anna Maria, Toronto.

Hughes, Elizabeth: Married William Oliver ; resides in Toronto.

Jackson, Anne E. : Taught for a few years ; now resides in Toronto.

Jackson, John E. : Clerk of Eldon Township, Victoria.

Jamieson, Edward, Toronto.

Johnson, Isabella : Taught in St. Catharines, Middlesex, and Lambton ; married Mr. Hamilton Tripp ; still lives, a widow, at Forest, Ontario.

Junor, Catharine : Taught some time ; turned her attention to painting ; is a recognized artist of superior merit.

Keddie, Eliza Wilson : Taught for some time in Oshawa ; married ; died in 1854.

Kennedy, Harriet Evelyn, York ; Kennedy, Margery Muter, Middlesex ; Kerr, Bernard S., York.

Livingston, John, Simcoe.
McCrady, Melissa : Died about thirty-five years ago.
McLean, Thomas Ferguson : Taught for a few years ; studied Medicine in Queen's University ; practised in Goderich ; went to Florida some years ago.
McLennan, Christy, Huron.
McNaughton, John : Entered the medical profession in 1866 ; practises in Durham.
McNaughton, Margaret, Peel.
Megaw, Samuel : Taught in Durham and Huron Counties until 1882 ; was superannuated ; resides in Goderich.
Noden, William : Practised Medicine ; now deceased.
O'Connor, Thaddeus, Hamilton.
Piper, Lucinda, B.Sc., M.D.: Taught in Woodstock and Toronto ; married Mr. Aaron Griffith in 1861 ; taught a year in St. Mary's, and afterwards several years in Ohio, U.S.A.; was graduated M.D. in 1874 by the Cleveland Homœopathic College; now resides at Thorndale, Ontario.
Plunkett, William : Taught several years in Owen Sound ; became a medical practitioner ; resides in Dakota, U.S.A.
Reynolds, Parmenius : Left Prince Edward County about thirty years ago.
Shearer, Mary ; Married T. Hall, B.A., of the fifth session ; resides in California.
Shrigley, Margaret : Married Mr. Seam; lived in Buffalo.
Snyder, Lizanna S., Oxford : Somerville, Robert, Simcoe : Stevens, Elizabeth, Kingston ; Stevens, Mary, Simcoe; Stevens, William, Kingston.
Sproat, Marion, Halton : Married Dr. Douglas ; deceased.
Sproat, Eleanor, Halton : Married Mr. T. Rome, Grimsby.
Storrie, Josephine : Taught for some time ; married Mr. Henry Glackmeyer of the Canadian Civil Service; still living in Quebec City.
Sudborough, Mary E.: Taught a number of years in the Hamilton Public Schools ; married Rev. Mr. Armour, a Congregationalist minister in Vermont ; now resides in Northfield, Massachusetts, U.S.A.
Terrill, John : Farming near Picton, Ontario.
Walkingshaw, Cecilia Mary Anne: Now Mrs. Jeffrey of Toronto.
Willson, Mary Anne : Married a farmer in Binbrook, Wentworth County.

TWELFTH SESSION.

(May, 1854—November, 1854.)

Armstrong, Agnes, Wellington.
Barkley, George Abraham, Dundas County.
Chisholm, Allan, Victoria ; Clark, Helen Elizabeth, Haldimand.
Craig, Francis Josiah: Taught writing in the Normal and Model Schools from November, 1854, to April, 1855 ; taught in the public schools of Belleville and London till 1857; spent ten years in the United States, and the remainder of the time till 1892 in business in London, Strathroy and Sarnia ; now Town Clerk of Strathroy.
Dingman, Absalom : Was a journalist in Strathroy and Stratford ; was for some time an Inspector of Indian Agencies.
Dorothey, Susan, Toronto ; Douglass, William, Peterboro'.
Foggin, Alice : Taught two years in Toronto ; married Mr. John Turner, once an Alderman of Toronto; died in 1873.
Fotheringham, David : Taught as assistant and also as third Head Master of the Provincial Model School, 1856-58; resigned and taught in Hamilton for two years; was a student at Knox College and University College during 1860-63 ; travelled in Europe and the United States from 1864-71 ; was appointed Inspector in the County of York in 1871 and is still so employed.

Gould, Amos, Hastings: Taught for some time; now deceased.
Hackett, William, Toronto.
Holmes, Ninian Leander: Taught for many years in Haldimand County; superannuated and now living in the United States.
Hurlburt, John A.: Resided at Warkworth, Northumberland; now deceased.
McDonald, Elizabeth: Taught in rural schools and in Oakville; wife of Mr. S. B. Ganton of that town.
McElderry, Margaret Teresa, Toronto.
McKay, Alexander: Taught a number of years in the County of Stormont; graduated in Medicine; practised at Beaverton, Ontario; died in 1882.
McKee, Davis, Oxford.
McLean, John: Taught in St. Thomas and Port Stanley; studied and practised Law for thirty years; has been Inspector of schools in St. Thomas for twenty years.
McNaught, Elizabeth: Taught for several years in the vicinity of Brantford, Paris, Galt and Fergus; went to Australia in 1861; married Mr. John Boyd, of Ballarat, and still resides there, since his death with her uncle, Mr. David McNaught.
McPherson, Alexander: Taught till 1863; was then appointed Clerk and Treasurer of Etobicoke Township, which office he still holds.
Mowat, Jane: Taught five years in the John St. School, Toronto: married Daniel Rose, publisher; still living in Toronto.
Nash, Samuel: Studied Medicine and took his degree in 1865; now practising in Milford, Ontario.
Patton, John, York; Preston, Annie, Wellington.
Robinson, Sarah Agnes, Toronto.
Scott, Richard William: Taught in Oshawa and on the Grand River; became English Master in the Toronto Grammar School.
Stephens, James: Taught school in Kent for five years; turned to farming in 1860, and filled an office in the Division Court till 1878; farmed again till 1885; is now a private banker in Dresden, Ontario.
Strickland, Margaret: Taught in Oshawa; married Mr. Burnett; died in Oshawa.
Strickland, Nancy: Died in Oshawa.
Weir, William: Taught some years in Eramosa, Wellington; now book-keeper for Goldie & McCulloch in Galt.
Wilkinson, Caroline: Taught in Oxford and York Counties, and in a private school in London: in 1860 married Rev. James Goodwin, a Methodist clergyman; living in Grimsby.

THIRTEENTH SESSION.

(November, 1854—May, 1855.)

Adams, Joseph Fellows, Toronto.
Alexander, Robert: Taught in Newmarket till 1874; has been Principal of Galt Public School since 1875; was largely instrumental in organizing the Provincial Teachers' Association, now the Ontario Educational Association.
Armstrong, Ann Musgrove: Taught two years in Wellington County; married Mr. Alexander Bruce of Morris Township; died in 1867.
Arnold, Emma, Toronto.
Backhouse, Matilda: Taught for some time; married Mr. Isaac Foster, a farmer.
Bigg, William Reader: Taught public school in Lincoln and Elgin Counties; was Mathematical and Science Master in the Galt Grammar School; Principal of the United Grammar and Common School of Brockville till 1871, when he was appointed first Inspector of Leeds County; took up mercantile business in 1884 and still follows it in Brockville.
Brown, Mary, Halton; Brown, Mary Frances, Ontario.
Campbell, Elizabeth, Toronto; Campbell, Peter, Carleton.

Ford, Angeline Brown, Toronto; Forsyth, Edward Lee, Welland; Fuller, Sarah Anne, Ontario.

Gick, Henry: Taught in Hamilton Central School.

Gunn, Catharine: Taught in London; married Mr. Agnew.

Lind, Harriett Ann: Afterwards Mrs. Drake of Montreal; now deceased.

McGrigor, James, Perth.

McKerchar, Colin: Taught in public schools in Victoria, Ontario, Glengarry, Essex, Stormont, Middlesex and Oxford Counties, and in a private academy in Glengarry—over twenty years in all; studied for the Presbyterian Ministry, and has spent over five years in home mission work in Manitoba, Algoma and Argenteuil.

MacMurchy, Archibald: Opened the first public school in the town of Collingwood in 1855; graduated as Mathematical medallist in the University of Toronto in 1861; joined the staff of the Toronto Grammar School, and became Rector of it in 1872; is still Principal of the Jarvis Street Collegiate Institute, Toronto.

Minions, James, Lanark.

Morton, John: Taught in Halton, Oxford, Brant, Prince Edward and Hastings Counties; retired in 1863; now living in Belleville.

Munday, Lydia Sophia, Hamilton; Munn, Donald, Wellington: Deceased.

Murray, Mary Ann: Taught in Perth; married Mr. Bates; went to Calgary.

Myers, Julianna: Taught for a time; married Mr. Thomas Hales of the township of Otonabee; after the death of her husband in 1868 she resumed teaching in the County of Leeds; has now retired from teaching; resides at Forfar.

Plunkett, Thomas: Taught seventeen years; was in business in Meaford for some years after 1863; is now Division Court Clerk in that town.

Porter, Louisa, York; Porter, Mary, York.

Raine, John, Toronto.

Rogers, Adelaide, Prince Edward.

Shenick, Henrietta: Taught seven years in the Provincial Model School, Toronto, from April, 1855, to December, 1862; married Mr. Pearson, who died in 1864; taught in San Francisco, and then went to Australia; was drowned near San Francisco on her return in 1867.

Shepard, Mary, Oxford; Sweeny, Mary Anne, Toronto.

Van Every, Adeline: Taught six years; married Mr. J. Campbell; living in Parkdale, Toronto.

Van Every, Emeline: Taught four years; married Mr. W. Hill; still living at Bond Head.

Wright, John Horton, York.

FOURTEENTH SESSION.

(May, 1855—November, 1855.)

Adams, Elizabeth: Taught in Hamilton till 1861, and in Woodstock till 1864; taught more recently in Oxford County and the District of Muskoka.

Allison, Andrew: Taught many years; now farming in the Township of Pickering; takes a keen interest in educational matters.

Blain, David: Entered the legal profession; graduated in the faculty of Law in 1860 in the University of Toronto; represented West York for some years in the House of Commons of Canada; still resides in Toronto.

Bowerman, James: Taught in Prince Edward County; engaged in farming and lumbering in Frontenac; Principal of the Public School in Napanee, except for one brief interval from 1876 to 1896; now living retired in Toronto.

Campbell, Alexander, Lanark: Died about twenty-five years ago.

Carlyle, James: Was fourth Headmaster of Boys' Model School from 1858 to 1871; graduated M. D. from Victoria University; became Mathematical Master in the Normal School in 1871; retired in Dec., 1893; is now living in Toronto.

Clarke, Henry S., Ontario: Became a lawyer.

Clarke, Josephine Witmore, Toronto.

Comfort, John Harris: Taught for some time; practised Medicine in St. Catharines; was for some years Inspector of Public Schools in that town; is now Police Magistrate.

Crane, Duncan, Elgin.

Cressman, Noah, Lincoln: Deceased.

Danard, William Bernard: Taught several years; became a Methodist Minister; now superannuated; resides in Grey County.

Flood, Elmira, Hamilton.

Foster, Mary: Taught continuously in the Brantford Central School till 1864; married Mr. Francis Ellis in that year; has lived in Brantford ever since.

Hay, James: Taught in several schools, one of which was the Common School at L'Orignal; now deceased.

Hicks, Henry M., B.A.: Taught for a time in Prince Edward County; studied Law in Montreal, but abandoned it to return to teaching; after a public school experience of some years, took an Arts course in the University of Toronto, graduating in 1871; afterward taught High School in Trenton and Colborne till 1885; now farming in Haliburton District.

Johnston, David J.: Taught in Haldimand Township until 1860; taught in Cobourg continuously till his resignation in 1879; appointed to the staff of the Ontario Department of Agriculture in 1883; resides in Toronto.

Keating, James, Victoria.

Kellock, John D.: Taught for two years; studied Medicine; has practised successfully for nearly forty years in Perth, County of Lanark, where he still resides.

Kennedy, Elizabeth Eleanor: Taught a number of years in the Public Schools of Toronto.

Leech, Eleanor, Toronto.

Lester, Mary: Taught a few years in London; went to Scotland; married Mr. Rainsford; lived afterwards in Montana, U.S.A.

McDonnell, Margaret Catherine, Lanark; McLean, Sophia Caroline, Leeds; McPherson, John, Lanark.

Munyard, Mary Ann: Taught in St. Vincent and Meaford in Grey County; retired from professional work and now resides in Meaford.

Ormiston, David: Taught in the Provincial Model School, from November, 1855, to August, 1857, and in the Normal School; took an Arts course in the University of Toronto, graduating in 1861; taught Grammar Schools for several years in Waterdown, Berlin, Cobourg and Brantford: entered the legal profession, and still practises in Whitby.

Osborne, Alexander Campbell: Taught for many years, and now lives in Penetanguishene.

Platt, Gilbert Dorland, B.A.: Taught in Ottawa, Gananoque and elsewhere; graduated in Arts; has been Public School Inspector of Prince Edward County since 1871; resides in Picton.

Roberts, Samson: Taught till superannuated; died at Columbus, Ontario, in 1876.

Robertson, Amelia, Welland; Robinson, Susannah, Toronto.

Shadd, Emmeline: Taught in Peel and Kent Counties for several years; married, and taught afterward in the Normal Department of Howard University, Washington, D.C.; went to Savannah, Ga., and taught there till 1876; returned to her home in Kent, Ontario, and lived on a farm until killed while driving over a Michigan Central Railway crossing three years ago.

Simpson, Henrietta, Hamilton; Simpson, Samuel, Hamilton.

Steele, Thomas O.: Appointed Inspector for Prescott County in 1871, and held that office till 1880; subsequently Model School Principal in Perth, Barrie and Simcoe; served as Inspector of part of Norfolk County till his death a few years ago.

Taylor, John, Ontario.

Tewksbury, Sarah Elizabeth, Hamilton: Deceased.

Thompson, Alexander, Toronto.

FIFTEENTH SESSION.

(November, 1855—May, 1856.)

Andrews, Martha Gilbert: Taught in Elgin County; now deceased.

Badgerow, Justin: Taught about eight years, including two short terms in the United States; entered the legal profession in that country, and has filled various public offices in Kansas; now resides in Michigan, U.S.A.

Bettie, Jane: Married Mr. Julius Duncan; died at Lynchburg, Va., U S.A.

Brown, David, Lincoln.

Brown, John; Brown, Robert: Twin brothers; they attended the Normal School, and the Congregational College together, graduating from the latter in 1861; Robert was a pastor in Garafraxa for eleven years, and in Middleville, Lanark, for nine; John was a pastor for a time in Eramosa and afterwards in Lanark Village; John migrated to Manitoba in 1880, and Robert in 1882; they both entered the Presbyterian Ministry there at the same time, and both went afterwards to Washington Territory, where they died.

Buchanan, Elizabeth: Taught in Halton, Haldimand, and Oxford, married about 1880; now deceased.

Button, Anna Amelia: Taught a short time; now lives at Locust Hill.

Churchill, Charlotte Madeline: Has spent all her teaching years in Toronto.

Crawford, Eliza Anne, Toronto.

Dadson, Stephen: Taught twenty years, mostly in Brant County; is now Town Clerk of Paris, and Secretary of the Board of Education.

Dew, Mary Avis, York.

Dodds, William: Taught in Collingwood, Southampton and Thornbury; farmed and taught in Lambton; died about 1880.

Gill, Mary Ann Elizabeth: Married Mr. Davis; died some years ago at Brantford.

Gordon, Fanny, Toronto; Goouch, Thomas, Victoria; Green, Thomas, Hastings.

Hamilton, Susan, Toronto.

Harley, Rachel Strong, Brant: Married Mr. John Hunter.

Hoig, Mary Turner, Toronto.

Houlding, Mary: Taught privately for some years; married Mr. W. S. Whittaker; still living in Brantford.

Hunter, John: Taught in Stratford for fourteen years; went into business in Guelph; taught afterward at Oil Springs and in Ottawa; died in 1885.

Hunter, Margaret: Taught four years; married Mr. Andrew W. Knox in 1860, and lived in St. Mary's; now resides in Toronto.

Husband, George E.: Taught a short time; entered the medical profession; practised thirteen years in Galt; has practised in Hamilton since 1874; was for fifteen years a member of the Medical Council of Ontario.

Irvine, Margaret: Now Mrs. Davidson, on the staff of the Collegiate Institute, Hamilton.

Jack, Margaret: Taught three years; married Mr. J. Mather, Angus, Simcoe; now resides at Kincardine, Bruce.

Jones, Amy Caroline, Durham.

Kennedy, Catharine Ainslie: Married Mr. Cooper, Chatham.

Kerr, Hannah Clarinda, Russell; Kerr, Mary, Russell.

Livingstone, Dugald, Simcoe.

McGregor, Alexander, Peel.

McIntyre, Duncan : Now practising Medicine in Glencoe.

McLean, Jane, Toronto.

McLellan, Mary : Married Mr. J. Wiley ; has taught for many years at Richmond Hill, York County.

McNiece, Catharine ; Taught in Perth, Lanark ; married Mr. Thomas Coulter in 1858 ; still resides in Almonte.

Magan, Kate Theresa, Hamilton : Deceased.

Marlatt, Mary Maria : Taught in Elgin and Oxford ; married Mr. F. H. Tufford, and resided on a farm near Aylmer till 1888 ; now resides in Brantford.

Milliken, William : Taught for a short time in Pickering Township ; has since been engaged in farming in Markham ; has been since 1884 postmaster at Hagerman.

Minshall, Mary Anne : Taught some years in rural schools and in Chatham ; still resides at Thamesville.

Mitchell, John : Left the profession many years ago ; has been a farmer near Watford, Lambton County.

Moore, Lewis Corydon : Taught in the Central School, Galt, and elsewhere ; studied Law and practised in Huron County ; now deceased.

Moyer, Samuel Nash : Taught for some years in the County of Bruce ; entered the ministry of the German Evangelical Association, and was presiding elder at the time of his death in 1895.

Mulhern, Catherine : Taught till 1859, when she married Mr. John Wood of Sydenham ; died in 1894.

Murchinson, Margaret, Glengarry.

Paul, Anna Maria : Now Mrs. Crosley, Thornhill, York County.

Pickersgill, Sarah Ann : Taught a private school ; now Mrs. Thomas Brooks.

Pratt, Abraham : Taught five and a half years in Ottawa ; spent six years in business and then entered the Civil Service of Canada ; has been since 1876 Assessment Commissioner of Ottawa.

Rich, Esther, Welland : Became Mrs. Keltie ; now deceased.

Robertson, Hannah, Hamilton ; Ruthven, William, Simcoe ; Rutledge, Fanny Anne, Wellington.

Ryan, Catherine : Taught in Toronto till 1866 ; married Mr. Rowland who died in 1872 ; taught till 1883 ; married Mr. Joshua Woodland ; died in 1889.

Shenick, Adeline : Has taught ever since the completion of her Normal School course ; took the degree of B. Sc. at Victoria University in 1887, and that of B. A. at Queen's University, in 1891 ; taught at Kingston, Port Hope and Cobourg ; is now Head Mistress of the Girls' Provincial Model School, Ottawa.

Shirreff, Benjamin Clarence : Taught for some time in Russell County ; went into farming ; lives near Owen Sound.

Shortt, Charles, Middlesex.

Sinclair, Mary Anne : Resides at Poplar Hill, Ontario.

Smith, George Young : Taught ten years in Whitby Grammar School ; graduated in Law in the University of Toronto in 1864 ; has practised Law in Whitby since 1867.

Sweetin, Agnes, Toronto.

Thomson, Hugh, York.

Walker, Catharine : Married Rev. John McMillan ; died about seventeen years ago.

Walker, Isabella : Married ; resides in Montreal.

Webster, Anne, Hamilton.

Wharin, Anne : Taught for a short time in Kingston ; married Mr. Gardiner ; resides in Kingston.

SIXTEENTH SESSION.

(May, 1856—November, 1856.)

Agnew, Eliza : Taught in Toronto till 1861 ; retired in that year.
Armstrong, Joseph, Toronto.
Austin, Gilbert : Resides at Portland, Ont.
Barnard, Sarah, Russell.
Bingham, James William : Taught in the Township of St. Vincent, County of Grey.
Bisbee, Gertrude Melinda, Toronto.
Borthwick, Anna : Taught one year in Toronto, and one in Perth, Lanark County ; married, in 1858, Rev. J. B. Duncan ; both now reside in Galt.
Boyd, Thomas, York.
Brebner, John : Taught in London, Sarnia and Ottawa till his appointment as Inspector for West Lambton and the Town of Sarnia in 1871 ; still discharging the duties of that office, which now includes also the Town of Petrolia and the villages of Oil Springs and Point Edward.
Bruce, James : Taught a number of years in Brant and Wentworth, and in Waterdown High School and Ridgetown Collegiate Institute ; now deceased.
Burden, Samuel : Taught eleven years in Darlington Township ; went into business in Bowmanville, where he filled various municipal offices, and was for nineteen years a member of the School Board, of which he is now Secretary.
Cameron, John M. : Entered the Presbyterian Ministry ; was pastor many years of a Toronto congregation.
Chisholm, Allan : Taught a short time in Ottawa ; long deceased.
Churchill, Mary Anne, Toronto : Has been dead many years.
Clark, Helen Milliken : Went to San Francisco with her mother, Mrs. Dorcas Clark.
Cody, James, Oxford.
Cosby, Alfred Morgan : Taught for some time ; went into business in Toronto ; is now manager of an investment company in that city and Colonel of the 48th Highlanders.
Cross, J. Fletcher : Taught a year and a half at Port Robinson, Welland ; graduated in the Faculty of Law of Toronto University in 1862 ; practised Law in Wellington County till 1872 and in Toronto till 1882 ; entered the Dominion Civil Service and remained in it till 1891 ; resides now in Toronto.
Dadson, Mary Anne : Married Mr. William West, merchant, in Toronto ; at present lives at Eglington.
Dobson, Robert : Taught Public School for a time ; graduated in Arts in Victoria University in 1880 ; has filled in succession the Headmasterships of Bradford, Lindsay and Picton High Schools ; still holds that position in Picton.
Duff, Daniel : Taught some time at Paisley and in other parts of Bruce County ; graduated from Knox College in 1863 ; spent three years as a missionary in British Columbia, going and returning by Panama ; has since been in one pastoral charge for twenty-nine years in the County of Bruce.
Fayette, Emilie Augusta, Grey ; Ford, John, Peterborough.
Fraser, George : Taught for a time ; now a leading merchant at Picton.
Gorsline, William Edwin, Lincoln.
Harlow, James, Ontario.
Hegler, John Hind : Taught for several years in Western Ontario ; went into mercantile business, and afterwards practised Law at Ingersoll ; died in 1889.
Huff, Elizabeth : Married Rev. Mr. Corbett ; resides in Picton.
Huff, Mary Vandusen : Married Rev. A. D. Miller ; resides in Picton.
Jackson, Bertha : Taught in Markham and Scarboro', in York County, and in Uxbridge Township and Town in Ontario County until her retirement from professional work in 1881 ; resides now in Toronto.

Jacques, John : Taught for two years in the Union School, Scarboro' and Pickering; then became a journalist; edited the *Halton Journal*, *Hamilton Times* and Parliamentary Reports ; died in 1864.

Johnston, Elizabeth : Married Mr. Garrett ; now deceased.

Laduc, Thomas, Wentworth.

Little, James : Taught a short time in Wentworth ; entered the Presbyterian Ministry in 1866 ; was Local Superintendent of Schools in Nassagaweya Township while pastor there ; transferred to Hamilton, and afterwards to Oxford, Bruce and Middlesex Counties ; still resides in the last named.

McConnell, John, York.

McKay, Jane : Married Inspector McNaughton of Stormont and Cornwall ; now deceased.

McKay, John : Taught six years in the Cayuga and Cornwall schools ; studied Medicine in McGill University and in London and Edinburgh : has practised in Woodville, Ontario, for twenty-five years ; has represented West Victoria in the Legislative Assembly of this Province since 1890.

McKee, Thomas : Taught in Oshawa, Ottawa and Kingston, and in the Hamilton High School ; studied Medicine, but afterwards entered the Presbyterian Ministry ; was appointed Inspector of Schools in West Muskoka in 1878, and in Southwest Simcoe in 1881 ; the latter position he still holds, residing at Barrie.

McMillan, John : Taught in Ottawa for a number of years ; took a distinguished course in Arts in the University of Toronto, graduating in 1864 as Prince of Wales Prizeman ; has been Principal for many years of the Ottawa Collegiate Institute.

Main, Jane, Northumberland ; Misener, George, Welland.

Musgrave, Peter : Taught seven years ; entered the Presbyterian Ministry in 1867, and was for a time a pastor at Milverton : is now in a like position in McKillop Township.

Ramsay, Marjory Jarden : Taught in Whitby for a short time ; married Archibald MacMurchy, M.A., Principal of the Jarvis St. Collegiate Institute, Toronto ; now deceased.

Richards, Amanda : Taught in Toronto ; retired in 1866.

Richards, George, Elgin ; Ross, John Simpson, Ottawa.

Robertson, Dorcas D. : Taught for a time ; was superannuated ; has since resided in London, Ontario.

Russell, Elizabeth : Taught in the Central School, Hamilton ; married Rev. William Troup ; after his death resided in Hamilton.

Soper, Jasper : Taught in Ottawa ; now deceased.

Stone, Newton Ransome, Welland.

Thompson, Elizabeth, Haldimand.

Vandewater, Samuel : Taught till 1877 in Fredericksburgh, Oro, and East Gwillimbury Townships ; retired on account of ill health ; now resides at Mount Albert in North York.

Walsh, Thomas, York.

Webster, Helen : Taught in Hamilton ; now deceased.

Weir, Andrew : Now resident in Walkerton.

Wilson, Thomas C. : Taught in the Kingston Grammar School ; was Principal of one of the Kingston Public Schools ; retired in 1878 ; has been for many years a member of the Kingston Board of Education.

Zimmerman, Isaac J. : Now Assistant Postmaster in Beamsville, Lincoln County ; taught only a few months ; spent several years in business in various parts of the United States.

SEVENTEENTH SESSION.

(November, 1856—May, 1857.)

Bell, Helen, Peel ; Bell, Janet, Peel.
Bissett, Mary : Went to Honolulu, and there married.
Bowles, Peter Langlois, Toronto.
Brookfield, Jacob: In business at Niagara Falls, N.Y., U.S.A.
Brown, Lillis, Ontario.
Calvert, Joseph, Elgin.
Campbell, Neil Moore : Taught for a number of years in Lambton and Middlesex ; became Principal of the St. Thomas Public Schools in 1876, and of the Elgin County Model School in 1877 ; still holds both positions.
Carey, Eleanor Harriett : Taught in Ottawa ; married Mr. Soper, one of the teachers there.
Chesnut, Thomas George : Took a course in Theology, and then established a private school in Toronto, which he maintained until 1868, when he become English Master in the Hamilton Collegiate Institute ; after filling this position for some time, he again took up private teaching, and continued at it in Hamilton till his death in 1881.
Clifton, Henry S., Oxford.
Cull, Alice : Taught for a time ; now lives at Aylmer, Ontario.
Dance, Ann : Taught for some time in Middlesex and Elgin ; married in 1860 Mr. Elijah Gray ; taught for a time in Iowa, U. S. A.; returned to Canada in 1863, and died in 1864.
Demill, Ervin : A farmer at Northport.
Dewar, Archibald : Taught in various Public Schools until appointed Inspector for East Huron in 1871; resigned that office a few months before his death in 1884.
Doon, George Henry : Studied Medicine ; now deceased.
Duff, James, Renfrew.
Dunn, Barbara Morrison : Taught in Niagara ; married Rev. R. Hall, a Presbyterian minister; died at Thorndale in 1877.
Elston, Faith, London.
Fleming, James : Taught three years in Paris, Ontario ; studied Law and practised for many years in Brampton ; represented Peel in the Canadian House of Commons from 1882 to 1887, when he became Registrar of Peel County ; was appointed in 1892 Inspector of Legal Offices for the Province of Ontario, which office he still holds ; resides in Toronto.
Fletcher, Charlotte, Kent : Died in Nebraska, U. S. A.
Foster, Ralph, Essex : Taught chiefly in Essex County ; retired in 1881 ; died in 1888.
Gardiner, Jane, Toronto.
Gillies, Mary, Toronto : Died about twelve years ago.
Gurd, Dorah : Taught in London several years ; married Mr. Pegler, of Port Stanley.
Haggerty, James : Taught for several years in North Hastings ; afterwards farmed ; represented North Hastings in the Ontario Legislative Assembly from 1891 till 1898.
Hamm, Thomas Edwin, Elgin : Died in Idaho, U.S.A.
Harley, John, Waterloo ; Hume, Mary Miller, Toronto.
Irving, George : Became a Presbyterian minister ; now deceased.
Jenner, Sarah Anne: Taught some years in Raleigh ; married Mr. S. J. Harvey, Treasurer of that township ; still living at Charing Cross, Ontario.

Johnston, Hugh : Taught a public school for a short time in Lambton County, and gave it up to take charge of a select High School at Arkona ; entered the Methodist ministry as a probationer, and in 1865 graduated with distinction from Victoria University ; after filling many pastoral positions in Ontario and Quebec he was called to take charge of the National Memorial Methodist Church at Washington, where he still ministers to a distinguished congregation, including President McKinley.

Jones, Jonas, Toronto.

Keown, Adelaide : Taught in Port Hope and afterwards in Toronto, married Mr. Wallen ; now deceased.

Kilpatrick, George, York.

Kniseley, Owen F. : A farmer and agent at Port Colborne.

Laughlin, William, Addington.

McBride, Sarah : Taught in the Toronto Public Schools for many years ; resigned to start a private kindergarten ; is now connected with the Young Women's Christian Guild.

McCammon, James : Taught in Kingston, studied and practised Medicine ; was Mayor of Kingston in 1884, and died in that year.

McKechnie, Mary Gray, Wentworth ; McKerchar, John, Stormont.

McMurray, Elizabeth Jane : Taught in Toronto ; retired in 1862 ; married Mr. Turnbull.

McNaughton, Janet, Brant.

MacWilliam, William : Graduated in Theology and entered the Canada Presbyterian Church in 1859, and in Arts in Toronto University in 1862 ; taught Norwood Grammar School from 1859 to 1863 : held Presbyterian pastorates successively in Harwood, Streetsville, Prince Albert (N. W. T.), and Port Hope, till 1893 ; is at present Librarian in Knox College, and lecturer in the Toronto Bible Training School.

Milne, Elnora, Ontario ; Miller, Janet, Brant.

Moore, Richard, Perth : Now deceased.

Munson, Charlotte : Married Mr. Mitchell ; now deceased.

Nichol, William : Taught Burford Village School, Brant County, for eight years; graduated in Medicine in 1869, and has ever since practised in Brantford ; has for most of that time been closely connected with the management of the Brantford Young Ladies' College.

O'Reilly, Robert, Ottawa.

Preston, James : Was Head Master of Owen Sound High School, and also of Goderich High School ; died in 1871.

Robertson, John, Welland.

Robertson, Martha : London ; married Mr. Hardy ; now resides in St. Louis, Missouri, U. S. A.

Rodgers, John : Taught in Glenmorris ; resides in Toronto.

Sarvis, George C., Oxford.

Shoff, Ann, London : Now Mrs. Shannon, Brantford.

Shurtleff, George : Taught in Lambton ; became Mathematical Master in Napanee High School; superannuated.

Shurtleff, Robert Fulton, Addington.

Sinclair, Lauchlin : Now practising Medicine at Tilsonburg.

Smith, Andrew, Peel : Now deceased.

Smith, Margaret, Lincoln ; Steacy, Jane, Toronto ; Thompson, George Washington, Welland.

Tisdell, John Cassie : Practised Medicine ; now deceased.

Turnbull, John, Toronto.

Veit, Annie, York.

Waters, George : Taught a few years, and then entered the medical profession ; commenced practice in 1868 in Cobourg, where he still resides ; in his boyhood in Middlesex he was a fellow pupil of the Hon. G. W. Ross, Minister of Education, their teacher being the late Rev. David Waters, his elder brother.

Wilkes, Margaret, Toronto.

Yeomans, Silas P., Elgin.

EIGHTEENTH SESSION

(May, 1857—November, 1857.)

Agar, Ellen, Norwich.

Armstrong, Jemima : Taught for some time in Toronto.

Armstrong, John, Oxford : Now deceased.

Ashall, Eliza : Taught four years ; has been twice married ; now conducting a general store in Greensville, Ontario.

Baikie, John : Taught several years ; was Principal of Galt Central School ; entered the Presbyterian Ministry ; became the first pastor of the West Presbyterian Church, Toronto, in 1866 ; died one year afterwards.

Barrick, Eli J. : Continued teaching until 1863 ; studied Medicine in Rolph's School, then affiliated with Victoria University ; graduated in 1866, and after spending a year abroad became a practitioner in Toronto and a teacher in the school which he had formerly attended ; since its discontinuance he has remained in Toronto, keeping up a close connection with Victoria University, and taking an active and prominent part in civic affairs.

Baumwart, Owen : Became a farmer ; went to Michigan twenty years ago.

Black, Davidson : Taught for some time ; graduated in Arts in Toronto University in 1867 ; practised Law for many years in Toronto ; died suddenly some years ago.

Blackburn, Mary, Hamilton : Now Mrs. Mitchell ; resides in Toronto.

Boag, Joseph : Was teaching in the west twenty years ago ; now deceased.

Book, Eli G. : Became a physician ; died at Niagara Falls South.

Brown, Isaac : Became a physician ; died at Ingersoll.

Brown, James, Ontario ; Brown, James, Oxford.

Brown, Maria : Taught in Halton and Welland Counties ; married in 1864 Rev. J. C. Wilmott, M.A., Methodist Minister ; died in 1889 at Newtonbrook, York County.

Brown, William, Hamilton ; Bryant, John Henry, Oxford.

Campbell, Robert, Welland ; Campbell, Sarah Anne, Wellington.

Cattanach, Anne Jane : Taught one year ; married Mr. E. A. Perry ; lived at Valleyfield, Montreal, Hamilton, Ottawa, and Winnipeg ; now resides with her son, Rev. E. G. Perry, at Wellington, Vancouver Island.

Clark, Ashbel Bowes : Taught till about 1880 in York County ; died in Toronto in 1885.

Clinton, John W. : Entered the Ministry ; lived at Vinton, Iowa ; now deceased.

Coady, Harriet Esther, Toronto : Married in California.

Cooper, Elizabeth, York ; Cremin, Daniel, Longueuil, Quebec ; Cummings, Margaret J., Toronto.

Currie, Menzies, Wellington : Deceased.

Dodds, William, Wentworth ; Dougherty, Isaiah, Onondaga.

Duff, Charles : Now a minister of the Congregational denomination.

Dundas, Lydia ; Taught a few years ; married Mr. McGuire ; resides in Toronto.

Eaton, Elizabeth Cecilia, Sophiasburg, Prince Edward.

Farrow, Elizabeth : Now Mrs. W. H. Pars of Buffalo, N. Y., U. S. A.

Frisby, Edgar : Took an Arts course in Toronto University. graduating in 1863 ; taught High School in several places until 1867 ; in that year and 1868. taught Mathematics in the Northwestern University at Evanston, Ill., U. S. A ; has been since 1868 an assistant in the United States Naval Observatory at Washington, and since 1878 a professor of Mathematics in the United States Naval College.

Gordon, Annie, Essex ; Grant. Alice, Welland.

Henderson, Jemima : Taught several years in the Central School, Hamilton ; married Mr. Grant ; now lives in Hamilton.

Hood, Jane : Taught in Quebec, Glengarry, and Kingston ; married Captain Thomas F. Taylor : died in 1897.

Kennedy, Susie, Toronto.

Kinney, Robert : Taught in Beamsville ; studied Medicine, and continued teaching ; was appointed, in 1871, one of the Public School Inspectors for Leeds and Grenville, which office he still holds.

Legerwood, Daniel : Died in Renfrew County.

Lester, Margaret. London.

Lucas, Thomas Dennis : Became a physician ; died at Stratford in 1878.

McCalla, John : Is now a merchant in St. Catharines.

McDiarmid, Duncan : Practised Medicine at Scarboro ; died in 1897.

McDiarmid, Peter : Graduated in Medicine from Toronto University in 1866 ; is now practising at Elmira, Ill., U. S. A.

McDougall, John, Carleton.

McElroy, Maria : Married Mr. George Elliott ; now resides in London, Ontario.

Mackenzie, John : Is a farmer in Glengarry County.

McLean, Archibald : Taught till 1864 ; studied and practised Medicine till 1891 in Sarnia ; is now Registrar of Deeds for Lambton ; lives in Sarnia.

McLean, Peter, Waterloo.

McMaster. John : Resides near Laggan, Glengarry.

McPherson, Catharine, Halton.

McVean, John : Studied Medicine ; practised for years in Carleton Place ; died long ago.

Millard, Rosa Scott : Taught five years in Bowmanville ; married Mr. McGee in 1863 ; lived in Oshawa until 1890 ; resides now in Toronto.

Miller, Isabella Brown, Hamilton.

Montgomery, Mary Jane : Now Mrs. Street of Port Arthur.

Morton, Frances Elizabeth : Now Mrs. Greer ; is Principal of one of the Public Schools in Hamilton.

Newman, Mary Hargrave : Now resident in Buffalo, N.Y., U.S.A.

Nicol, Peter : Taught at Port Ryerse ; became a Presbyterian minister ; resides at Unionville, Ontario.

Noxon, Isaac James, Sophiasburg.

O'Connor, Thaddeus James : Taught in St. James parochial school ; died in 1886.

Preston David Hiram : Taught for a short time ; studied Law, and served in the volunteer militia in 1866 ; in that year was admitted to practice, which he has ever since carried on at Napanee.

Price, Robert, Leeds : Now deceased.

Purslow, Adam : Taught from May, 1858, to September, 1858, in the Provincial Model School, Toronto ; became second and afterwards Head Master of the United Grammar and Common Schools of Port Hope ; graduated in Arts and Law in Victoria University ; resigned his Headmastership in 1894, after thirty-eight years of teaching ; still lives in Port Hope and is Secretary of the High School Board.

Riddell, Andrew, Durham ; Robertson, Magdelene, Welland ; Robinson, Eliza, York.

Roche, Mary Elizabeth : Taught for several years ; now married.
Rogers, Christina, Toronto.
Scott, Agnes : Taught three years in Martintown, Glengarry ; married in 1861 Mr. William McIntosh ; now living on a farm near Martintown.
Scott Elizabeth, Lanark : Deceased.
Smith, John Darling : Taught different schools in Norfolk County ; now a retired farmer.
Sturk, John Dunn : Graduated in Medicine in Victoria University in 1867.
Stevenson, Samuel, Prescott ; Sutherland, Anne, Huntingdon, Que.
Sweet, Orison David : Resides at Nelson, British Columbia.
Thompson, Rebecca : Has taught in Toronto continuously till the present time.
Tracy, Mary, Ottawa.
Webster, Charlotte, Durham.
Welbanks, Hiram : Taught in several schools in Prince Edward County ; followed journalism in Picton for two years, and carried on a hardware business in the same place for sixteen ; now lives in Toronto.
Wilson, Annie : Taught for a time on Wolfe Island, near Kingston ; married in 1861 Mr. C. W. Coates ; now lives in Montreal.
Wolverton, Daniel, Walsingham, Norfolk.
Wright, Eliza Jane : Married and lives in Orono, Durham County.
Young, Thomas : Now resides in Rossburn Township, Manitoba.

NINETEENTH SESSION.

(November, 1857–May, 1858.)

Adams, Lucinda Ruth : Married Rev. Mr. Wilkinson.
Anderson, William Walker : Taught in the Newmarket High School for a time.
Armstrong, Martha : Taught a few years in Lanark ; married Mr. Greer of Toronto ; is on the Public School staff of that city.
Betts, Eliza Ann : Taught some years in Norfolk County ; married Mr. Keys of Oakland ; died about 1880.
Blackburn Jane : Married Mr. G. J. Waugh ; resides in Stratford.
Blain, Kate : Taught in London till 1860 ; married, in 1861, Dr. J. L. Stevenson, who died in 1865 ; taught in Toronto from 1870 to 1888.
Bond, William, Toronto.
Brine, Henry James : After teaching for some time he became a general agent of the Ontario Life Assurance Company.
Burns, Robert : Taught for four years in Lanark, Frontenac and Oxford Counties ; entered the medical profession ; has practised since 1865 in Carleton Place, in Pakenham and in Almonte, where he still resides.
Burr, Hester J., E. Flamboro'.
Chesnut, Harriet Henrietta, Kingston ; Clark, Annie Lydia, Toronto ; Currie, Mary, Toronto ; Currie, Peter, Toronto.
Dickinson, Eliza, King, York.
Doan, Robert Willson : Taught till 1872 in East Gwillimbury and Aurora, York County ; has been Principal of schools in Toronto for over twenty years ; was Principal of the city Model School from 1881 to 1888 ; has been Secretary for several years of the Ontario Educational Association, and is a member of the Educational Council of the Province.
Duncan, James : Taught in Georgetown, Blenheim, Thamesville and Dresden, before going to Windsor : was Principal of the Essex County Model School there for thirteen years ; superannuated ; living in Windsor.
Elliott, Thomas, Albion, Peel ; Evans, Jessie. Guelph.

Forrest, John, Ottawa : Foster, Jesse, Etobicoke, York.

Fraser, Mungo, D.D.: Taught some years in Public Schools; entered the Free Church Presbyterian Ministry in 1867, after a course in Knox College and Toronto University; has since been pastor successively of three congregations, one in Barrie, one in St. Thomas and his present one in Hamilton.

Fraser, William : Taught three years at Woodbridge ; became a physician ; practised for a time in Nova Scotia ; moved to La Salle, Illinois, U.S.A., where he is still living.

Good, Rosa : Spent three years as a governess in London, Ontario ; married Mr. Grinton ; resides in Illinois, U.S.A.

Grant, Robert : Taught at various times in Wellington and Welland Counties, and in Brockville Central School ; superannuated in 1896.

Hamilton, Sarah Maria : Taught in the Toronto Public Schools from 1868 to 1886 ; still resides in Toronto.

Hamilton, Susan Georgiana : Taught in the Toronto Public Schools from 1858, and still resides in that city.

Hayes, Almira, Toronto.

Henderson, Gregg : Entered the medical profession in 1867 ; now practising in Strathroy.

Hillock, Moses : Now farming near Melville Cross, Peel County.

Irwin, James, Toronto.

Kean, John Russell, Innisfil, Simcoe.

Kelloch, Agnes : Has taught in the Toronto Public Schools since 1861, with the exception of an interval of three years.

Liddell, Christina Blair : Taught three years in the Toronto Public Schools ; married, in 1862, Mr. John Young, now in charge of the Depository of the Upper Canada Bible Society ; resides in Toronto.

McBean, Janet: Taught three years on Amherst Island ; now retired ; lives at Napanee.

McCallum, Elizabeth : Married Mr. McDonald ; deceased.

McCann, Susan : Taught for some years ; now Mrs. James Harrison : lives at Milton.

McGee, Alexander, Merrickville.

McKay, Dorothy : Taught some years ; married Mr. Josephus Rose of Matilda ; now a widow ; resides in Cornwall.

McKay, John Wood, W. Gwillimbury ; McLelland, John, Darlington.

Maxwell, Henry William : A Methodist Minister ; now deceased.

Maxwell, James : Taught Public School for over eighteen years ; has been superannuated for nearly twelve ; resides at Melville Cross, County of Peel.

Morgan, Augusta Ann : Taught for many years in Goderich and Ingersoll ; died a few years ago.

Morgan, Eliza : Taught only a few months ; is now Librarian of the Public Library of St. Thomas, which city has always been her home.

Morgan, Eliza Sarah : Married Mr James Preston, then a High School Master ; after his death, in 1871, married Rev. John Carry, who died recently at Port Perry ; now a widow residing at Millbrook.

Morris, James, Toronto.

Newman, John Byron, Tecumseh.

Nichol, Margaret Elliott : Taught for some time ; married Mr. John Brebner, now P. S. Inspector of West Lambton ; resides in Sarnia.

Patterson, James Centenary, Toronto ; Proctor, Sarah Ann, W. Gwillimbury.

Pysher, David : Taught many years in Lincoln County ; is now a farmer at Rat Portage.

Rothwell, William : Taught Public School for some years ; graduated in Queen's University ; was Principal of the Perth and Dutton High Schools ; is at present a School Inspector at Regina, N. W. T.

Robinson, John, Whitby.

Scholes, John, Manvers ; Snell, Charles, Stephen.

Stevenson, Mary Elizabeth : Taught for two years in Hamilton Central School ; taught two years, 1884-6, in Orillia Public School ; moved to Toronto ; now Mrs. Hay.

Sudborough, Esther, Toronto ; Sudborough, Sarah Ann, Toronto.

Thompson, Alexander : Now a physician practising at Strathroy.

Thompson, James, Hamilton ; Thompson, Jane, Scarboro'.

Tidey, Martha Victoria ; Married Rev. Mr. Huff ; died years ago.

Wilson, Margaret : Married Mr. Grant of St. Mary's.

Windsor, Francis, Rochester, Essex.

TWENTIETH SESSION.

(May, 1858—November, 1858.)

Allan, Mary Kennedy . Taught in Port Rowan ; married Mr. Lamport ; now lives in Toronto.

Allen, Maria, Hamilton.

Baird, Alexander Kennedy, Toronto ; Bates, James Marshall, Clinton, Lincoln ; Beach, William Godkin, Toronto.

Be'hell, Sarah : Taught in Bobcaygeon and Toronto till 1890 ; died June 5, 1893.

Bielby, William, Toronto ; Bisbee, Julia Elizabeth, Toronto.

Blackwood, Robert : Was Principal of Waterloo Central School for many years ; afterwards taught in Galt Central School ; retired from teaching ; resides at Galt.

Brodie, James, Toronto.

Bruce, George : Taught five years in Markham and Whitby ; took an Arts course in the University of Toronto, graduating in 1868 ; entered the Presbyterian ministry in 1871 ; spent four years in mission work about Aurora and Newmarket ; seven as pastor in St. Catharines, and sixteen in charge of a congregation in St. John, N.B., where he still resides.

Cann, Samuel Bragaten, Hope, Durham.

Clark, Charles : Taught in London Central School ; retired ; resides now in London.

Curry, Robert Nicholas : After some years' experience in Public Schools, established " Komoka College," which he maintained for several years ; in 1878 became a Model School Principal ; is now a broker in London, Ontario.

Davis, Jane Eliza, Toronto.

Disher, John Clark : Taught from October, 1858, till his death in 1864, as second master in the Provincial Model School.

Duncan, Alexander, Thurlow.

Fairbairn, Robert, Peterborough.

Forster, Mary Rachel : Married Mr. A. S. Holmes of Chatham ; still resides there.

Foster, Richard, Nepean.

Galloway, William, Hamilton.

Ganton, Stephen : Taught in Peel and Halton till 1871 ; now a merchant in Oakville, Ontario.

Gardiner, Ann, Niagara ; Gardiner, Elizabeth, Niagara.

Guthrie, Margaret : Now Mrs. Watt of Guelph.

Hankinson, Thomas, Malahide.

Harper, Jane : Married Rev. Mr. Gray ; now resides in Toronto.
Hatton, Mary Victoria : Taught in Port Hope High School ; married Mr. R. Fleming, who then taught in the same school ; now deceased.
Hayne, Caroline, Hamilton.
Henderson, Rubina Isabella, Hamilton : Died in 1860.
Hewson, Edmund Thomas, Seneca : Entered the medical profession.
Hodgins, Thomas : Taught eight years ; entered mercantile life in Lucan, and still follows that occupation there.
Holmes, Emma Elizabeth : Married Mr. J. Stalker ; resides in Toronto.
Hurd, Helen M. : Taught a few years ; married ; now resides near Rochester, N.Y.
Jenkins, John Fletcher, Thurlow ; Johnston, Martha Jane, Etobicoke.
Kellough, Thomas : Entered the Presbyterian ministry, and was settled at Trenton ; afterwards went into Medicine, and practised in the United States ; died at Chicago in 1895.
Kennedy, Alexander : Taught for some time as assistant in the Ottawa Grammar School ; for five years in rural schools in Quebec and Ontario, and for twenty-three years as Principal of the Glengarry County Model School in Martintown : resides now on his farm near Vernon, Ontario.
Kessack, Lydia Jane ; Taught in London until 1887 ; now resides there.
Knight, James Henry : Taught in Waterloo, Durham and Victoria, till 1861 ; taught music and filled municipal offices for ten years ; has been Inspector of Public Schools in East Victoria since 1871.
Lamb, Martha, Toronto.
Lloyd, Charlotte, S. Dumfries.
Luton, James Lyman : Taught in Elgin County till his death, in 1859.
Luton, Leonard : Taught in Elgin, and was for some time Local Superintendent of part of the County ; entered the medical profession, and has practised continuously in St. Thomas since 1867.
McCaig, Donald : Taught for a number of years in Ottawa, and in the Rockwood Academy, a private institution near Guelph ; became Principal of the Galt Central School ; has been since 1886 Inspector of Public Schools in the District of Algoma ; is an author of a volume of poems.
McCulley, Alfred : Taught for years in Kent County ; went to Kansas, U.S.A., where he is still in business.
McCulley, Esther : Taught till 1868 ; married Mr. Waterworth ; lives in Ridgetown.
McDavid, Mary, Markham ; McEachren, Donald, Eldon.
McGregor, Norman R., Huron: Died many years ago.
McLaughlin, Mary Ann : Now Sister M. Aloysius ; has taught in the Separate School at Niagara Falls and at Loretto Academy, Guelph, Belleville, Hamilton, and Toronto ; has now charge of the High School at Loretto Convent, Toronto.
McLennan, Simon, Puslinch : Now a farmer in Wellington County.
Macoun, John : Taught in Belleville Public School till 1874 ; resigned to become Professor of Geology and Natural History in Albert College ; retired in 1879 to take charge of an exploring party sent out by the Dominion Government ; has been for many years Botanist to the Department of the Interior, and is now Assistant Director of the Geological Survey of Canada ; resides in Ottawa.
Magan, Frances Ann : Now Sister Mary of Mount Carmel ; has taught in connection with Loretto Convents in Lindsay, Quebec, Toronto, Hamilton, Guelph and Niagara Falls.
Magan, Mary Josephine : Taught in Lower Canada ; entered Loretto Convent as Sister Mary Nativity ; continued to teach in Loretto Academy, Joliet, Ill. U.S.A., Belleville, Toronto and Hamilton, till her death in 1889.
Maguire, Anna Margaret, Cavan ; Malloy, Alexander, Vaughan ; Martin, Elizabeth, Yorkville ; Matthews, William Loader, Toronto ; Milne, William, Markham.
Morton, Mary : Is Principal of one of the Hamilton Public Schools.

Murdie, Mary Jane, Moulton ; Murray, Elizabeth, Toronto.

O'Leary, Mary, Toronto.

Patterson, James : Taught two years in Almonte ; entered the medical profession and practised in the same place from 1864 to 1882 ; moved to Winnipeg, where he has practised ever since ; was for some time a Professor in the Manitoba Medical College, and is still Chairman of the Provincial Board of Health.

Pearce, Thomas : Was first assistant in the Berlin Central School from 1858 to 1864, and was Principal of the same school from 1864 to 1871, when he was appointed Public School Inspector for Waterloo County, which position he still holds.

Peters, Henry S., Pickering : Now deceased.

Porter, Agnes, London : Resides in Toronto.

Pratt, Cornelia Augusta : Taught in Chatham for many years ; died in 1881 shortly after retiring from teaching.

Ranney, Cynthia, Hillier.

Robertson, John Palmerston : Taught in Ottawa and its neighborhood for thirteen years ; retired to enter business ; was at various times a School Trustee and Alderman of Ottawa and took a very active part in securing the Normal and Model Schools for that City ; went to Manitoba in 1879 and was appointed Librarian of the Legislative Assembly in 1884, which position he still holds. He was for many years, both in Ontario and Manitoba, connected with the press.

Robinson, Mary : Taught a number of years in Toronto ; now Mrs. Lamb of Toronto.

Rolls, Alfred : Became a physician ; was surgeon in the Confederate Army, and married a Confederate officer's widow ; practised his profession until his death twenty-five years ago.

Rose, Catherine : Taught several years ; married Mr. Colin Macdougall, Q. C. : lives in St. Thomas.

Rose, John George, Cornwall ; Rutledge, James, Clarke, Durham.

Serson, Mary, Fitzroy ; Slocombe, Mary Ann, Hamilton ; Stewart, Margaret Elizabeth, Guelph.

Tye, George Archer : Became a physician and practised in Thamesville and Chatham ; died in 1892.

Walker, Mary : Married the Rev. P. Currie, a Presbyterian minister ; died many years ago.

Walker, Thomas, Chinguacousy, Peel.

Warburton, George Henry : Retired from teaching ; resides at Stratford.

Way, Daniel Sherman, Cayuga ; Wilson, Agnes Rachel, Toronto ; Wilkes, Marcella, Toronto.

Wright, George Wesley : Taught for eight years in Eglington and Yorkville ; entered the medical profession in 1867 ; has practised in Berlin for twenty-eight years, during twenty-five of which he has been a Coroner for the County of Waterloo.

Young, Caroline, Nelson : Married Mr. Charles King, a farmer.

TWENTY-FIRST SESSION.

(January, 1859—June, 1859.)

Adams, Martha : Taught in Woodstock till 1862 ; as Mrs. Cullen was Head Mistress of the Girls' Model School in Toronto from 1867 to 1883.

Armitage, John Robinson : Taught several years, and then entered mercantile life, which he still follows in Lucan, Middlesex County ; was local Superintendent of schools, and a member of the County Board of Examiners for some years.

Armstrong, Mary, Guelph ; Atkin, Ellen, St. Catharines.

Atkinson, Edward Lewis : Taught in Gananoque, Galt, and Yorkville, till he entered the medical profession in 1866 ; practised at Freelton, and afterwards in Gananoque, where he has conducted a manufacturing business since retiring from professional work.

Banan, Ellen Olivia : Now Mrs. Boottan, Toronto.

Beam, Rebecca Anne, Willoughby ; Beckstedt, Joseph M., Williamsburgh.

Boyes, James Stephen : Retired from teaching some years ago, and died in Chatham in 1897.

Buchanan, John Calder, Tuckersmith ; Buchanan, Robert, Tuckersmith.

Campbell Alexander R.: Taught from August, 1859, till May, 1864, in the Provincial Model School, Toronto ; went to France, and became English master in a school in Paris.

Carrie, James : Taught a short time ; became an Anglican clergyman in 1866 ; now resident at Goderich.

Code, John Richard, Elma Tp.

Cowan, Elizabeth : Married, in 1867, Rev. James Little, a Presbyterian clergyman now resident in the County of Middlesex.

Cowan, Sarah, Toronto.

Dow, John : Taught for some years ; went into the manufacture of agricultural implements at Gananoque.

Edmison, Alexander Rickerston : Taught several years in Peterboro'; subsequently practised Law ; died a few years ago.

Fenney, Jane Parker, Blenheim.

Flood, Louise, Hamilton : Now deceased.

Fraser, Mary Ann, Kincardine : Now deceased.

Frood, Thomas : Taught in Halton and Elgin Counties, and in the Hamilton Central School ; took part in the Ridgeway campaign of 1866 against the Fenians ; went into the drug business in Clifford, and afterwards into general business at Southampton ; served on the Canadian Pacific Railway construction staff, and went into business at Sudbury, where he still resides.

Garden, Mary Louise, Toronto ; Gordon, Eliza, Toronto.

Hay, Eliza Augusta : Taught in Port Hope ; married Mr. Bodwell, who was afterwards a member of the House of Commons for South Oxford ; moved to British Columbia.

Hornell, Mary Johnstone : Taught several years, part of the time near Paisley in Bruce County ; married Mr. D. B. Wylie ; conducted a Kindergarten for some time in Brantford, and subsequently established a private one in Buffalo, where she still resides.

Howell, Lewis, Brant.

Irwin, Margaret : Taught some years in the Hamilton Public Schools ; married Mr. Davidson, and on the death of her husband resumed teaching ; is now on the staff of the Hamilton Collegiate Institute.

Johnston, Robert, Gloucester.

Kennedy, Jessie Alison, London.

Kidd, William G. : Taught near Walkerton in Bruce County, and afterwards in Fergus, County of Wellington ; was Principal of one of the Kingston schools from 1871 to 1875, and has ever since been Inspector for that city ; is well and widely known as a geologist and naturalist, and for his unique collection of crystallographic specimens.

Kitchen, Edward, Dumfries.

Kitchen, Samuel : A Physician in Michigan, U. S. A.

Leitch, Alexander : Retired ; living in Strathroy.

Little, Archibald M., Chinguacousy ; Livingston, Lewis, Markham.

McArthur, John : Became a farmer in Lobo, Middlesex.

McCarthy, Mary Ann, Toronto ; McClure, Robert, Howard ; McCorkindale, Mary, Guelph.

McDiarmid, Donald : Taught in Huron County ; was Principal of Cornwall Public School ; entered the medical profession in 1867 ; was appointed, in 1874, Public School Inspector of Glengarry, which position he still holds ; holds the ank of Major in the Active Militia.

McDonald, Alexander : Entered the Baptist ministry and is now in Manitoba.
McKay, Elizabeth, Hamilton : Married ; now deceased.
McLellan, Archibald : Went long ago to Michigan, U.S.A.
McPhail, Margaret, Osgoode.
Magee, Phœbe Sumner, Etobicoke.
Mickleborough, John : Went to the United States and has filled there several educational positions ; was from 1878 to 1884 Principal of the Cincinnati Normal School ; from 1885 to 1895 was Principal of one of the Grammar Schools in Brooklyn, N.Y. ; since 1895 has been Principal of the Boys' High School in Brooklyn.
Millar, Arnoldus : Was for some years Head Master of the Walkerton High School ; entered the Anglican ministry ; was for a time on the staff of King's College, Windsor, N.S.
Moore, James Samuel, Lanark.
Neelands, Joseph, Chinguacousy
O'Brien, Patrick, Norwich.
Peters, George, Toronto.
Robinson, Mary Ann, West Gwillimbury.
Robertson, John Pushman, Tp. of Gloucester.
Rose, Mary Jane, Rainham : Died about 1890.
Saunders, James : Taught for several years in and near Paisley, in Bruce ; went into business there, and served for many years as Post Master and Treasurer of the village ; died about ten years ago.
Sharp, Sarah Ann, Cavan.
Shaw, Alexander : Taught several years in Lanark ; kept a drug store in Almonte ; disappeared years ago and has not been since heard of.
Sinclair, John : Now a farmer in Whitby Township.
Smith, Francis, Zone ; Smith, Rachael Ann, Louth ; Smith, William Wakefield, Toronto ; Smith, Mary Catharine, Louth Township.
Sullivan, Dion Cornelius : Taught some years ; took the degree of LL.B. in the University of Toronto in 1868 ; spent some time in journalistic work in Walkerton, Bruce County ; taught subsequently in Brantford ; now deceased.
Tasker, James ; Taught in Wellington and Halton Counties ; conducted a business college in Montreal from 1866 till 1881 ; has ever since been actively and prominently engaged in financial business in that city.
Topping, William : Taught in Galt Grammar and Public Schools ; was for a time editor and part proprietor of the *Galt Reformer* ; taught for three years in Brant County, and was for twenty-five years private secretary for Goldie & McCulloch, Galt, where he still resides.
Wark, Alexander : Taught for some time in Peel County, and afterwards for three years in Enniskillen, in Lambton ; has taught ever since in Sarnia, where he has been Principal of the County Model School since 1877.
White, William Henry : Taught some years ; became Assessor and Collector of Raleigh Township in Kent ; was killed in a railway accident at Charing Cross in 1894.
Willson, Benjamin Franklin, Wainfleet.
Winlaw, Isabella, Hamilton : Now deceased.
Wright, Fannie Mary, Toronto.

TWENTY-SECOND SESSION.

(August, 1859—December, 1859.)

Armstrong, Annie L. : Taught in Toronto Public Schools till 1882 ; has been ever since Principal of the Protestant Orphans' Home School, in the same city.
Armstrong, Helen, Hamilton.

Ball, Martin Edward, Grantham.

Beer, William Charles : Taught in Durham County for three or four years ; entered the Bible Christian ministry, and has ever since been engaged in that calling ; since 1884 he has been a Methodist Clergyman ; is at present in Dutton, Ont.

Brown, Elizabeth Jeffrey : Taught in Huron County some years ; married Mr. D. McLaughlin in 1865 ; she still lives near Seaforth.

Carnochan, Janet : Taught till 1866 in Brantford and Kingston ; was Principal of the Niagara-on-the-Lake Public School till 1872, and has ever since been assistant in the High School in the same town ; has for many years past given much attention to the History of Ontario, and especially of the Niagara Peninsula, and has written many monographs on the subject.

Carroll, Charlotte Jane, Oakville : Now deceased.

Chaisgreen, Charles : Taught in different parts of Ontario till 1883, seven years of that time assistant master in the Brantford Central School ; was in business in St. Thomas from 1883 to 1893 ; taught in Parry Sound till 1897 ; now retired, living in St. Thomas.

Childs, Sarah Elizabeth : Married ; resides in London, Ontario.

Chambers, Mary, Toronto.

Charlton, Mary Ellen, South Dumfries : Now Mrs. (Rev.) J. Donald, California, U.S.A.

Clare, Samuel : Taught in Waterloo County, and afterwards in Port Hope and Cobourg : was Commercial and Writing Master in the Provincial Model and Normal Schools from 1867 to 1884 ; now retired and living in Toronto.

Clark, Maria Chapman, Toronto ; Clarke, William Andrew, King ; Collar, Eliza, Hamilton.

Collins, Joseph Jonathan : Taught for ten years ; is now engaged in farming and fruit growing near St. Catharines.

Cranfield, Richard E. : Taught in Hamilton till 1875, first in the Central School, and afterwards in the Collegiate Institute.

Duncan, Alice : Taught for several years ; married ; went to the Southern States.

Fitchett, David : Died many years ago at Marmora, Hastings.

Fleming, Robert McMillan : Taught in Port Hope ; went into the legal profession ; practised in Toronto ; was accidentally killed.

Fraser, Catharine, York.

Freeland, Henrietta : Married Mr. J. H. Thompson of the Printing Bureau, Ottawa.

Granger, Mary Jane : Married Mr. T. W. Charlton of St. George, Ontario.

Greenlees, Andrew : Graduated in Arts in Toronto University in 1866 ; entered the legal profession ; has practised for many years in London, Ontario.

Haight, George Lester, Brantford ; Hall, Agnes, Toronto ; Harris, Fanny Jane, Toronto ; Henderson, Elizabeth, Brampton.

Jackson, Donald : Entered the medical profession, and went to Texas, U.S.A.

Jackson, Duncan, Eldon : Now deceased.

Keam, Peter, Cobourg ; Kennedy, John, Southampton.

Leggett, Joseph : Taught as Assistant Master in Whitby High School, and afterwards as Head Master of Oakville High School ; is now a lawyer in San Francisco.

McHale, John : Resides at Lakeport in Northumberland.

McKellar John Archibald : Taught several years, part of the time as Head Master of the St. Mary's Public School ; was killed in a railway accident at Komoka.

McLean, Peter, Cobourg.

McLean, Archibald : Entered the Presbyterian ministry ; now resides at Blyth, Huron County.

McNabb, John : Taught two years in Victoria County ; entered the Presbyterian ministry in 1867 ; was missionary to the Red River District from 1869 to 1874, and pastor at Beaverton from 1874 to 1882 ; now resides at Lucknow, and is Clerk of the Maitland Presbytery.

Malloch, Donald McGregor : Taught various Public Schools, and was Principal of the Clinton Public School when he was appointed, in 1884, Inspector of East Huron, which position he held till his death in 1890.

Messmore, Alexander, Blenheim ; Munn, John, Erin.

Paterson, Elizabeth C., Streetsville.

Platt, George Albert : Taught a number of years in Ontario ; is now teaching in Manitoba.

Platt, John Milton : Taught for some time ; entered the medical profession, and has ever since practised in Picton ; represented Prince Edward County for two terms in the Canadian House of Commons.

Rattray, Jessie Sophia, Cornwall.

Ridgway, Robert : Was for some time engaged in the publishing business in Toronto.

Robertson, Margaret, Hamilton ; Robinson, Grace, Toronto.

Scarlett, Catherine, Toronto ; Shurtleff, Mary Jane, Whitby.

Sparrow, Caroline, Galt : Died in 1888.

Vanalstine, William H., Prince Edward : Died in California.

Wilcox, Richard Jefferson, S. Dumfries : Entered the medical profession ; now deceased.

TWENTY-THIRD SESSION.

(January, 1860—June, 1860.)

Anderson, William : Taught for some time ; studied Medicine.

Barefoot, Isaac : An Indian from the Mohawk Reserve ; became an Anglican Missionary and Inspector of the Six Nation Schools in Brant County.

Bedell, Sarah Melantha : Taught for several years in Wentworth ; married Mr. Alexander McDougall, and went to the North-West.

Bethell, Dorinda Graham : Taught for some time ; married Mr. Geo. H. Stewart ; resides in Winnipeg.

Bourke, Barbara Anne, Toronto.

Brierly, Charles : Became a Baptist Minister ; was killed at Notfield, Glengarry, by a fall from his horse.

Buckland, Henry, W. Zorra.

Cannon, George, Marysburgh ; Chisholm, William, Brant ; Corrigan, Augusta Margaret, London ; Coulter, Margaret, Toronto.

Craig, George : Taught three years ; entered mercantile life, and after some years started his present prosperous business in North Gower, Carleton County.

Craigmile, Elizabeth Wilson, Hamilton ; Cummins, Margaret, Toronto ; Cuthbertson, Edward Greer, Toronto.

Dunn, Hannah Olivia : Has taught continuously in the Toronto Public Schools since 1864.

Farewell, George McGill : Taught at Raglan, Walkerville and other places ; became an M.D. ; practised until recently in Oshawa.

Farquharson, Georgiana, Whitby.

Fleming, William : Taught near Owen Sound till disabled by ill-health in 1864 ; resumed teaching in 1868, and taught in Scarboro' and Markham till 1881, when he went into business in Markham Village, where he still resides ; he has filled various local public offices, has been an earnest promoter of education, and is widely known as a champion Checker player.

Ford, Julia Cadman, Newmarket ; Foster, Mary Louisa, Toronto.

Fotheringham, Andrew Thomson : Now a Presbyterian minister in Blanshard, Perth County.

Fraser, Charlotte, Yorkville.

Goodfellow, Elizabeth, Brantford ; Gowanlock, Janet Kidd, S. Easthope.

Groce, Martha Zenobia : Taught almost continuously in Middlesex County till her marriage, in 1874, to Mr. William Booth ; now resides near Belmont.

Gunn, Jane : Taught in Woodstock, and is still teaching in the Toronto Public Schools.

Hammond, William, Elma.

Hay, Angus Cameron : Taught in Cornwall ; went to California, was elected to the Senate of that State ; returned to Cornwall and died there.

Healey, Michael, Asphodel.

Hendershott, Melissa Frances : Taught for a few years ; married a Methodist minister and went to Michigan.

Hill, Alfred : Taught for some years ; is now a merchant and farmer at Bear Brook in Russell County ; has filled various municipal positions.

Hill, Charlotte Mary : Married Dr. J. Smith ; now deceased.

Hipple, Jacob : Taught many years in rural sections in Lincoln, and also in St. Catharines Collegiate Institute ; retired in 1893 ; died in 1895.

Keffer, Thomas Dixon, Vaughan.

Kiernan, Thomas : Taught in Sarnia ; now a physician.

Lloyd, Eliza Jane, Toronto.

McAllan, Annie : Married Mr. William G. Dow of Whitby, and went to Manitoba.

McCamus, William : Taught in Fairmont, Ashburnham, and Glanford ; became a physician in 1869 ; practised Medicine twenty years at Bobcaygeon ; is now a druggist in the same place.

McFarlane, Laughlin : Studied Medicine, graduating in the University of Toronto in 1867 ; was for many years a member of the teaching staff of Toronto Medical School, and, when it became affiliated with the University of Toronto, he was appointed one of the professors of Surgery, and remained so till his recent death.

McGregor, Robert Campbell : Taught for some time in Osgoode and in Cornwall ; resides on a farm near Sandringham, Stormont.

McKay, Hugh M., E. Zorra.

McLennan, Margaret, Cornwall : Now deceased.

McMillan, Malcolm Cameron, Yarmouth.

McMillan, Susan Maria : Taught a few years in the Township of St. Vincent ; married Mr. Hiram Brown, a teacher ; now resides at Wiarton in Bruce.

McRae, Alexander, Kincardine.

Margach, John Lewis : Taught in Ontario County and in Brockville ; is now in business.

Moore, Charles Boyle, Goderich.

Millard, Alice Gay : Taught ten years in Bowmanville Public School, three years in the Methodist College at Stanstead, Que., and a number of years in the Indian mission schools at Hiawatha and Alderville in Northumberland, and the one on Walpole Island in the St. Clair ; retired from the profession two years ago.

Mullin, Sarah, Dumfries : Taught for many years in Brant County.

Mulloy, Nelson : Taught for a short time ; entered the medical profession, graduating in 1866 ; has practised at Preston, Waterloo, ever since.

Murray, John : Entered the Presbyterian ministry ; now and for many years past, pastor of a congregation in the Town of Kincardine.

Mutton, Ebenezer, Toronto.

Richardson, James : Taught for a time ; entered the Methodist ministry ; on account of failing health turned to farming ; taught some time in Wisconsin ; became a minister of the Methodist Episcopal church ; now deceased.

Rogers, Ellen, Toronto ; Rouse, William Hiram, Whitby ; Russell, Mary Jane, Stamford.

Sanders, Harriett Louisa, Barrie ; Scollon, John, Toronto ; Shepherd, Anne Eliza, Port Hope ; Shepherd, Mary Elizabeth, Port Hope ; Sinclair, John, Blanshard.

Sing, Samuel : Taught seven years ; entered the Methodist ministry in 1867 ; is still on circuit.

Stewart, Annie : Went to Winnipeg, Manitoba.

Stewart, Thomas, Toronto.

Thompson, Alexander, Ross.

Treadgold, George : Taught many years in Peel and York ; retired about 1881 ; died at Beeton in 1896.

Umney, Lilly : Married Mr. Leadley ; taught in Toronto Public Schools from 1872 till her resignation in 1888.

Walker, Thaddeus, Toronto.

Whiteside, Jacob Lemon : Practised Law in Lindsay from 1876 to 1879 ; was Stipendiary Magistrate of Haliburton for three years ; was four years a Clerk of the Queen's Bench at Osgoode Hall ; died in 1886.

Wilson, George, Mosa.

Wright, Meade Nisbett : Taught twenty-five years in various parts of Middlesex ; superannuated in 1886 ; resides now at Thorndale ; is Treasurer of W. Nissouri Township.

Yeats, Elizabeth : Taught in Dundas and Woodstock ; now deceased.

TWENTY-FOURTH SESSION.

(August, 1860—December, 1860.)

Andrew, Archibald : Taught eighteen years ; retired in 1879 ; resides at Skead's Mills, near Ottawa.

Beckett, Emma : Taught six years at Holland Landing ; married Mr. Allen ; now resides in Toronto.

Bell, Robert : Taught in Chatham ; was one of the founders of the Bell Organ Company in Guelph ; resides in California, where he has a large fruit farm.

Beattie, Grace Shepherd, Toronto ; Beattie, Jeremiah, Westminster ; Bishop, Maria Agnes, Woodstock ; Blanchard, Samuel Gray, Percy.

Bolton, Jesse Nunn : Taught two years in Peel County ; went into land surveying, and practised in Grey and Simcoe ; after a brief return to teaching, went into business in Bolton village in 1870 ; moved to Toronto in 1892 and still resides there.

Clement, William, Rawdon ; Cummings, May Elizabeth, Toronto.

Davidson, Archibald, Dalhousie.

De St. Remy, Harriet Annie Angélique le Lièvre ; Taught in Woodstock till 1864 ; married Mr. James Beard of that place ; resides in Kingston.

Dean, Andrew Daniel, Dereham.

Emery, Marion, Toronto.

Gerrie, James, Ancaster.

Glashan, John C. : Taught in the Provincial Model School from 1864 to 1867 ; was Inspector of Public Schools in West Middlesex ; is now Public School Inspector for the City of Ottawa ; has at various times been a member of the Central Committee of Examiners ; is the author of a number of works on Mathematics.

Graham, Charles, E. Gwillimbury : Now deceased.

Graham, John, Toronto ; Graham, Mary Caroline, E. Flamboro' ; Griffin, Ellen, Dumfries.

Hanlon, Ellen Victoria, Hamilton.

Hanly, John : Taught till 1867 ; entered the medical profession and practised at different places, being at Waubaushene from 1871 to 1896 ; now living retired at Midland.

Hills, Isabel, Hamilton ; Hocking, William Francis, Brantford.

Johnston, John : Taught from 1857 to 1871 ; was appointed in the latter year Inspector for South Hastings, and in 1873 for Belleville ; these positions he still holds.

Jones, Ann Elizabeth : Taught some years in York County ; married Mr. Robert Lackey of Toronto.

Keddy, John : Taught for some time ; kept a sheep ranch on San Juan Island near Vancouver ; is now a merchant in Brandon, Manitoba.

Kermott, Charles, Newmarket.

Kerr, Marion : Taught in Toronto from 1862 to 1867, and again from 1882 to the present time ; now Mrs. McGregor.

Kiernan, William M. : Taught several years ; superannuated ; now farming at Mansfield.

Lusk, Charles Horace : Taught Public School for a few years ; taught in the Provincial Model School, Toronto, from Aug., 1864, till Feb., 1867 ; graduated in Medicine in Victoria University in 1867 ; has been for many years Assistant Master in the Oakville High School.

McCarthy, Catherine, Toronto ; McDougall, Duncan, Erin ; McGrath, Patrick, Mono.

Moffatt, Susan Wait, Orillia.

Morrison, Adam : Taught in York County till 1864 ; spent six years teaching in the Sherbrooke Academy, and in gold mining ; taught four years in Peel and York, and has been on the Toronto Public School staff since 1875.

Pollock, Jane : Married ; resides in Bowmanville.

Reed, Georgina : Taught private school for a time ; married Mr. W. H. Riches in 1867 ; began teaching in Toronto in 1874 ; is now Principal of Sackville Street Public School, Toronto.

Rogers, George : Taught a few years ; became a Methodist minister.

Smith, Jenny, Dumfries ; Smith, Sarah Anne, Chinguacousy.

Switzer, Parmenio Alvan : Taught in Cobourg ; graduated in Victoria University in 1872 ; taught in the Oakville High School and in Elora ; became Public School Inspector of the District of Algoma ; died about 1882.

Turner, Elizabeth Ann, Toronto.

Vallance, Margaret : Taught for a short time in Wentworth ; married Thomas Wardlaw Taylor, then of Toronto, now Sir Thomas Taylor, Chief Justice of Manitoba ; resides at Winnipeg.

Wickson, Emma : Taught for some years in York County ; married Mr. Miatt, of Buffalo, N.Y., and lived there till her death.

Wood, Mercy, Westminster.

Young, Egerton Ryerson : Taught two years in Madoc ; entered the ministry of the Methodist church ; was missionary for five years among the Indians at Norway House in the North-West Territory, and in 1874 began a similar mission at Beren's River ; returned after a few years more to Ontario, and has since given up much of his time to lecturing in Canada, United States and Great Britain on behalf of Indian missions ; lives in Toronto.

Young, William Howie : Became an undertaker ; was at one time Mayor of Oakville, where he still resides.

TWENTY-FIFTH SESSION.

(January, 1861—June, 1861.)

Armitage, Margaret, Toronto.

Brown, Alick Howard : Taught Public School for several years ; spent some time in the foundry business ; went to California and died there.

Burk, Ada : Now Mrs. N. H. Stevens, Chatham, Ontario.

Chisholm, James, Chinguacousy ; Christie, Augusta, Toronto.

Christie, Caroline : Taught near Port Hope ; died in Australia.

Crawford, Agnes : Teaching Elocution in New York.

Cruickshank, Margaret F., Toronto ; Cumming, Margaret. Owen Sound.

Devlin, John, Whitchurch.

Duck, Mary Jane : Taught in St. Catharines ; married ; died about sixteen years ago.

Dunseith, David, Blanshard.

Easton, Robert : Taught five years, and then retired from the teaching profession on account of his health ; is now living in Toronto.

Elliott, John Charles : Taught continuously till his superannuation, the last ten years in St. George, County of Brant, where he still resides ; during this long period he taught in Puslinch. Paisley, Mount Forest, Fenelon Falls, Bath, and Cannington, before going to St. George.

Gott, Benjamin : Taught eight years ; commenced the practice of Horticulture near Arkona, in Lambton County ; followed this pursuit continuously till 1893, when he retired, and took up his residence in Strathroy, where he still lives.

Graham, Adelaide, Walpole.

Groat, Stillman P.: Taught Public Schools for a few years ; was appointed Inspector for East Middlesex in 1871 ; resigned to devote himself to journalism ; afterwards went to the United States.

Hammond, Joseph : Taught some years in the Township of Arran ; became a Baptist minister, and is now preaching near Boston, U. S. A.

Harper, Wm., Whitby.

Henderson, David : Taught for a time ; is now a merchant and banker in Acton ; has represented Halton for some years in the Canadian House of Commons.

Howland, Francis Lamb : Entered the medical profession in 1867 ; lives at Huntsville, Muskoka.

Hyde, Levi Thaddeus : After teaching for a time, went west to farm.

Jackson, Henry H., N. Dorchester ; Johnston, Arthur, Caledon.

Laidlaw, Janet : Taught for many years in the Dundas Public Schools ; now lives retired in the same town.

Laird, Jane, Harwich ; Lanton, Kate Simpson, Peterboro'.

Lloyd David : Taught till 1870 ; retired to take a position in the North York Registry Office ; was appointed Division Court Clerk in 1883, and still holds that office ; is also Clerk and Treasurer of Newmarket, and Treasurer of the Public School Board there.

Love, Mary Ann : Taught till 1865 ; married Mr. Carrier ; resides at Woodstock, Ontario.

McCully, Robert : Taught several years ; was for some time in business ; is now an Accountant in St. Thomas.

McDonald, Robert, W. Zorra.

McDougall, Elizabeth : Taught a short time in Kenyon Township ; married Rev. John Keone ; died in 1868.

McKellar, Catherine : Married Mr. Alexander McArthur of Westminster in Middlesex County ; her present residence is London.

McLennan, Andrew : Taught in the County of Glengarry ; now resides in Ottawa.

McShea Royal : Taught several years in the County of Huron ; entered the medical profession, and is now practising in the United States.

Marshall, Agnes, Stratford ; Muir, Agnes Eliza, Grimsby ; Muir, Orpha, Grimsby.

Murdoch, Andrew, M.A.. LL. D.: Taught two years, then prepared for an Arts course which he completed in Toronto University in 1868 ; entered the Baptist Ministry, and filled various pastorates in the United States and Canada ; has charge at present of a congregation in Waterford, Ontario.

Murray, David L., W. Zorra.

Neilson, William : Taught several years ; went to Cleveland, Ohio, where he is still engaged in business.

Owen, John : Taught for a time ; became a photographer in Stratford and Detroit ; died some years ago.

Owen, William Jerrold, Downie.

Parrott, Amanda, Ernestown.

Perry, Robert S. : Teaching and farming near Drayton.

Raney, William, Whitchurch.

Reid, George, Erin : Now farming.

Rowland, Fleming : After teaching for a time, chiefly in Kingston Grammar School, was appointed Collector of Inland Revenue at Kingston, which office he has held for twenty-two years.

Rundle, Richard Folly, Darlington.

Smith, Joseph Henry : Taught Public Schools in Huron and Wentworth ; spent some time in the lumber business ; resumed teaching in Halton ; was appointed Inspector of Public Schools for Wentworth in 1871, and this position he still holds ; is the author of a history of Wentworth County.

Starratt, Hannah, Chinguacousy.

Suddaby, Jeremiah : Taught six years in Leeds, and the remainder of the interval to 1877 in various schools in Waterloo County, including Galt Central School ; in that year he became the first Principal of the County Model School in Berlin, which position he still holds.

Taylor, Henry G., : Left the profession in 1865 ; now in business in Wyoming.

Turnbull, Jessie : Taught three years in Brantford Central School ; was appointed second teacher in the Girls' Model School at Toronto, in 1865, and held the position for three years until she retired to marry Mr. D. McEwen ; has since lived in Toronto, Montreal, and Cornwall, and is now living on a farm near Brandon, Manitoba ; has always been active in promoting movements for the improvement of the position of woman in society.

Unsworth, Anna H., Guelph : Now married.

Vardon, Anthony D., W. Oxford.

Vining Eusebia B., : Taught in Fergus from 1862 to 1871, and afterwards near Thorndale ; married in 1873 the Rev. D. Oliphant ; resumed teaching in 1879, and has ever since taught in London, Ontario.

Winans, William Henry : Entered the Methodist ministry ; died about 1866.

Woodward, George W., : Taught in Elmira, Waterloo County ; entered the Inland Revenue Service twenty years ago ; lives in Waterloo.

TWENTY-SIXTH SESSION.

(August, 1861—December, 1861.)

Bancroft, Asa M., W. Hawkesbury ; Bartlett, Wm. Edward, Percy.

Beaton, Harriet : Taught on Long Island and in Pittsburgh Township, both near Kingston ; married Mr. William Vanhorn in 1867, and still lives on a farm near her last school.

Bethell, Maria : Never taught ; resides in Toronto.

Boddy, Sophia Louisa : Taught continuously in Toronto from 1865 to 1873 ; married Mr. Henry Lowry of Lockport, Ill. ; now deceased.

Bruce, William Fraser, Thorah : Now deceased.

Brundage, Candace, Toronto.

Buik, Margaret : Taught many years in the Toronto Public Schools ; now retired and living in London, England.

Bull, Corey, Hallowell : Now deceased.

Cherry, William : Studied Medicine ; settled in Cleveland, Ohio.

Clark, Annie: Has taught continuously in the Toronto Public Schools since 1863; now Mrs. Carey.

Clark, Sarah Haley, Toronto; Collar, Leonora, Toronto.

Cork, George: Has taught continuously to the present time, in Prince Edward, Lincoln, Welland and Waterloo Counties, has been Principal of the Central School in Waterloo Town for ten years.

Dean, Sarah Jane Cavan; Dewart, Samuel H., Dummer.

Evans, Robert: Now practising Medicine in Dakota, U.S.A.

Fletcher, William, E. Gwillimbury.

Flynn, Daniel: Taught in York County till 1883; is now Inspector of Weights and Measures in Toronto.

Fraser, Alexander: Now superannuated; resides at Campbellville, Halton County.

Gibson, Rachel, London; Greer, Mary Anne, Kingston.

Guthrie, Grace: Married Mr. Wm. MacLeod of Woodstock.

Hardie, Ellen, Warwick; Hemenway, Sinia Amanda, Kemptville.

Hicks, David: Taught various Public Schools in Prince Edward and Hastings Counties till 1868; taught as assistant in the Colborne High School, 1876; completed his Arts course in Toronto University in 1881; has since been Head Master, successively, of the High Schools in Newburgh, Beamsville, Vienna and Port Dover, where he still teaches.

Holmes, Robert, Kitley; Horner, Esther Anne, Brockville.

Hughes, Amos J.: Taught Public School for two years; went into farming in East Gwillimbury Township, of which he has been Reeve, and is still Clerk and Treasurer; resides at Sharon.

Hughes, James Henderson: Taught Public School for two years; took an Arts course in Toronto University, graduating in 1869; was Principal of Markham High School for some years; went into business; died in 1892.

Jeffers, Emma, Toronto.

Kane, Mary Ann, Toronto.

Kidd, Alexander Brown, Dummer: Now deceased.

Knowlson, Mary I., Cavan.

McColl, Hugh: Taught till 1868; went into journalism, and followed that calling for seven years in Strathroy; was appointed Postmaster of that town in 1875, and still fills the position; has always taken an active interest in education.

McEachren, James, Toronto.

McDiarmid, Donald, Beckwith: Now deceased.

McDonald, Duncan Forbes, Lobo.

McDougall, Catherine: Taught in the Public Schools of Glengarry for several years; married Mr. John W. Kennedy; lives near Apple Hill, Ontario.

McGregor, Charles, Caledon; McHardy, Norman, Colborne.

McIntyre, Duncan J.: Taught two years; began to prepare for the study of Law, and was called to the bar in 1871; has since practised in Lindsay, of which he has been Police Magistrate since 1892; represented South Victoria in the Ontario Legislative Assembly from 1883 to 1886; resides in Lindsay.

McKay, Archibald, Brock.

MacPherson, Crawford: Has taught continuously since 1861, with the exception of an interval of three years in business; has been Principal of the Public Schools in Durham and Harriston, assistant master in the Elora High School, and Principal for sixteen years of the Public and Model Schools in Prescott, Grenville County, where he still lives.

Maloy, Hiram: Taught for some time near Mount Albert; was for a time License Inspector of North York.

Moran, John M.: Taught several years; was appointed Inspector for South Perth; resigned to go into journalism; taught for a time in Barrie; went to Kansas, U.S.A.; now deceased.

Meech, Thomas English, Oxford.

Nash, Charles Walter, Pickering.

Nichols, Wilmot M. : Took a University Arts course ; became Public School Inspector for West Kent ; died in 1894.

Nicholson, Thomas : Went to Vancouver Island in 1862 ; taught there, and in Oregon and California until 1879 ; engaged in mercantile business for nine years in Victoria ; taught again for eight years, and still resides there.

O'Flaherty, Edith, Toronto.

O'Neill, Margaret : Taught Roman Catholic Separate School in Hamilton for two years ; entered the Community of Loretto, and has been teaching under its auspices ever since ; her work for the last fifteen years has been preparing candidates for the Departmental Examinations.

Parkhurst, Etta C., Bowmanville.

Reeves, Mary Maria : Taught in a private school in Toronto till 1865 ; continued teaching in Woodstock till 1867 ; married Mr. Ross.

Rogers, Jessie : Taught for a time in Toronto.

Ross, John Cameron, Toronto.

Saunders, Matilda J. : Taught six years in Pickering and Markham Townships ; married Mr. John Millard, after whose death she resumed teaching, and has continued the work till the present time, the last nine years in Orillia.

Scott, James G. : Taught in Lambton and Huron Counties for some time ; entered the medical profession, and commenced practice at Bluevale in 1870 ; three years afterwards went to Seaforth, where he still follows his professional calling.

Sinclair, James C. : Taught for two years in Cayuga ; took a partial course in Toronto University ; taught eleven years in Stratford ; resides on his farm near Guelph.

Smith, Abram, N. Easthope ; Smith, Sarah, Toronto.

Theal, Nelson, Grantham.

Thetford, William Henry : Taught Public Schools in Grenville, Bruce and Wellington Counties ; went into business, but has since taught for a time in Manitoba ; now resides in Toronto.

Troy, William Dennis, Brantford.

Vance, William : Taught in Bobcaygeon, Mount Pleasant and Millbrook till 1879 ; carried on mercantile business in the last named place till 1893 ; is Postmaster of Millbrook.

Van Slyke, George W. : Taught in London and in the Hamilton Collegiate Institute : was afterwards Principal of the Woodstock Public and M del Schools ; went into the medical profession, and now practises in Detroit, Michigan.

Warburton, William : Taught continuously till 1880 ; retired on account of failing health ; resides in Hamilton.

Willis, Robert : Taught many years, for some time past in Whitby ; now superannuated, and living in that town.

Wilson, Hercules, Richmond ; Wood, Benjamin Wills, Mann, Quebec ; Woodington, Minnie, Toronto.

TWENTY-SEVENTH SESSION.

(January, 1862—June, 1862.)

Acres, Jane, Wentworth.

Allan, Absalom Shade : Taught two years and then went into business, first as an Accountant in Elora and afterwards as general merchant in Clifford, where he has resided since 1868 ; has filled various municipal offices, and represented West Wellington in the Ontario Legislative Assembly from 1886 to 1893.

Anderson, John : Taught in Peel County.

Anker, Mary Ann : Now Mrs. Goldman of Toronto.

Armstrong, Mary E. : Teaches in one of the Hamilton Public Schools.

Bates, Mary Jane : Taught for twenty-three years, the last six in Brantford Central School, from which she retired on account of ill health in 1887 ; has since resided in Prince Albert.

Boake, Sarah Anne, Toronto ; Boldrick, Richard Henry, Hastings ; Brown, Sophia Georgina, Perth.

Buchan, Mary : Now Mrs. William Francis of Mitchell, Ontario.

Campbell, Mary, Kent.

Campbell, John Munro : Entered the medical profession ; practised for a time at Seaforth, Huron County; now resides in Brooklyn, New York.

Davis, Ruth, Carleton.

Green, Philip : Taught many years in Wentworth, Waterloo and Brant ; has become a farmer and cheese manufacturer at Sheffield, Wentworth County.

Greene, Martha, Wentworth ; Griffin, Walter, Durham.

Halls, Samuel Pollard : Taught a rural school in Huron County for several years ; was Science Master in the Goderich High School from 1876 to 1892 : has been since 1895 Principal of the Goderich Public and Model Schools.

Henderson, Isabella P., Wentworth.

Henning, Amelia : Taught in one of the Toronto Public Schools from 1864 to 1870 inclusive ; now Mrs. A. H. Welch ; resides in Toronto.

Hilliard, Thomas : Taught till 1866 ; followed journalism as an occupation till 1886 ; has since that time been engaged in the business of insurance ; has been since 1876 P. S. Inspector for the Town of Waterloo, where he resides.

Hunt, Robert : Taught for some time ; went into the medical profession ; deceased.

Hutchison, William, Quebec.

Kennedy. Eliza Jane, Lincoln ; Kenny, Elizabeth, Wentworth.

Langdon, John : Taught for many years at Prince Albert in Ontario County ; is still teaching in the County of Victoria.

Ley, Theresa Georgiana, Toronto.

Lloyd, Agnes : Taught ten years in Ontario ; married Mr. F. W. Holtzhausen, a Baptist minister ; has resided for the past ten years at Marquette, Michigan.

Lundy, Sarah, Peel.

McCausland, Robert : Taught for many years in Toronto ; died in 1897.

McCausland, William J. : Became a Physician ; died some years ago in Pennsylvania.

McIntosh, Angus, Glengarry.

McLaren, Alexander : Taught in Carleton and Halton Counties, and from 1870 to 1876 in Toronto ; entered the medical profession ; practised for a time at Delaware, Middlesex, but is now in London.

McPherson, Finlay ; Became an Accountant in Chicago.

McPherson, Moses M. : Graduated in Arts in Victoria University in 1869 ; was for many years Head Master of the Prescott High School ; recently retired.

Maybee Euphemia A., Northumberland ; Metcalf, Hiram, Prescott.

Millar, John : See Biographical Sketches.

Miller, John R. : After teaching for some time was appointed in 1871 Public School Inspector for West Huron ; retired to enter the legal profession, and practised for some years in Toronto ; died in 1896.

Monkman, James Matthias : Taught continuously for twenty-three years ; has been, since his retirement in 1885, clerk of Arran Township, Bruce ; resides at Arkwright.

Morrison, Margaret Ellen, Lambton ; Morton, John Brown, Hastings ; Munson, Charles Francis, Durham.

O'Grady, Patrick John, Lanark.

Powers, Henry A. : Taught almost continuously for twenty-one years ; now farming in London Township ; resides near Maple Grove.

Richardson, Isabella: Taught for two years at Keswick, York County; married Mr. A. Barber, who is now Principal of the Brampton County Model School.

Roberts, Sarah Ann, Hastings ; Robinson, Annie, Middlesex.

Summerss, George, Middlesex.

Schmidt, John Henry : Taught for several years ; has published since 1872, in Stratford, the *Kolonist*, a German Newspaper.

Sullivan, Daniel : Taught three years in Peel County, and has ever since been engaged in mercantile business in Brant Township, Bruce ; has held various local public offices ; lives at Elmwood.

Tapscott, Samuel : Taught two years in Peterboro' ; went into the drug business, and has continued at it in Brantford for thirty years.

Taylor, Walter : Taught in Peel County for several years ; is now in business in the Village of Bolton.

Taylor, Susannah, Durham ; Thompson, Charles, Welland ; Thomson, Matthew, York.

Treadgold, Manton : Taught one year in Weston High School, and ten in a Public School ; went into business in Brampton, where he still resides.

Wager, Reuben Lewis : Is now a Methodist Minister in the United States.

Ward, James Henry, Northumberland.

Welsh, John : Taught in the Township of Dover from 1864 till 1870 ; was engaged in mercantile business from 1870 till 1876 ; resumed teaching ; retired in 1892 ; has been Township Clerk for the past twenty-two years.

Williams, Eliza Ann, Toronto ; Wilson, William, Durham.

Wilson, Edward Sutton : Taught school a number of years ; graduated in Medicine in 1880 ; practised in Bobcaygeon, Fenelon Falls and Lindsay, is now practising in Buffalo, New York.

TWENTY-EIGHTH SESSION.

(August, 1862—December, 1862.)

Adams, Agnes Maria : Taught at Acton ; married a merchant.

Bruce, King : Taught in Kent rural schools till 1877 ; went into business ; resides in Chatham ; is about to resume teaching.

Cole, Lucinda A., Simcoe ; Corbett, Richard. Simcoe ; Crawford, Margaret, Hamilton.

Crane, George Toronto : Has taught in the Toronto Public Schools for twenty-two years ; is now Principal of Lansdowne School.

Dodson, Richard Elisha : Taught in Tilbury West ; is now farming near Comber, Essex County.

Ewing, John, Richmond, Quebec.

Fansher, Lucretia, Lambton ; Ferrell, Kate Walker, Toronto.

Foreman, Fanny : Taught in Etobicoke till 1868 ; married Mr. C. Webb.

Fowler, Henry, Northumberland ; French, Sarah Toms, Paris, Brant.

Giffin, Willard Morse : Taught nineteen years in Lambton ; became a merchant in St. Thomas ; resides now in Sarnia.

Gillin, Catharine, Brantford ; Gillin, Ellen, Brantford ; Gillin, Margaret J., Brantford.

Graham, Dugald, Peterboro' ; Graduated B.C.L., McGill University, Montreal ; became a successful merchant ; deceased.

Grant, Elizabeth : Taught many years resides in Lancaster, Ontario.

Greenlees, Margaret : Taught several years in Toronto Schools, and in 1873 married Mr. Samuel Crane ; died in 1890.

Hardie, Robert, Victoria.
Henderson, Margaret A., : Taught for several years in the Hamilton Public Schools; married, and now resides in Toronto.
Henry, Rebecca : Teaching in one of the Hamilton Public Schools.
Hill, John Neilson, Lennox.
James, Lucy, Peel ; Johnson, Frances, Brockville.
Keam, Reuben, Northumberland.
Kessack, Elizabeth : Taught in London and Strathroy ; is now teaching in Toronto.
Lanton, Annie, Bath ; Lawson, George Dudley, Norfolk.
McDonald, James, Carleton.
McGrath, John : Taught for a short time in Kingston ; now deceased.
MacPherson, Archibald, Waterloo : Taught in Wellington and the Town of Galt for many years ; deceased.
Martin, John : Now an Actuary in Toronto.
Morris, John George, Ontario ; Muirhead, Maggie, Oxford ; Mulcahy, Mary, Toronto.
Oates, Isabella A., : Taught for three years in York County ; has taught in Toronto Public Schools since 1884.
Pepper, John : Taught a short time, and then took an Arts course in Toronto University, graduating in 1868 ; was Head Master of Oakville High and Public Schools for two years ; became a Methodist Minister, and is still on circuit.
Poole, Edward : Taught in both Public and High Schools ; is now practising Law.
Powell, Francis Cox : Taught in Thornbury, Southampton, and Port Elgin, till 1877 ; was appointed the first Principal of the Kincardine County Model School, and still fills the position.
Rose, Amos William, Peel.
Ruby, Daniel Christian : Practised Law in Texas for over thirty years ; died in 1896.
Sanderson, Robert : Has taught, with intervals of cessation, from 1863 to the present time, in a considerable variety of schools, among them the Drayton Public Schools, the Mount Forest High School, the Sutton West Village School, the Harriston Public School, and the Orangeville High School ; now resides at Grand Valley.
Sinclair Angus : Graduated in Arts in Toronto University in 1870 ; was for many years Head Master of Windsor High School ; retired, and lives in Toronto.
Sinclair, Jane, St Mary's ; Stevenson, Ruth Badelia, Brockville ; Stewart, Isabella Nesbitt, Cayuga.
Trenholme, Clarissa Jane, Toronto ; Turney, Melissa, Newcastle.
Wiggins, Henry, Simcoe ; Wilkinson, Hannah, Toronto.
York, Frederick E., Carleton.

TWENTY-NINTH SESSION.

(January, 1863—June, 1863.)

Allen, Mary, Middlesex.
Banks, Richard, Wellington.
Barr, William : Taught in Dorchester Township for over twenty years, almost until his death.
Bell, William : Has taught, with brief intermissions, in rural and town Schools of the County of Middlesex ; is at present teaching at Ailsa Craig.
Bell, Mary Anne, Toronto.
Berney, William Henry, Middlesex : Now deceased.
Burrows, Frederick : Taught continuously till 1871, when he was appointed Public School Inspector of Lennox and Addington.

Butler, Richard Charles : Began the practice of Medicine in 1869, and resided at Coldwater, Prince Edward County ; recently deceased.

Cain, James : Went to practise Medicine in the United States.

Cameron, Thomas : Died at Arkona, where his family still resides.

Campbell, Aaron Jesse : Taught, with occasional interruptions, till 1872 ; graduated in Medicine in Toronto University in 1874 ; has since practised in various places ; resides now in Gravenhurst, Muskoka District.

Carlisle, Jane, Norfolk ; Cash, Charlotte, York.

Craig, Elizabeth : Married Mr. Owen of California, U.S.A.

Dick, Margaret Elizabeth, York.

Elder, Jane, Perth County.

Elder, Christina H. : Married Mr. W. Thomson, Mitchell.

Fawcett, Simon Wesley : Now in business in London, Ontario.

Frampton, John : Taught in Halton and Kent ; died about 1895.

Galbraith, Daniel : Taught in Elgin till 1867 ; graduated in Medicine in Toronto University in 1868 ; has practised in Dresden, Ontario, ever since.

Goldsmith, Perry David : Taught several years ; practised Medicine in several places ; is now in Belleville.

Grabell, Ladonia Maria Emeline, Welland ; Guthrie, Jane, Oxford.

Hamilton, Alexander : Entered the Presbyterian ministry.

Hamilton, Sarah Jane : Taught in the Toronto Schools from 1867 till her death in 1881.

Hannah, William George ; Now a practising lawyer in Toronto.

Harbottle, Charlotte : Taught eight years in Hamilton ; married Mr. Ronan in 1873 ; still resides in that city.

Hare, George Washington, Middlesex.

Helson, Thomas Henry, Durham : Taught in Durham County ; died many years ago.

Herrick, Alvan Corson : Was Principal of the Owen Sound Public School ; is now in business.

Hodge, George : Taught two years ; entered the medical profession and has since 1870 practised in Lakefield, Mitchell, and London ; is now Professor of Clinical Medicine in the Western University at London.

Horgan, Mary Rebecca, Toronto ; Horner, Esther, Lincoln.

Jordan, Thomas, Peel.

King, John S. : Taught in Wentworth and Waterloo Counties till 1869 the last three years as Principal of the school in Waterloo Village : spent five years in journalistic work on the Hamilton *Times* and Toronto *Globe* ; entered the medical profession, and has been practising in Toronto since 1876 ; has been Surgeon to the Mercer Reformatory since it was established.

Lamb, Susannah, Toronto.

Langdon, Richard Vickery ; Taught in Prince Albert, Ontario ; went to Michigan to practise Law.

Lowe, Peter, Huron ; Lymburner, Eliza, Wentworth.

McArthur, Alexander, Peel.

McBrayne, Dugald : Taught in Elgin and Middlesex till 1879 ; went to Denver on account of failing health, and died there in that year.

McDonald, William, Oxford ; McKay, Andrew, Oxford.

McLaren, Alexander Lumsden : Taught five years ; prepared for the practice of Medicine by attendance at teaching institutions in Toronto, New York, London, and Edinburgh ; practised for some years at Point Edward, Lambton, and then moved to Port Huron, Michigan, where he still resides.

Martin, Elizabeth, Toronto ; Matheson, John Hugh, Oxford.

Moment, Alfred Harrison : Taught a few years in Ontario ; entered the Presbyterian ministry in the United States in 1876, and has spent his time since in New York and Brooklyn.

Moyer, Eli Nash : Has gone into business, with headquarters in Toronto.

O'Brien, Eliza : Entered St. Joseph's Convent, Toronto, in 1866, and died there in 1881.

O'Flaherty, Annie Maria ; Taught in Toronto from 1864 till 1870 ; married Mr. W. J. Thorald ; resumed teaching in 1881, and is still on the Toronto staff

Palmer, Geo. Alex., York ; Peden, Jessie, Hamilton.

Rider, Thomas, Oxford.

Rockwell, Ashbell S. : Taught till 1872, and began in that year to practise Medicine ; is still in active practice in Rochester, N. Y.

Rose, Leonard Alfred : Taught in Lanark some years ; superannuated and living near Arnprior.

Ross, John, Oxford

Simons, Theresa, Essex.

Swan, Thomas : Taught in Glenmorris, Brant, till 1866, practised Medicine in Preston and Hespeler, Waterloo County, till his death in 1887.

Taber, Jacob Russell, York ; Twohey, Ellen, Toronto.

Welsh, Jane, Leeds ; Wright, Mary Eleanor, Grey.

THIRTIETH SESSION.

(August, 1863—December, 1863.)

Abbott, John Thomas Victoria.

Alexander, William : After teaching several years was appointed, in 1871, Public School Inspector of Perth County, and he still holds that position.

Allen, John : Taught several years, went into mercantile business at Mono Mills, Ontario.

Archibald, Charles : Studied Medicine for a time in New York ; taught in Oxford County, and afterwards in the Provincial Model School, Toronto, from Jan., 1868, until Sept., 1869 ; completed his medical studies and went into practice there ; died about ten years ago.

Atkinson, Mary ; Taught at Chatham ; retired in 1894 ; resides near Florence, Ontario.

Ayers, William : Now in business in Beamsville, Ontario.

Baldwin, Louise, Durham ; Bales, Annie, York ; Barnes, Annie, Wentworth.

Belfry, Sarah Ann : resides near Newmarket.

Bogart, George A. : Moved to Kansas, U.S.A.

Braiden, Wilson : Taught for several years in Halton County, chiefly at Oakville and Burlington ; entered the medical profession ; now deceased.

Brown, Livius ; Died in Manitoba in 1896.

Brown, Miles : Taught four years ; took a medical course, and has practised since 1871, partly in Leeds and partly in Dundas County, where he still resides at Chesterville.

Cameron, Annie Isabella : Has taught continuously in Toronto since completing her Normal School course ; has been Principal of various schools since 1885.

Campbell, Mary, Toronto.

Capsey, Mrs Margaret : Taught in Elgin County, and afterwards in Chatham, till 1881 ; was appointed Lady Principal of Alma College, St. Thomas, when it was established, and filled that position till 1892 ; now resides at Odell, Ill., U.S.A.

Cartmell, Martha Julia : Now a missionary to Japan.

Carter, Wm. Henry Perry, Brant ; Christie, Elias, Perth.

Churcher, Annie : Taught in different positions in the London Schools till 1868, when she married Mr. J. C. Glashan, Public School Inspector of Ottawa, where she is still living.

Clark, Clara Jane: Taught for a short time in Woodstock, and in the Girls' Model School, Toronto, from Aug., 1865, until April, 1869; married, in 1869, Mr. John D. Nasmith; still resides in Toronto.
Cochran, Charles, Grenville.
Coyne, Annie: Taught in London Public Schools; married Mr. Elliott; resides in London.
Coyne, Maria Hamilton: Taught in London since 1866; now Principal of one of the schools in that city.
Crawford, Grace, York.
Dobie, Isabella McCreath, Brant.
Donnelly, James: Taught in several places, mostly in Peel County till 1881; is now engaged in mercantile business in Toronto.
Elliott, George, Durham.
French, William Wilson, Prince Edward.
Gerow, Arthur Martin, Hastings.
Gibson, James: Taught for a number of years; afterwards engaged in farming in the Township of Athol; has been active in Municipal affairs.
Girdwood, Alexander, Brant: Now deceased.
Hall, Asa, Peel.
Harcourt, Luke Arthur: Taught for three years in Wellington County; entered the medical profession; practised in Chicago, and more recently in Sacramento, Cal., U. S. A., where he still resides.
Hay, Janet Kenrick, Halton; Heaslip, Nelson, Lincoln.
Irvine, Eliza, Wentworth.
Jones, Rebecca: Taught a very short time in Toronto; married; now resides in England.
Kahler, Emma Amelia, Perth.
Lovett, William: Taught several years in Wentworth; went into the medical profession, and is now practising in Ayr, Ontario.
McArthur, Robert Blair, Perth; McCabe, Margaret, Toronto; McFarlane, George, Perth; MacGregor, Mary, Leeds.
McKellar, Hugh: Taught till 1868 in Lambton County; entered the Presbyterian ministry; spent four years as missionary in the North-West, and ten years as a settled pastor in Manitoba; has been since 1888 in a pastorate near Mount Forest.
McKay, Jessie, Wentworth; McMahon, Michael, York; McTavish, Douglas, Perth.
Mills, Margaret, Perth; Monkman, John Gordon Lawrence, Peel; Mullin, Charlotte Ann, Brant; Murphy, John Joseph, Peel.
Narraway, John Wesley: Taught in Oshawa and Belleville; has been for several years on the teaching staff of Toronto.
Oles, John Whiting, Norfolk.
Parsons, John, York; Peart, William, Ontario; Pritchard, James, Wellington.
Reeves, Ellen, York; Robbins Helen Gertrude, Wentworth; Rutherford, James, Oxford.
Rutherford, James, Durham: Now practising Medicine in Orono, Ontario.
Scott, Eliza Patton, Toronto; Simpson, John Wm., York; Sinclair, Janet, Toronto; Squire, William, Bruce; Stanley, Catharine Penelope, York.
Titchworth, Ira Cyrus, Brant.
Wait, Lucien Augustus: Returned to Vermont his native state; took an Arts course and graduated in Harvard University; became Assistant Professor of Mathematics in Cornell University in 1870, and has since 1895 been in entire charge of that department; during 1873-74, filled the post of United States Consul at Athens.

Warburton, Lucinda : Taught till 1875 in various schools in Elgin, Middlesex, and Huron ; moved to Stratford and taught there for over seventeen years till her retirement in 1891.

Webb, Joseph Hughes : Taught for a number of years ; entered the medical profession ; practised in Ayr and New Dundee, then removed to the Town of Waterloo, where he is still in practice ; is a Coroner for Waterloo County and Medical Referee for one of the Waterloo Insurance Companies.

Williams, Wm., Carleton.

Young Sarah, Wentworth.

THIRTY-FIRST SESSION.

(January, 1864—June, 1864.)

Agar, Jane, York.

Aitken, Jeanie: Taught a number of years; resides at Simcoe, Ontario.

Arthur, Samuel, Wentworth : Now retired.

Balderson, Thomas, Lanark.

Braiden, Richard: Taught for some time in Halton County; went into the medical profession; practised in Michigan, U. S. A.

Brown, James Burt: Now a missionary in Nebraska, U. S. A.

Burwash, Mary, Prescott.

Callinan, Thomas, Haldimand ; Campbell, James, Elgin ; Campbell, Mary Anne, Wellington; Campbell, Sarah Annie, Middlesex.

Cantlon, Elizabeth : Married a clergyman ; now deceased.

Clark, James Fred., Northumberland.

Cusack, Amelia: Now Mrs. Webster of Hamilton.

Donohoe, Anne, Leeds.

Earl, Barton : Taught many years in the Peterboro' Collegiate Institute ; went into business about ten years ago ; now resides in Peterboro'.

Elliott, Margaret: Taught in Toronto from 1867 to 1871.

Ellis, John Allen: Taught in York County; spent some years in the wholesale stationery business in Toronto, and became afterwards manager of a Life Insurance Company.

Ellis, Fred. Llewellyn, Ontario.

Ewan, Janet: In 1866 married Mr. Daniel McCraney, who subsequently represented East Kent in the Ontario Legislative Assembly for several parliamentary terms ; after his death moved from Bothwell to Collingwood, where she still resides.

Farrington, James: Taught for a short time ; became a Dental Surgeon, and practised in Oxford County.

Fraser, George James: Taught in both Public and High Schools in Woodstock ; became an officer of the Inland Revenue Service ; resides at Woodstock.

Fraser, John : Taught for a short time; entered the medical profession ; was appointed to the teaching staff of Rolph's Medical School, and after it became defunct he continued to practise in Toronto.

Fry, Menno Simon, Haldimand.

Gemmell, Jessie: Taught some years in Toronto; married ; now deceased.

Gregory, Thomas : Was Principal of the Exeter Public School from 1876 to 1889, when he resigned on account of failing health.

Haggerty, Hugh, Wentworth.

Harcus, Mary: Taught for a short time in Grey County, and afterwards in Oakville until 1871, when she married Mr. C. W. Coote ; still resides at Oakville.

Harper, Robert, Ontario.

Houston, William: Taught Public School for a short time; took an Arts course in Toronto University, graduating in 1872; was Head Master of the Beamsville High School during 1873-4; engaged in journalism on various papers till 1883, when he was appointed Librarian to the Ontario Legislative Assembly; has held, for the past four years, the position of Director of Teachers' Institutes for the Province.

Jackson, Ellen, York.

Jennison, Reuben Robinson: Taught in Milton, Sharon, Stayner, Barrie and Baden; now engaged in business in Toronto.

Legge, Isabella: Resides near Cherry Grove, Ontario.

McBean, Isabella: Taught in Napanee Public School; married Mr. McGee; died in 1878.

McCallum, Malcolm, Middlesex: Now deceased.

McColl, Hugh: Taught in Perth County and in London; entered the medical profession, and has since 1874 practised in Lapeer, Mich., with the exception of two intervals of special professional study in Europe.

McDonald, John James: Oxford.

McIntosh, Margaret: Taught one year and a half; married Mr. J. D. Cameron; resides in L'Orignal, Ontario.

McIntyre, George, Durham.

McLean, James, Wellington: Now retired.

McLean, Peter: Taught in Milton; was Public School Inspector for Algoma; died at Milton.

McLeod, Mary, Stormont: Taught at Cold Springs; married Rev. Mr. Robertson.

McLim, William Andrew: Taught many years, a large part of his time in the Orangeville Public School; died in Toronto after his retirement.

Mainprize, Sarah: Taught six years in North Gwillimbury, York; married Mr. Mann; now resides in Newmarket.

Marling, Mary Ellen, Toronto; Metcalf, John Henry, Dundas.

Murch, Thomas: Still teaching at Holmesville, Huron.

Rae, Alexander Marshall: Taught seven years in York, and one in Ontario; went to Port Perry in 1873 to teach in the Public School; has been Principal of the County Model School since 1877.

Ross, Catherine McCandie: Taught in Oxford County, in the Ingersoll Collegiate Institute, and afterwards in Mount Forest; married, in 1875, Rev. D. McDonald, for the past twenty-one years Presbyterian minister at Glenarm, Victoria County; still takes an active interest in educational matters.

Russell, John Rowe, Brant.

Scott, Jane, Lanark.

Sidway, Elizabeth: Taught at Fenton, Black Creek and elsewhere; married Mr. Alexander England; now resides near Port Dover.

Smith, James, Ontario; Smith, Wm. Charles, Wellington; Sullivan, Annie, York.

Trout, Harriet Ann: Married Mr. Duncan, Sterling; now resides at East Toronto.

Turner, Maria Jane, Ontario.

Wright, George Catley, Northumberland.

Wright, Aaron Abel: Taught a few years; went into mercantile business in the Town of Renfrew, where he still resides.

THIRTY-SECOND SESSION.

(August, 1864—December, 1864.)

Banan, Jane Anne: Taught Public Schools in York, Oxford, Huron and Durham Counties until 1872; since 1874 has taught continuously in the Toronto Public Schools; now Mrs. J. A. McBrien.

Brown, George, York.

Carley, Abram : Has taught continuously in Public Schools in Middlesex and York for thirty-one years.

Cavanagh, William Herbert : Taught in Selkirk, Ontario, for many years ; now practises Medicine in Michigan.

Chambers, John : Was for some years Head Master of the Walkerton Public School ; went into business there, and filled the office of Town Clerk until 1896.

Cone, Julia, York.

Crawford, Allan : Entered the medical profession in 1870 ; died at Alvinston, Ontario.

Crawford, Elizabeth, Wentworth.

Dingman, Margaret Mahalla : Went as a Missionary Teacher to Africa ; came back in poor health, and died while teaching in the Indian School near Southampton.

Dobbin, Emma Walker, Wentworth ; Dodds, Margaret, Brant ; Dunn, Robert, Simcoe.

Eccles, Daniel : Taught several years in Lambton ; went into the drug business in 1870 in Parkhill, but resumed teaching in 1879 ; retired from teaching in 1881 to enter the insurance business ; has been in a mercantile house in Toronto since 1891.

Ellis, Hannah, Norfolk : Now deceased.

Forster, Mary Telfer, York.

Gray, Samuel, Peel ; Greeve, Ellen, Wentworth.

Gilfillan, James : Taught rural schools in Durham County and the Orono and Bowmanville Public Schools as Head Master ; in 1880 was appointed Assistant Master in the High School in the latter town, and became its Principal in 1897, having taken an Arts Degree in Queen's University the year before.

Harman, Reuben Powell : Taught Public Schools in Ontario County for about six years ; went into business in Uxbridge, where he still takes an active interest in public affairs.

Hay, Andrew : Taught some time in St. Mary's, and has since taught in the Barrie High School as Mathematical Master.

Henderson, Margaret Jane, York ; Hodgins, Jane, York.

Jennings, Hannah Augusta, Oxford.

Jessop, Elisha : Taught for some time ; entered the medical profession, taking his degree in Toronto University in 1875 ; practised at Jordan for ten years and more recently in St. Catharines.

Johnson, Chas. Richard, Peel.

Jupp, William, Simcoe : Entered the Anglican Ministry.

Kennedy, Jane, Wentworth.

Lees, Henrietta : Taught for some time in Public Schools ; kept a private school, with one interval of a few years, till 1889 ; now Mrs. Parker.

Lewis, Richard : Taught Public Schools in different parts of the Province until his death at Winona in 1887.

McCrimmon, Angus : Taught in St. Thomas ; now practising Law.

McNaught, Frances : Taught till 1873 in the Central School, Galt ; has since that time made her home with her sister, wife of the Hon. James Young, Ex-M.P.

McNaughton, Margaret, Durham.

Masales, George Washington : Taught several years in Halton and Huron Counties.

Montgomery, Esther Emma : Taught for many years ; was at one time on the staff of the Institute for the Blind at Brantford ; died many years ago.

Morton, Andrew, York ; Moulton, Proctor, Durham.

Murray, John : Went into the medical profession ; practised in Fingal, Ontario ; long dead.

Nixon, Kate, Wentworth.

Page, Thomas Otway : Taught for a time in the Belleville Seminary, and afterwards in various Public Schools till 1876 ; graduated in Arts in Toronto University in 1877 ; taught in several High Schools successively as Head Master until his retirement in 1896 on account of ill health ; now resides in Woodstock.

Palmer, Sarah Anne, York ; Pettinger, Mary, Wentworth.

Rawson, Elizabeth Anne, Simcoe.

Reed, Isabella, Wentworth : Now deceased.

Richard, Alexander, Huron ; Richardson, Joshua John, York ; Robertson, James, Perth.

Scobie, Sarah Emily Alexandrina : Taught in Public Schools in Hamilton till 1879 and in Toronto till the present time.

Sefton, Annie Maria : Taught in Uxbridge till 1875 ; has taught in the Toronto Schools since 1877.

Short, Mary, Northumberland.

Strickland, Elizabeth : Married Mr. J. L. Smith ; now resides in the Township of Whitby.

Smith, Thomas, Perth.

Sutherland, Annie Agnes : Taught in a private academy and in the Provincial Model School in Toronto till 1869 ; married in that year Mr. J. L. Hughes, now Public School Inspector for Toronto ; died in 1884.

Sutherland, Jennie H. : Taught in Toronto from 1869 to 1872 ; resides in that city.

White, Eleanor : Teaching at present in the Murray Street School, Hamilton.

Wilkins, David Francis Henry : Graduated in Arts in Toronto University in 1869 ; taught in various High Schools till his death in 1892, while Head Master in Beamsville.

Wilson, Josiah, Oxford ; Wilson, Samuel, York.

THIRTY-THIRD SESSION.

(January, 1865–June, 1865.)

Agnew, James, York.

Bentley, Kate : Taught in the Toronto Public Schools from 1872 till her resignation in 1876 ; married Mr. Carswell, and went many years ago to the North-West.

Black, Mary E. : Taught three years in Penetanguishene ; married Mr. Walter Bell of that place ; moved in 1881 to Grand Marais, Michigan, where she has at different times served the public as Postmaster and Inspector of Schools, while assisting to carry on a mercantile business.

Blain, Hugh : Went into mercantile business, and is now partner in a large wholesale firm in Toronto.

Brown, John Thompson : Died recently in Essex County, where his family still reside.

Bullock, Mary Cecilia, Oxford.

Carscadden, Thomas : Taught Public School and as Assistant in Chatham High School and Woodstock College, successively ; graduated in Arts in Toronto University in 1875 ; taught a year in Prince Edward Island and some time in Upper Canada College : went to the Galt Collegiate Institute in 1881 as Assistant, and has been Principal for thirteen years.

Cartmell, Amelia Isabella, Hamilton ; Conkley, Henry, Middlesex.

Dawson, Cornelius, Northumberland ; Dawson, George, Carleton ; Dolmage, Florence Marion, Toronto ; Drew, Ellen, Toronto.

Ferguson, Margaret, Toronto.

Fisher, Simeon : Now a Presbyterian minister, pastor of congregations at Flamboro' and Linden.

Foreman, William : Taught for six years in Ontario, and afterwards at different places on Long Island, New York ; went into business some time before his death in 1896.

Forster, Mary : Taught in Hamilton till 1877, and in Toronto till 1879 ; married Mr. Frederick Swannell ; has taught in Toronto since 1888.

Foster, Margaret Jane : Taught six years in Fergus ; married, in 1871, Mr. R. H. Perry, a druggist in Fergus ; died there in 1885.

Graham, Andrew, Perth ; Graham, Simon, Grey ; Goldsmith, Stephen, Northumberland.

Hamilton, George : Has taught uninterruptedly since 1865, the last twenty-one years as Master of the Sebringville School.

Jackson, Thomas : Taught in the Counties of Durham and Waterloo ; entered the Wesleyan ministry in 1867 ; was secretary of Conference in 1884 ; was a member of the General Conference in 1890 and 1898 ; is now stationed at Elora.

Kessack, Margaret : Taught in London High School ; now living in retirement in that city.

Lanton, Emilie, Elgin : Taught for some time in Vienna.

Leslie, Eliza Jane, Barrie.

Lawrie, Elizabeth : Taught for a time in Oxford, Peel and Halton ; married Mr. Colin Smith, and lives on a farm near Oakville.

McLean, Daniel : Went into the legal profession ; has practised for many years in the city of Ottawa.

McNair, Alexander, Huron ; McNaughton, Duncan, Cobourg ; Macniven, Susan, Ingersoll.

Martin, John Anthony, Northumberland.

Meldrum, Norman William : Taught a short time in Brant and Oxford ; graduated in Medicine in Toronto University in 1873 ; has practised ever since in Ayr, Ontario.

Metcalf, Josias Richey, Renfrew ; Moran, Mary Frances, York.

Nuthall, Phillis : Married Mr. Willis Coates ; died in Brockville in 1882.

O'Connell, Margaret, Toronto.

Osborne, Edward : Spent the years from 1865 to 1881 in periods of teaching, alternating with mercantile employment, journalism and the study of Medicine : has been practising since the latter year in Mason City, Iowa, U.S.A.

Page, Mary Jane : Taught in the Township of Bertie until her marriage to Mr. Wilson Bowen in 1871 ; resides near Ridgeway, Ont.

Perkins, Maria Olivia, Elgin.

Porter, Margery : Taught from 1865 to 1869 ; married Mr. Richard Benson, a farmer and cheese manufacturer ; resides near Picton.

Preston, Victoria Elizabeth : Married Mr. Fairchild.

Reed, Almida Cordelia, Oxford.

Reynolds, Mary Ann : Has been for some years a teacher in the Cobourg School.

Risk, William Henry : Taught till 1883, mostly in Kent, Lambton and Norfolk ; retired and went into farming near Alvinston, where he still resides.

Ross, Arthur Wellington : Taught for a time ; took an Arts course in Toronto University, graduating in 1874 ; was for a few years Public School Inspector of Glengarry ; entered the legal profession and practised in Winnipeg ; represented Lisgar District, Manitoba, for several years in the House of Commons ; spent some time in business in British Columbia ; now resides in Toronto.

Russell, James : Taught two years in Wentworth ; entered the medical profession and practised at Binbrook in that county till 1887, when he was appointed Medical Superintendent of the Hamilton Asylum for the Insane.

Sefton, Martha E : Taught in the Counties of Grey and Ontario till 1875, and has been on the Toronto teaching staff since 1876.

Shewan, Jennie : Taught privately ; married in 1875 ; died in 1896.

Smith, Peter : Now engaged in farming in the Township of Downie, of which he is Clerk.

Somers, Harriet Christina, Oxford ; Spencer, Percival Lawson, Grey.

Spotton, Charlotte E.: Teacher in the Toronto Public Schools.

Swayze, George Albert : Has been Principal of Commercial Colleges in London, Belleville and Kingston ; is now in New York State.

Switzer, William Haw : Now a druggist in Dresden, Ontario.

Thomson, Alex. Galloway, York.

Tier, Helen : Taught two years ; married Mr. Robert Davis in 1869 ; died in Cleveland, United States, in 1880.

Tytler, Barbara : Taught several years in Public Schools in Lambton and Wellington ; married Mr Kirkman in 1874 ; has taught, since his death, in the High Schools of Elora, Richmond Hill and Seaforth ; still on the staff of Seaforth Collegiate Institute.

Wallace, David, York.

Weese, Redford Colborne : Prince Edward.

Wegg, David Spencer : Went into the practice of Law ; is now a prominent business man in Chicago.

Whillans, Robert : Taught for a few years ; graduated in Arts in McGill University in 1872 ; entered the Presbyterian ministry, and is now in the pastorate at Hintonburg.

White, Humphrey Albert Lucas : Went into the legal profession ; now Postmaster of the Town of St. Mary's.

THIRTY-FOURTH SESSION.

(August, 1865 —December, 1865).

Adams, Richard, Huron.

Armstrong, Thomas Clinton Little : Taught in Durham County till 1870, took an Arts course in Toronto University, graduating in 1875 ; was Modern Language Master in the Hamilton Collegiate Institute till 1881 ; entered the legal profession, and has practised ever since in Winnipeg and Toronto.

Baxter, Louisa : Taught in Toronto from 1879 to 1885 ; married Mr. W. C. Tolton ; resumed teaching in 1893, and has taught ever since in Toronto.

Beattie, William : Taught ten years in Northumberland, two years in Peterborough, and three winter sessions in Toronto, where he still resides.

Bell, Emma Elizabeth : Now Mrs. A. T. Gregory, of Toronto.

Bell, Sarah, Wentworth : Bredin, Wilson Watson, Halton.

Chambers, Elizabeth, Haldimand ; Clark, Robert, Oxford ; Comfort, Sarah, Middlesex ; Cooley, Robert, Welland.

Couzens, Emily : Taught four years in Woodstock ; married Mr. Frederick Welford and moved to Brockville ; has taught there continuously since resuming her profession in 1877.

Croll, David : Taught continuously in rural schools in Carleton County till his retirement in 1896 ; lives on his farm near Ottawa.

Davey, Peter Nicholas : Taught in the villages of Lyn, Perrytown, Brooklin, and Millbrook, in the Port Hope High School, and the Provincial Model School from January, 1879, until August, 1884 ; entered the medical profession and has practised ever since at Duart, Ontario.

Douglas, William Alexander ; Taught two years, and then took an Arts course in Victoria University, graduating in 1873 ; was Head Master of Mount Pleasant High School for one year and of Orangeville High School for two ; has since followed the occupation of Accountant in Toronto.

Drury, Martha Jane, Middlesex.

Gage, William James : Taught for a short time ; went into business in connection with the publishing firm of Adam Miller & Co., of Toronto ; has long been principal of the firm which is now distinguished by his own name.

Gibbard, John : Taught one year near Napanee ; went into the drug business in Strathroy and afterwards in Toronto, where he died in 1874.

Gillan, Mary : Now Mrs. Matheson, of Helena, Montana, U.S.A.

Hamilton, Agnes Victoria, Welland ; Hamilton, Jessie, Wentworth ; Harbottle, Mary Ann, Wentworth ; Harris, Augusta Julia, Wentworth.

Hatton, Emma : Taught some years in Halton County ; married Mr. John Willmott of Milton ; has resided many years in Toronto.

Hendry, William John : Taught one year in North York ; became Head Master of the Yorkville School in 1873, and has occupied the same position ever since except for two years, during which he acted as the first Superintendent of the Industrial School at Mimico ; has been for many years Treasurer of the Ontario Educational Association.

Huggins, John Rutledge, Oxford.

Hughes, James Laughlin : Taught at Frankford for a short time ; was appointed second assistant teacher in the Provincial Model School, Toronto, in 1867 ; became Head Master in 1871 ; resigned in 1874 to become Inspector of Public Schools for Toronto, which position he now holds ; is a distinguished lecturer and author.

Hutton, Benjamin Lowe : Now Superintendent of Passaic City Schools, New Jersey.

Laing, Helen : Taught till the end of 1872 ; married Mr. Robert Alexander, now Principal of the Galt Central School ; still living in that town.

Lawrence, Fannie Helena : Taught one year in Toronto ; married Mr. James Price, still resides in that city.

Lemon, Kate : Married Mr. Bowden ; formerly taught in Toronto ; now deceased.

McCausland, Caroline Elizabeth : Taught in the Provincial Model School from 1868 to 1871 ; married Dr. Sangster, formerly Principal of the Toronto Normal School ; lives at Port Perry, Ontario.

McEwan, Findlay : Taught for some time in Lanark County ; entered the medical profession ; practised in Carleton Place until his death five or six years ago.

McFarlane, Archibald : Died at Forest, Ontario.

McGregor, John, Wentworth ; McKellar, Archibald, Middlesex.

McLean, William Jenkinson : Taught at Palermo in Halton County ; became a Methodist minister ; long dead.

Malcolm, Fullerton Boyd, Carleton : Now deceased.

Mark, Kenward : Taught at Castleton, Blairton and Keene ; lives at Peterboro'.

Medley, Emma : Taught a few years ; married ; resided in Toronto ; now deceased.

Moore, Martha, Wentworth.

Mundell, John : Taught a short time in Teeswater and Wingham ; went to California on account of ill health ; taught there one year and then went to Vancouver Island ; taught almost continuously in different parts of British Columbia till his retirement in 1889 ; now resides in Comox, B.C.

O'Brien, Rebecca : Married Rev. Mr. Paradis, Port Stanley.

Pattison, Joseph Wilford, Haldimand.

Payne, Louisa : Taught in Toronto from 1865 till 1895.

Percival, Margaret, Middlesex.

Riddell, Mary Anne : Married Mr. Davidson of North Gwillimbury.

Ritchie, David Scott Ferguson : Has taught continuously in the County of Bruce, mostly in Southampton and Chesley, as Head Master ; has in the last named place a " Continuation Class."

Russell, Marian Agnes Blanche, York.

Scales, Sophia Eliza: Taught about ten years in Kingston; married Mr. J. S. Duncan; went to Manitoba several years ago; resides at Portage la Prairie.
Scarlett, Mary Elizabeth: Taught in Belleville; married Mr. Alexander McDonald; lived some time in Guelph; now resides at Fenelon Falls.
Sharpe, Adam Middleton, Halton; Snell, Elias Benson, Peel; Stalker, Mary, Elgin.
Sutherland, Margaret: Taught in Toronto from 1869 to 1877; married Rev. Cecil Harper; died in 1882.
Tilley, William Edward: Taught Public School for three years; was for several years Assistant Master in Bowmanville and Port Hope High Schools, successively; was Head Master of the Lindsay High School from 1880 to 1884, and was appointed in the latter year Public School Inspector for Durham County, which office he still holds; graduated in Arts in Victoria University in 1875; received the degree of Ph.D. from Bloomington University.
Tobias, Esther, Essex.
Walker, Eliza Allan: Married; lives at Guelph.
Worth, Mary Anne: Taught in Haldimand for two years, and ever since in Toronto.
Young, Mary: Taught some years in the Dundas Schools; now lives in retirement.

THIRTY-FIFTH SESSION.

(January, 1866—June, 1866.)

Bailey, Eliza: Never taught; resides in Cornwall, Ontario.
Barrett, Thomas, Waterloo; Barrie, George, Waterloo: Now deceased.
Becket, Elizabeth: Is still teaching in the city of Peterboro'.
Becket, Lucy M.: Taught in a private academy in Georgetown; then in the Yorkville School, now Jesse Ketchum School; then in the Toronto Public Schools from 1880 to 1885; since then has been Assistant Superintendent of the Andrew Mercer Reformatory in Toronto.
Blatchford, William, Huron.
Boyce, Martha Jane: Taught in the Toronto Public Schools from 1876 till her death in 1879.
Brooks, Henrietta: Taught a number of years; married Mr. Blott; resides in Wardsville, Ont.
Brown, Martha Eva, Elgin; Butler, Harriet Jessie Edith, York.
Campbell, Jane Ann Jamesina: Taught in rural schools of Halton, and in the Oakville Public School; married Captain Street, and since his death has continued teaching in Oakville.
Campbell, William, Oxford; Campbell, James, Perth.
Clarkson, Charles: Taught as Assistant Master in the Paris and St. Mary's High Schools; graduated in Arts in Toronto University in 1876; was first Principal of the Brockville Model School and the first Head Master of the Seaforth High School; was Headmaster of the Boys' Model School, Toronto, from 1882 to 1886, and then returned to Seaforth as Principal of the Collegiate Institute.
Clendinning, William Scott: Taught in Point Edward and afterwards in Walkerton; was appointed Public School Inspector for East Bruce in 1873, and still fills the position; resides in Walkerton.
Dygert, Anna Maria, Oxford.
Donelly, Joseph Henry: Taught in Mitchell; died in 1874.
Ebbels, Walter Dennis, York.
Fairgrieve, Agnes, Wentworth: Married Mr. Duncan; now deceased.
Filer, Alexander David: Taught in Leeds County for two years; went to the United States; died at Lockport in 1895.
Flavelle, Minnie: Taught in Public Schools in Omemee and Lindsay for nearly five years; has ever since been head book-keeper in a large mercantile house in Lindsay.

Gunn, Sarah Sophy, Middlesex.

Harris, Frances Josephine, Wentworth.

How, Frances Esther : Has been in the service of the Toronto Public School Board since 1875 ; is now Principal of the Elizabeth St. School.

Hugill, Joseph, Perth ; Hurlburt, Maria Almyra, Lambton.

Kennedy, Neil : After teaching some years, went to California on account of failing health, and died there.

Kenny, Christina : Now Mrs. Kelly, Parkdale.

Leitch, Thomas : Taught five years in Public Schools in Elgin ; was Science Master in the St. Thomas Collegiate Institute for twenty-one years ; resigned in 1893 to go into business in Hamilton, where he still lives.

Luttrell, William : Now engaged in manufacturing.

McCallum, John Sangster : Taught in Uxbridge Township for a short time ; entered the medical profession ; practises at Smith's Falls, Ontario.

McCormack, Colin : Taught several years and in several schools in Kent County ; entered the medical profession in 1872, and has practised ever since in Michigan ; resides at present at Owosso, where he has filled several local public offices.

McDonald, Isabella, Wentworth.

McGill, Anthony ; Taught Public Schools in Waterloo, Perth and Muskoka ; graduated in Arts in Toronto University in 1880, and in Science in Victoria in 1882 ; taught Science in the Ottawa Collegiate Institute till 1887, when he was appointed to his present position, Assistant Analyst to the Inland Revenue Department at Ottawa.

McIntyre, Annie : Married Mr. George Archer Tye of the twentieth session of the Normal School ; has since his death in 1892, lived in Chatham.

McKay, Hugh : Taught for some time in Oxford Co., studied for the ministry in Knox College ; labored as a home missionary for some years in Manitoulin Island ; was appointed in 1884 to the Indian Mission at Round Lake, Assa., which position he still holds.

McKay, Robert Peter : Taught two years in Oxford County Public Schools, and one year in Woodstock Grammar School ; graduated in Arts in Toronto University in 1875, and entered the Presbyterian ministry in 1877 ; has been since 1892 Secretary of the Foreign Mission Board.

McKay, William : Taught for some time in Oxford Co. ; entered upon a course for the Presbyterian ministry, but died before completing it.

McLaughlin, Elizabeth Anne : Has been in the service of the Toronto Public School Board for twenty-five years ; now Mrs. E. A. Green, Principal of the Alexandra Industrial School for girls.

McLaughlin, Margaret Elizabeth : Taught a short time : married Mr. E. F. Wheaton of Toronto ; resides in that city.

McMahon, Catherine : Taught in Ingersoll ; entered the Community of Loretto ; died in 1883.

Matthews, Agnes Olivia : Now Mrs. Joseph Quarrie of Hamilton.

May, Charles Henry, Ontario.

Meldrum, Margaret Jane : Married Rev. Mr. Stewart ; now deceased.

Moir, George : Taught in St. Mary's Public School ; spent some years in journalistic work ; entered the Dominion Civil Service at Ottawa.

Moore, Alvin Joshua : Was Principal of Georgetown Public School ; is now Mathematical Master in the Goderich Collegiate Institute.

Oliver, Edith, Stormont.

Palmer, John Henry, York ; Paterson, Mary Theresa, York.

Pentland, Jane Matilda : Taught several years in Wentworth ; married ; her husband is an extensive lumberman on the north shore of Georgian Bay, where she still lives.

Pollard, Ann, York ; Pritchard, John Frederick, Oxford.
Rankin, John Brown : Taught in several Public Schools, including the Hamilton Central School ; graduated in Arts in Toronto University in 1874 ; was Head Master of Chatham High School for two years ; entered the legal profession, and is now head of a law firm in Chatham.
Ridley, Alexandrina Sophia : Now Mrs. Lousley ; teaches in the United States.
Rutherford, Peter : Now a book-keeper in Chatham, Ontario.
Saunders, Anna Maude : Taught two years ; married Mr. A. McMartin ; resides near Evelyn, Middlesex.
Slaven, Edward : Taught for a time ; is now Roman Catholic Parish Priest at Galt, Ontario.
Somerville, Agnes, Hamilton ; Sparling, Mary Jane, Perth.
Thompson, Mary Jane, Durham ; Tremeer, Thomas, Durham.
Turnbull, Sarah Annie : Married Mr. Andrew Jeffrey, now a druggist in Toronto
Walshe, Margaret Elizabeth : Teaches in the Institute for the Blind at Brantford.
Weed, Mary Jane, York.
West, Eliza Jane : Teaches in one of the Hamilton Public Schools.
White, Hester Ann, Wentworth.

THIRTY-SIXTH SESSION.
(August, 1866—December, 1866.)

Armstrong, Andrew, Kent.
Beattie, Mary, Toronto.
Bennetto, Susan Elizabeth : Has taught in the Hamilton Public Schools since 1867, with an interval spent in Winnipeg.
Brown, Margaret : Married the Rev. John Robbins ; resides at Wetford, Herts, England
Carlaw, Davidson : Taught a short time ; went into financial business in addition to agriculture ; still resides on his farm near Warkworth.
Clarke, Jane, Frontenac ; Costin, William, Brant.
Duncan, Helen : Taught in Strathroy ; married Mr. S. Wilkins ; resides in London.
Forsythe, Annie Dawson, Middlesex : Died in 1868.
Gillespie, Catharine, Grenville.
Harris, Benjamin Wesley : Taught for some time in Oxford and Middlesex ; went into business ; now resides at Sault Ste. Marie.
Hendry, Andrew : Taught rural schools in York and Wentworth till 1874 ; has since taught continuously in Toronto ; is now Principal of Parkdale School.
Herner, Samuel Shantz : Taught in Waterloo County till 1897 ; is now farming in the Township of Wilmot.
Jardine, William Wilson : Taught in several Public Schools in Ontario and Durham ; graduated in Arts in Toronto University in 1883 ; has since that time been Principal of various High Schools ; is now at Omemee.
Kellogg, Charles Palmer : Taught in Chatham ; died about fourteen years ago.
Lean, John : Entered the medical profession ; now deceased.
Leslie Alexander : Taught in the London Public and High Schools till 1872 ; took an Arts course in Toronto University, graduating in 1875 ; entered the Presbyterian ministry ; is now pastor of a congregation in Oxford County.
McDiarmid, John : Died some years ago while preparing for the Presbyterian ministry.
McFaul, John Henry : Taught in the Peterboro' and Brockville High Schools ; was the first Principal of the Lindsay Model School, and taught in the Lindsay High School ; was five years Public School Inspector in St. Catharines ; was Drawing Master in the Normal School, Toronto, from Feb., 1884, until Dec., 1891 ; now practises Medicine in that city.

McGeorge, Mary : Taught fourteen years in Mitchell and Ayr Public Schools ; married Mr. Thomas McDonald ; now resides in Mitchell.
McInnes, Alexander, Ontario ; McMillan, Donald, Elgin.
Milne, Walter Baird, Perth.
Moorcraft, Sarah Esther : Has taught continuously in the Bowmanville Public School.
Patterson, Clara Amelia, Durham.
Redditt, Thomas Henry : After teaching for a time took an Arts course in Toronto University, graduating in 1880 ; was Head Master of the Aurora High School and is now Principal of the Barrie Collegiate Institute.
Riddell, Elizabeth : Taught Public Schools in Kent for six years ; married Mr. James Hamilton, a farmer ; still lives at Ravenshoe, Ontario.
Robbins, Clara : Now Mrs. Eldon Bull of Hamilton.
Robertson, Margaret Gordon, Toronto.
Rutledge, Rebecca, Toronto : Now deceased.
Scott, Margaret Taylor : See biographical sketches of members of staff.
Sylvester, Emily, Hamilton.
Wellwood, Nesbitt, John : Taught Public School two years in Kent ; graduated in Arts in Toronto University in 1873 ; has since that time been Principal in the High Schools of L'Orignal, Vankleek Hill, Streetsville and Oakville, the last for twenty years ; still holds the position.
Wilson, Jane, Middlesex ; Wood, Henrietta, Toronto.

THIRTY-SEVENTH SESSION.

(January, 1867—June, 1867).

Aird, Margaret : Now Mrs. McCuaig ; has taught in the Toronto schools since 1877.
Andrews, Abigail Wilkinson, York.
Armstrong, Elizabeth : Still teaches in Hamilton.
Britton, William : Taught in Public Schools in Manilla and Brantford, and in the Barrie High School ; entered the medical profession ; has practised in Toronto since 1875 ; represents the University of Toronto on the Council of the College of Physicians and Surgeons.
Cameron, Jane : Taught until a few years ago ; now deceased.
Clark, Alvina, York.
Coyne, Margaret Jane : Teaches in the Toronto Public Schools.
Dorland, Lydia Catharine : Now Mrs. Neilson, Calgary, Alberta.
Dowswell, Elizabeth, Norfolk ; Dowswell, Mary Jane, Norfolk.
Duffin, Mary Charlotte Jane : Now Principal in one of the Chicago schools.
Durham, William, Lincoln.
Edmison, Ralph Hetzlop, Peterboro'.
Fullerton, James S.: Taught at intervals till 1877 ; in that year was called to the bar ; has practised in Toronto till the present time, and has since 1894 been counsel to the city municipal corporation ; has been a Queen's Counsel since 1889.
Guillet, Mary Ann, Northumberland.
Harris, Elizabeth : Teaching in the Ryerson School, Hamilton.
Hatton, Sarah Adelaide : Durham ; Henderson, Robert : Bruce.
Hepburne, Rhoda : Now Mrs. James McPhail, Dakota, U. S. A.
Keam, Mary Roberts, Northumberland.
Linton, John A.: Taught Public Schools in Brant and Lambton until forced by declining health to retire ; was treasurer of Moore Township till his death.

Lowrie, Eliza Jane : Taught in London until 1875 ; married Mr. H. Baptie ; resides in London.

McAndrew, James : Taught several years in Huron County ; now farming near Fargo, in North Dakota.

McCrae, Mary Ann : Taught six years, the last in Orono ; married Mr. Isaac Jewell, a farmer ; now lives, retired, in Bowmanville.

McEachren, Charlotte Emma : Now Mrs. Charlesworth of Hamilton.

McFarland, Robert : Taught several years in Lanark County ; is now farming near Forest, in Lambton.

McKay, George Webster, Ontario.

Marett, Sebina, Oxford.

Mearns, Isabella : After teaching three years in Oshawa and London, has taught in the Toronto Public Schools since 1875.

Mills, Jane, Grenville.

Moore, Isabella : Married John S. Atkinson, M.D., of the thirty-eighth session ; has resided since his death, in Hamilton.

Moore, Sarah, Halton.

Nesbitt, Agnes : Taught in Oxford County till the close of 1875 ; married Mr. Waldock ; went to Winnipeg and afterwards to Medicine Hat, where she still resides.

Page, Minnie Emilie : Taught privately ; married Dr. John Ponsonby King, Dublin, Ireland.

Pollock, James Edward : Taught for some time ; graduated in Arts in Toronto University in 1878 ; taught in Public Schools, and as assistant in Vienna and Bradford High Schools ; retired owing to ill-health ; teaches Art in various parts of York County.

Preston, Elizabeth Jane : Has taught for many years in Ottawa.

Prior, Joanna Amelia, Victoria.

Ramsey, Mary Ann ; Now Mrs. T. A. Gregg ; was formerly Mrs. Fitzgerald, one of the Toronto teachers.

Rogers, Agnes, Toronto.

Rothwell, Peter D.: Taught in Ontario till 1871, and afterwards in various part s of the Northwestern States ; entered the medical profession, and has practised in Denver, Col., since 1881.

Silcox, John B.: Taught four years : entered the Congregational ministry ; was in the pastorate five years in Toronto, seven in Winnipeg, six in California, two in Montreal and two in Chicago, where he still resides.

Smith, Charlotte : Taught in Nissouri Township till 1871 ; now lives at Maple Lodge, Ontario.

Smith, Edward Saunders, Waterloo ; Stewart, Elihu, Kent.

Woodside, Mrs. Jane, Bruce ; Wright, Mary Anne, Penetanguishene.

THIRTY-EIGHTH SESSION.

(August, 1867—December, 1867.)

Ableson, Huldah Ann ; Married Mr. David Smith of Toronto.

Atkinson, John Sangster: Taught in the Hamilton Central School, and was afterwards Principal of the Prescott and Brockville Model Schools; entered the medical profession, and practised for the last ten years of his life in Gananoque; died in 1896.

Bonner, Horatio James: Entered the medical profession ; practised for many years in Chesley, Bruce.

Boyle, William S.: Entered the medical profession ; practised at Bowmanville from 1872 till his death in 1891.

Brown, Sophia Georgina, Perth.

Calder, Elizabeth: Taught several years; married, and now resides in Toronto.

Carson, Joseph Standish: Taught in several Public Schools in Simcoe County, and afterwards in Strathroy, where he was when appointed Public School Inspector of West Middlesex in 1876; that office he held till his death in 1889.

Corrigan, Augusta Margaret: Taught in London till the close of 1872.

East, Cornelius: Taught in McGillivray Township and Parkhill Village; entered the medical profession, and practised in Forest from 1873 till his death in 1883.

Ellis, Louisa Josephine, York.

Fletcher, Margaret: Taught a private school in Toronto till 1877; married Rev. J. H. Ratcliffe, a Presbyterian minister, now in St. Catharines.

Fraser, Margaret: Taught in Toronto; married Dr. A. R. Pyne, of that city.

Fraser, William, Oxford.

Frazer, Donald Blair: Entered the medical profession in 1874; practises in Stratford.

Fuller, Henrietta, Colborne.

Fulton, James: Taught a short time and went into business at Lynedoch in Norfolk; taught there from 1876 to 1880; went into business in the United States, and is now in Hartford, Illinois, a member of the City Board of Education, and its Secretary.

German, Mary Eleanor, Victoria.

Gibson, Margaret Agnes, Lanark: Now deceased.

Harris James H., Owen Sound.

Harney, Ellen: Taught privately for a time, and afterwards in the Chatham School for colored children; taught in the Toronto schools from 1881 to 1889; died in 1890.

Hogarth, Thomas: Taught in York County till 1883, and since 1886 has been teaching in the Toronto Public Schools.

Jones, Eleanor Josephine: Now Mrs. Parker Smith, of Fort William, Ontario.

Jones, James Robert: Now a physician in Winnipeg.

Jones, Louisa Harriet, Cobourg.

Kirk, William, Hastings.

Leitch, John McMillan, Lambton.

McDonald, Annie Jane, Toronto.

McDonald, Margaret, Woodstock: Now deceased.

McEwen, John: Taught a few years in Lanark County; is now in business in California.

McFarlane, Peter Alexander: Taught in the Jarvis St. Collegiate Institute till his death, about 1877.

Morton, Hester Amelia: Taught a short time in Port Dalhousie and in the St. Catharines Central School till the close of 1890; resides now at Newmarket.

O'Brien, William, Peterboro'.

Rannie, William: After teaching for several years became Principal of the Newmarket County Model School, over which he still presides.

Riddell, Mary Anne: Taught a short time, and has since lived privately in Toronto.

Robertson, Duncan: Taught for many years at Ottawa; now a resident of Victoria, British Columbia.

Scallion, James Wm., Middlesex.

Schmidt, George: Taught in the Berlin Central School till 1871; entered the medical profession; practised from 1874 to 1891 in Ontario; has practised since 1891 in Milwaukee, Wisconsin, U. S. A.

Schofield, Amelia Monro: Is still teaching in Brockville.

Simpson, Mary, Brockville.

Stahlschmidt, William: Taught in Preston, Waterloo, till 1884; went into the business of manufacturing improved school furniture in Preston, and still continues it in the same place.

Thompson, Charlotte Emily: Taught for many years in the Jarvis Street Collegiate Institute; resigned in 1897.

Tuttle, Alice Mary: Now Mrs. J. W. Sexsmith. living at Ebwinc in British Columbia.

Walker, James Taylor, Owen Sound.

THIRTY-NINTH SESSION.

(January, 1868—June, 1868.)

Batty, Alice P., Dunnville; Bodwell, Sarah Melinda, Oxford.

Boulter, Joshua John: Went to Nebraska; taught for a short time; went into business as an Accountant; is in the employ of the Union Pacific Railway at Omaha.

Brownlee, Marion: Taught some time in South Hastings; married Mr. S. A. Lazier.

Calder, Annie: Taught several years in Wentworth; married and went to Scotland.

Campbell, John Harkness, Grey.

Clark, William Reid: Became an Anglican clergyman; now at Ancaster.

Crawford, Duncan: Taught until 1878; went into business; now resides in Detroit.

Daville, Emma Julia, Hamilton.

Dennis, James Edwin: Taught in Oxford County; was Principal for a time of the Woodstock County Model School; now deceased.

Doupe, William: Taught in Perth County; went into the medical profession; now deceased.

Edwards, Thomas Albert: Was for a long time Principal of the Thamesville Public School; retired about eleven years ago to go into business.

Ferrier, Amos; Taught fourteen years in Peel County; now engaged in business.

Galbraith, William James: Taught in Oakville, Palmerston, and Hanover Public Schools, and in Streetsville High School, before taking his present position as Modern Language Master in Brampton High School; graduated in Arts in Trinity University in 1896.

Gill, Samuel Rea: Taught several years in Oxford County; became a farmer; died in 1896.

Good, Rebecca Ida: Now Mrs. Fletcher of Toronto.

Gorman, Jennie: Married Mr. Feeney; now deceased.

Hoggan, Eliza, Toronto.

Houston, John: After teaching for some time, graduated in Arts in Toronto University in 1877; was Principal of the Arnprior Public School, English Master in the London Collegiate Institute, Principal of the Portage la Prairie (Man.) Collegiate Institute, and Head Master of the Brighton High School, before becoming Principal of the Clinton Collegiate Institute, which position he still holds.

Hughes, Samuel: Taught in Public Schools in Belleville and Bowmanville; was for ten years English Master in the Toronto Collegiate Institute; went into journalism in Lindsay, and has represented North Victoria for several years in the Canadian House of Commons; is Colonel of the 45th Victoria Batt.

Hunter, Mary: Taught in Kingston; moved to Belleville; married Mr. T. M. Henry, now Principal of the Napanee Collegiate Institute.

Johnson, Sarah Edith: Has taught almost continuously in rural schools in Essex County for twenty-five years; married in 1869 Mr. Samuel Baltzer, then and now a farmer; resides at North Ridge.

Law, Benjamin, Lambton.

Lister, Jane: Teaching in the Queen School, Hamilton.

McBride, Charlotte Louisa : Taught for some time in the London Public Schools ; married Mr. Loftus ; now deceased.
McGurn, Mary Jane, Hastings : Taught in South Hastings.
McIlvaine, Samuel : Taught in Orillia and Meaford ; was in business in Manitoba from 1877 to 1885 ; taught two years in Oakwood High School, Ontario ; is now in business at Vernon, British Columbia.
McKay, David W. B. : Taught till 1884 in several parts of Ontario, and in Kansas and California in the United States ; farmed in Manitoba till his death in 1887.
McKellar, Hugh : Taught in East Zorra, Galt, Paisley, and Teeswater ; went to Manitoba in 1880 and engaged in business; acted as immigration agent for the Province in Toronto, and Moncton ; has been since 1892 in the Department of Agriculture at Winnipeg ; is Deputy Minister.
McMillan, John : Taught in Tiverton, Bruce County ; died twenty years ago.
Manley, Charles Lewis, Lincoln : Now deceased.
Mulloy, David Willson, Wellington : Now an Accountant in Chicago.
Nichols, Mary Anne, Peterboro' : Teaches in Peterboro'.
Preston, Sarah : Taught in Lindsay and Peterboro' ; went to British Columbia ; now teaching in Vancouver.
Reilly, Marlow M., Renfrew ; Robertson, Jane, Welland.
Rowland, Alice Jane : Taught for two years in the Toronto Public Schools ; married Mr. Woodley ; resides in Toronto.
Scott, William : See biographical sketches of the members of the staff.
Spread, Maggie, Toronto : Now deceased.
Tamblyn, Elizabeth Ann, Toronto ; Trott, Mary Ann, Collingwood.
Walkinshaw, Mary Ann : Teaching in the Toronto Public Schools.
Walsh, Mary Ann : Taught in Durham County, in the Provincial Model School at Ottawa, and in the Institute for the Blind at Brantford ; married Mr. Wickens, one of the Institute staff ; still resides at Brantford.
Ward, Edward : Taught in several places in York. Peel and Simcoe, and in the Collingwood Collegiate Institute before taking his present position of Principal of the Collingwood Model School, which he has filled for eighteen years.
Ward, Henry : Teaches at Thornhill in South York.
Watt, Elizabeth : Married Mr. Stephen Nairn, formerly of Toronto, now of Winnipeg.
Williams, James Richard : Taught about four years in Simcoe County ; died very soon after taking charge of the St. Thomas Public School.
Wilson, John : Taught in various Public and High Schools in Ontario ; removed to Winnipeg, where he taught in the Collegiate Institute until his death in 1894.

FORTIETH SESSION.

(August, 1868—December, 1868.)

Adkins, Frances Mary, Ingersoll ; Annis, Andrew Emerson, Scarboro'.
Boddy, James : Taught for many years in Toronto ; is now engaged in business there.
Brownlee, Hugh James : Taught for some time ; now resides at Hespeler, Waterloo.
Buckle, Frances Hannah : Has been teaching in the London Schools since 1869.
Burk, Mary Emily : Taught a few months ; married Col. Samuel Hughes, M.P., of the Thirty-ninth Session ; now resides at Lindsay.
Burriss, Mary Jane : Married Mr. Graham ; taught in Essex County for two years ; has taught in London since 1884.
Chadwick, Eliza Miriam : Taught in the Toronto Public Schools from 1876 to 1891 ; died in 1893.

Crothers, Thomas Wilson : Taught for a time ; now practises Law in St. Thomas.
Cockburn, Catharine, Niagara.
Clark, Jessie A. : Married Mr. G. H. Hodgetts in 1874 ; now resides in St. Catharines.
Dixon, Samuel Eugene : Taught eight years in Castleton, Northumberland, and has been teaching ever since—twenty-one years—in a rural school in the same county.
Drimmie, Daniel : Has taught at intervals in Grey County ; lives on his farm in Egremont Township.
Dundon, John Steven, Ancaster.
Gray, Emma, Toronto.
Hay, Janet R., Milton.
Hodge, Robert : Now practises Law in Toronto.
Holcroft, Margaretta Sarah, Ingersoll.
Joyce, Mary Greeves : Taught privately for four years, and in the Ottawa Public Schools till 1880 ; was then appointed to the position of assistant in the Provincial Model School, Ottawa, and still holds that position.
Kelly, John William, Oxford.
Kessack, Jessie : Taught in London High School ; died about twelve years ago.
Lundy, Louisa Elizabeth : Taught privately in the Town of Simcoe, and afterwards in High Schools in Ingersoll, Goderich, Peterboro' and Galt ; married Ivan O'Beirne in 1875, and after his death taught in private institutions till the close of 1881 ; has since lived retired, partly at Lundy's Lane and partly in Toronto.
McCausland, Fannie : Taught a short time in Woodstock ; married Mr. James McDonald ; still resides there.
McCreight, Sarah : Taught for some time in Perth County ; has since taught in the Toronto Public Schools.
McDowall, Joseph Wm., Owen Sound : Taught for several years ; died many years ago.
McKee, George, Perth ; McKenzie, Isabella, Madoc ; McKenzie, Mary, York ; McLeod, John, Huron.
Moore, Charlotte Elizabeth : Teaching in the Hamilton Public Schools.
Moran, Alicia, Georgina.
Mullin, Charlotte Ann : Taught in Brant County ; now deceased.
Mullin, Isabella : Taught in Brant County ; now retired.
Munro, Donald L. : Taught five years, part of the time as Principal of Lindsay Public Schools ; graduated in Arts in Toronto University in 1876 ; entered the Presbyterian ministry ; has done pastoral work at various places in the United States ; is now teaching in Stockton, California, U.S.A.
Munshaw, Matilda Caroline : Taught as a governess two years ; removed to Michigan and taught there four years ; married Mr. Ezra J. Demorest ; now resides in Saginaw City, Michigan.
O'Brien, Mary Josephine, Toronto.
O'Neill, Mary Anne : Married Dr. J. A. Wilson ; now residing in Toronto.
Palmer, Charles, Pickering : Died in Michigan several years ago.
Panton, Jessie Reid Hoyes : Has taught almost continuously, partly in Public and partly in High Schools ; was seven years on the staff of the Peterboro' Collegiate Institute, and has been since 1886 on that of the Oshawa High School.
Riddell, Margaret E. : Taught for a few years ; now retired.
Robertson, Jannet, Thorold.
Saxton, Josephine Jerusha : Married Mr. Duncan of Castleton ; now deceased.
Sinclair, Barbara, Toronto.

Somerville, Peterina : Taught one year in Galt, and twenty-five in Dundas ; retired on account of failing health.

Spink, Jane Elizabeth : Taught two years in Haldimand County ; married Mr. William Arthurs ; taught afterwards two years in Brockville, and from 1876 to the present time has been teaching in Toronto.

Telford, Marion, Oshawa.

Templeton, Sarah Jane : Taught in Belleville for many years ; is now a teacher in the Institute for the Deaf and Dumb, Belleville.

Thompson, John Nixon : Taught several years in Durham County ; entered the medical profession, and after practising in other places settled in Omemee, where he still resides.

Turnbull, Elizabeth : Is now teaching in the Hamilton Public Schools.

Vercoe, James, Elgin : Entered the medical profession.

Wallace, Jane : Taught about four years in Peel County ; married Mr. L. Cheyne ; resides in Brampton.

Weir, Sarah Emma : Married ; lives near Hamilton.

Wood, Frank : Taught in Waterloo and Simcoe Counties till 1877 ; was Principal of the Bradford Model School till 1884 ; has since that time been Principal of the Port Hope Model School.

FORTY-FIRST SESSION.

(January, 1869—June, 1869.)

Alford, William : Taught in the Provincial Model School, Ottawa from September, 1880, until August, 1881 ; now in the Civil Service of the Dominion.

Ashmore, Sarah Anne : Taught in the Brantford Young Ladies' College ; now deceased.

Bergey, David : Taught in Waterloo County till 1890 ; is now farming in Wilmot Township.

Bigelow, George : Taught in Public Schools in Stormont County till 1889 ; went into business in Cornwall, where he still resides.

Birchard, I. J., M.A., Ph.D.: Taught in Public Schools for some time ; graduated in Arts in Toronto University in 1880 ; was Principal of Perth Collegiate Institute for a short time, and Mathematical Master in the Brantford Collegiate Institute from 1882 to 1893 ; has been since the latter year Mathematical Master in one of the Toronto Collegiate Institutes.

Black, Annie : Taught till 1879 in Simcoe County.

Blatchford, Thomas : Taught for some time in Huron County ; is now in the Methodist ministry.

Bretz, Abram : Taught for some years in Tavistock ; now in business in Toronto.

Brotherhood, Amelia Eliza : Taught many years in Alma College, St. Thomas ; is now teaching in Salt Lake City University, Utah.

Brown, James : Is in the Customs Office at Niagara Falls South.

Buckle, Sarah Amy : Has taught in London from 1870 to the present time.

Campbell, Jane Ann : Now Mrs. Dr. Hurlburt of Mitchell, Ont.

Chambers, Annie Catharine, Peterboro'.

Clapp, David Philip : Graduated in Arts in Toronto University in 1877 ; has been for some time Public School Inspector for North Wellington.

Copeland, George : Taught two years ; entered the Methodist ministry ; is at present on the Deseronto Circuit.

Crane, Laura Cornelia, Elgin : Married to Mr. Cavers.

Crisp, Emma Matilda : Now Mrs. McArthur ; teaching in Hamilton Public Schools.

Crossley, Hugh Thomas : Taught four years ; entered the Methodist ministry and did pastoral work for five years ; has, with Rev. J. E. Hunter, been for the past fourteen years engaged in evangelistic work in Canada and the United States.

Cumming, Louisa Ellen : Taught in Simcoe and afterwards in Oxford ; has been teaching in Woodstock fifteen years.

Davis, Samuel Percy : Graduated in Arts in Toronto University in 1877 ; was Principal of Pickering College ; died while in that position.

Dickenson, Henry : Taught a number of years in Waterloo and Brantford ; was for a time Principal of the Stratford Model School ; went into the wholesale paper business in Toronto.

Dowswell, John, Ontario : Now farming in Manitoba.

Duncan, Eleanor : Teaching in Brantford Central School.

Emory, Cummings Van Norman : Taught till 1875 ; entered the medical profession and practised in Detroit and Galt before settling in Hamilton, where he has been since 1884.

Findlay, David : Taught for some time ; entered the Presbyterian ministry ; has charge of home mission work in the Ottawa Valley.

Fisher, John Henry Cole Fitzgerald : Entered the medical profession ; practising in Toronto.

Fleming, James Henry, Lanark.

Gunn, Mary : Taught in Woodstock till 1874 ; has taught in Toronto since 1875.

Harvey, Helen : Now Mrs. Herbert Marten, Hamilton.

Hodgins, William S.: Taught nineteen years, including three spent as Principal of Stratford Model School ; has been in business since 1883 ; resides in Berlin.

Holbrook, Robert, Lambton.

Howland, Mary Ann : Married Mr. H. J. Hurlburt ; resides at Mitchell, Ontario.

Huggard, Susan, Oxford : Married Mr. Matthieu.

Johnston, Sarah, York.

Kemp, Sarah Bianca, Hamilton ; Kennedy, Hugh William, Glengarry.

McCreary, James : Teaching in Peterborough.

McCreight, Isabella : Has been for some years teaching in the Toronto Public Schools.

McKenzie, Susan : Taught in Listowel for a time ; has taught in the Toronto Public Schools since 1872.

McLurg, James : Taught for a number of years in Perth and Lambton ; was one of the masters in the Provincial Model School in Toronto from Sept., 1884, until Aug., 1887 ; is now practising Medicine in Woodstock.

McNaughton, Jane, Glengarry.

McNeile, Mary Ann, Wentworth : Married.

Manning, Elvina Amelia, Simcoe : Married.

Marsden, Sarah, Wentworth.

Meldrum, Peter Gordon : Taught for a time ; entered the medical profession in 1885 ; is now practising in Whitby.

Mitchell, Mary Anne, Durham : Married.

Montgomery, Sarah : Married Mr. Earls ; now deceased.

Moore, Charles, Lambton ; Morton, Alfred, Perth.

Moule, Fannie Barbara : Taught a year in Michigan, and five in Hellmuth Ladies' College, London ; was Lady Principal in Woodstock College for a time ; married in 1880 Prof. Wells, Principal of that institution ; has lived many years in Toronto.

Murray, Adam : Taught at Southampton, Bruce, and in California, U.S.A. ; now deceased.

Murray, John L., Oxford : Died in 1870.

Nixon, Jane, Wentworth : Married.

Osborne, Walter Joseph : Has taught twenty-eight years, twenty-one in Prince Edward and the remainder in Hastings ; teaching now in Bloomfield.

Partington, Annie Levina : Married Mr. Kline ; resided in California ; now deceased.

Paterson, Andrew : Taught two years in Huron County, and two in the Hamilton Public Schools ; has been on the staff of the Hamilton Collegiate Institute for twenty-three years ; graduated in Arts at Trinity University in 1892 ; is at present Lecturer in History and Geography in the Ontario Normal College, Hamilton.

Payne, Edward : Taught in the Provincial Model School at Ottawa ; still resides in that city.

Powell, Joseph Gunne : Taught a short time in Haldimand County ; went into business ; died in 1872.

Proctor, Henry, Peel.

Ray, Agnes, Peterboro' : Taught in Ottonabee for two years and in Lakefield for one and a half ; married George Hodge, M.D., in 1873.

Richardson, Joseph : Has taught continuously since 1870, for a short time in Middlesex and Huron, and a quarter of a century in Oxford ; is still teaching in Tavistock where he has lived for ten years.

Sharpe, Jane Ann : Now Mrs. Mulligan, Millbrook.

Sheppard, George : Taught about twenty years ; is now in business in Goderich.

Silcox, Abner : Taught till his death, which took place many years ago.

Simpson, Jessie Ann : Has taught in London from 1871 to the present time.

Smiley, George, Russell.

Somerville, Elizabeth, Wentworth ; Stokes, Georgina, York.

Sutton, Marshall : Went into the medical profession ; practised both in Canada and in the United States.

Sylvester, Sarah, Wentworth.

Teskey, William, Simcoe : Now resides in Orillia.

Tibb, John Campbell : Taught till 1873 ; graduated in Arts in Toronto University in 1877 ; entered the Presbyterian ministry ; spent three years in mission work in Manitoba ; now pastor of a congregation in Eglington, near Toronto.

Walker, Elizabeth Laura, Perth : Teaching in Stratford.

Walker, Alexander, Peel.

Welsh, P. John, Huron : Taught many years in Scarboro' ; was a very successful lay preacher ; died in 1897.

Wilson, William, Ontario.

FORTY-SECOND SESSION.

(August, 1869—December, 1869.)

Adams, Annie : Taught in the Provincial Model School, Toronto, from Oct., 1871, until Aug., 1878 ; married Mr. M. J. Fletcher of that city ; resided for a time in Winnipeg ; has since taught in private schools in Toronto.

Adams, Thomas, Durham : Now deceased.

Armour, Samuel : Has taught continuously till the present time, rural schools for several years, and in Lindsay for the last eighteen.

Atkinson, Harriet Emma : Taught some time in Chatham ; married Mr. Malcolm Lamont ; now lives in Toronto.

Ballard, John Francis : Now Principal of one of the Hamilton Public Schools.

Beer, Henry : Was for some time Head Master of Carleton Place Public School, Lanark ; entered the Anglican ministry ; spent some time in Minnesota ; is now in Alaska.

Bell, William, York ; Brass, Annie, Wentworth.

Bowman, George Washington : Has taught for many years in various colleges in the United States.

Campbell, James, Lambton : Died in 1871.

Carney, Barbara Charlotte : Married and went to Manitoba.

Cody, Caroline S., Oxford : Married.

Cruise, Jane Ann : Teaches in the Toronto Public Schools.

Cusack, Margaret : Taught in the Provincial Model School, Ottawa, from 1880 to 1885 ; married Mr. Pierce.

Davis, Murdoch Lloyd, York.

Deacon, John Scott : Took part of an Arts course in Victoria University ; was Principal of the Ingersoll Public School from 1872 to 1884, and for the last seven of these years of the Model School also ; after one year's Principalship of Woodstock Model School, became Public School Inspector of Halton, which office he still holds.

Donovan, Mary, Toronto.

Durand, Emma Louise : Married Dr. S. J. Fraser of Detroit, Michigan.

Findlay, Isabella, Scarboro'.

Fulton, Mary Helen, Winchester : Married.

Good, Agnes Louise : Teaches in the Toronto Public Schools.

Guest, Joseph, Grenville.

Hanson, Fanny Mary Elizabeth : Taught continuously in London, in the Public Schools, till 1886, and in the Collegiate Institute since.

Hooper, Henry : Taught some time in Darlington; commenced the study of Medicine, but died before completing his course.

Johnson, Daniel, Elgin.

Kellogg, Charles Palmer, Hastings.

Kerr, George Jonathan : After teaching for a short time entered the Methodist ministry, and is still on circuit pastoral work.

Kinney, William Thomas : Taught in Prince Edward County ; went to the Northwest and engaged in journalistic work ; is now teaching in British Columbia.

Laidlaw, John Beattie : Taught in Middlesex ; became an Accountant in London, and is now partner in a business firm there.

Lightburne, Annie Eliza: Now in St. Louis, Missouri.

Lynn, John, Grey.

Lough, Mary : Taught two years ; married Mr. A. G. Cheney of Vankleek Hill.

McArdle, David : Taught in the Provincial Model School, Ottawa, for a short time ; studied Law and went to the North-West.

McDiarmid, Hugh : Was Principal of the Model School in Cobourg ; now fills a similar position in Ingersoll.

McIntosh, Angus : See biographical sketches of members of the staff.

McKenna, Teresa Maria, Brampton ; McMulkin, Martha Jane, Ingersoll.

McTavish, Margaret : Taught continuously twenty-two years, chiefly in village and rural schools in Dundas County ; was assistant for a time in Pakenham High School, and in Madoc High School ; retired in 1895.

Martin, Caroline, Dunnville ; Murison, Annie, Hamilton ; Murphy, Anne, Addington.

Nash, Samuel Shelly : Taught for many years ; went into business ; now resides in New York.

Nixon, Frederick, Peel.

Payne, Maria, Durham.

Ramsay, Annie : Teaching in Hamilton Public Schools.

Richardson, Caroline Amanda, Hamilton.

Richardson, Jemima : Teaching in Peterboro'.
Riddel, Sarah Jane : Taught for some time ; now Mrs. McLaren of Toronto.
Robertson, Jane : Now Mrs. Hilton of Benton Harbor, Michigan.
Robinson, Alfaretta : Now Mrs. Kilvington of Hamilton.
Ross, George William : See biographical sketches.
Rutherford, Grace, Hamilton.
Silcox, Fannie Allworth : Taught in Elgin several years ; married Mr. W. Burgess of Dresden, Ontario.
Struthers, Andrew Wotherspoon : Entered the medical profession ; is now practising in St. Louis, Mo.
Summerby, William Joseph : Taught in Victoria and Russell Counties ; was Principal of the Kingston County Model School from 1877 to 1880 : has since 1880 been Public School Inspector of Prescott and Russell.
Swallow, William Francis, Toronto.
Tonkin, Edward Albert : Now a Metaodist Minister.
Williams, Edwin Rice : Taught five years, till his death.
Wilson, Eliza, Toronto.

FORTY-THIRD SESSION.

(January, 1870—June, 1870.)

Addison, Ellen, Wentworth.
Allan, Kate M. : Taught in Clinton and Orillia ; has taught in the Toronto Public Schools since January, 1873.
Anson, James, Pickering.
Bailey, Emma Charlotte, Huron.
Bean, David : Taught in schools in Waterloo County till 1888 ; went into journalism in Waterloo Town, and is still in the same calling and place.
Berry, Jane, Toronto : Now deceased.
Bigger, Charles Albert, Brant.
Bowerman, Cornelius : Taught in various schools until 1892 ; graduated in Dental Science in Toronto University ; now resident in Beaverton.
Briggs, Addison Arnold, Toronto.
Campbell, Elizabeth : Taught in North Hastings ; died in 1883.
Campbell, Elizabeth : Taught in Oakville and vicinity, and also in Dakota ; married Mr. Alexander Wilson of Oakville ; now living in Dakota.
Campbell, Jessie : Teaches in the Toronto Public Schools.
Cradock, Agnes, Toronto.
Crawford, Margaret : Has taught continuously since leaving the Normal School in St. Catharines Public Schools.
Crawford, Wm. Henry, Mount Albert.
Crews, Lewis Warren : Entered the Methodist ministry ; now deceased.
Croley, Mary Francis, Tilsonburg ; Cummings, Wm. Richardson, Victoria.
Currie, Dugald : Taught for five years ; graduated in Arts in McGill University in 1880 ; entered the Presbyterian ministry, and has been pastor of a congregation in the Town of Perth for the past four years.
Dunlop, Elizabeth, Ontario.
Eastman, Samuel Henry : Taught in Lincoln County and in Fergus till the close of 1872 ; graduated in Arts in Toronto University in 1877 ; has been in the Presbyterian ministry since 1879 ; is now in pastoral work in Meaford.
Frisby, Adah, Welland.
Fullerton, Eleanor : Married Dr. J. A. Williams now of Ingersoll ; still lives there.

Gray, William: Taught in the Ingersoll Public School and the Chatham Central School; entered the medical profession; now deceased.

Hagarty, Kate, Toronto; Hall, Henry Walter, St. Mary's.

Hawley, Charlotte Cordelia: Taught two years; married Mr. Charles Cannon; lives in London.

Henry, Mary Jane: Married Mr. C. F. Fuller; resides in Florida, United States.

Horton, Rachael: Has taught in Port Perry for twenty years; is now on the staff of the County Model School there.

Kennedy, Alice Smart, Hamilton: Now deceased.

Kennedy, Emma, Whitby: Has taught continuously in the Toronto Public Schools.

Langford, Charles: Taught a short time; entered the Methodist ministry; has been on circuit ever since, with intervals spent in securing more thorough training.

Langrell, Edward Pierce Hopkins, Toronto.

McCamus, John Armstrong: Entered the Methodist ministry; still on circuit.

McCoy, Susanna: Married the Rev. Peter Musgrave of McKillop.

McDonald, Mary Ann, Oxford.

McGinty, Winifred Unity, Pickering; McGowan, Thomas Manson Kinney, Hastings; McIntosh, Isabella, Toronto; McKay, Murdock, Perth.

McKillop, Charles: Taught a few years in Lanark County; graduated in Arts in Queen's University; entered the Presbyterian ministry; is now in charge of a congregation in Lethbridge, N.W.T.

Mackintosh, William: Taught till 1874, and was in that year appointed Public School Inspector of North Hastings, which office he still holds, residing at Madoc; was President of the Ontario Educational Association for one year.

McPherson, Hughena Eugenie, Ops; McGladry, William, Eglington.

Mencilley, Julia Isabella: Taught in Public and Private Schools and in Hellmuth Ladies' College, London; was assistant teacher in the Provincial Model School for Girls at Toronto from 1880 to 1887; since that time, has conducted parties of young ladies on educational tours; resides in Toronto.

Metcalfe, Janet: Has taught for some years in Berlin, and is now Principal of a school there.

Minaker, William: Taught for a time; is now practising Medicine in Chicago.

Moffat, Eliza, Lanark; Morton, Alfred Clarence, Whitchurch; Mulholland, Sarah, York; Munro, Janet, Stormont.

Murphy, Edward Walker: Became a teacher in the Penetanguishene Reformatory.

Neilson, Isabella Helen: Married Mr. Brown; resides in Winnipeg.

Phillips, Mary Louisa: Taught in St. Thomas and Kingston; married Mr. George Macdonell, Q.C., of the latter city.

Purvis, William: Taught continuously, mostly in rural schools, in Haldimand and York till 1878; has since been in business in Columbus, Ontario, where he still resides.

Rich, Catherine, Grey; Roseburgh, Melvin Moe, Brant.

Rowe, Mary Ann: Taught in Guelph Public Schools a short time, and four years in the Sarnia High School; married Mr. Elgin Wood; lives in Sarnia.

Scilly, Samuel Thomas: Now practising Law in Toronto.

Shaw, Mary, Durham.

Sheppard, Daniel Erastus: Taught in Public Schools in Brockville, Newmarket and Ottawa, and in High Schools in Hamilton and Carleton Place until he entered the legal profession; practised till 1891 in Carleton Place and ever since in Gananoque.

Smith, Sylvester: Taught in Stamford Village till 1878; now resides there in retirement.

Steele, Andrew Cheeseman, Perth ; Stewart, Margaret, Toronto ; Stuart, Farquhar McRae, Huron.
Thompson, Emily Clara : Now Mrs. (Rev.) Charles Shutt, St. Catharines.
Thompson, Jane, Ontario.
Twohey, Eleanor Teresa : Married ; resides in the Township of Monteagle.
Wellwood, Richard : Farming near Mono Mills.
Williamson, Eliza Moneta Leavens : Taught in Galt, Clinton and Strathroy ; married Mr. D. McKenzie in 1875 ; now living on a farm in the Genesee Valley, New York.
Woods, Maria : Teaches in the Toronto Public Schools.
Yorke, Lucinda Elma, Wardsville.
Zeigler, Elizabeth : Has taught continuously in Waterloo County, since 1874 in the Town of Waterloo.
Zeigler, Lydia Ann, Berlin.

FORTY-FOURTH SESSION.

(August, 1870—December, 1870.)

Abbott, Mary Caroline : Married and living in the United States.
Boyle, Kate : Taught in St. Catharines ; still lives there as Mrs. Pay.
Barber, Mary, Willowdale ; Bolton, John, Huron ; Braithwaite, William, Grenville ; Burkholder, Hannah D., Winona.
Campbell, Maggie Ellen, Grey.
Carey, Dominick Hugh : Entered the medical profession ; practises now in Detroit, U. S. A.
Carey, Robert : Entered the legal profession ; practises in Upper Sandusky, Ohio.
Chapman, William Francis : Taught in Berlin as assistant master in the Model School and assistant master in the High School, and in Waterloo as Principal of the Public School, until he went to Toronto in 1888 ; after that he was Principal till Dec., 1891 ; was appointed one of the Public School Inspectors of Toronto ; began his duties in Jan., 1892.
Clark, William, Toronto ; Clarke, Anna Mary, Toronto.
Comrie, Peter : Taught several years in Lanark County ; now superannuated ; lives at Carleton Place.
Cruise, George : Taught in Norfolk for fifteen years ; has since farmed near Wyecombe.
Emerson, Samuel, Kincardine.
Farrow, Harriet Amelia : Taught in Elora ; now Mrs. Pars.
Girardot, Ernest Joseph : Taught some time ; is now in business in Sandwich ; has been Mayor of that town for several years
Gray, Caroline Martha : Taught for a time in Wentworth ; has been, since 1873, teaching in the Toronto Public Schools.
Harrison, James M. : Taught a short time in Oxford and Durham ; entered the Methodist ministry, and has been since 1874 in Manitoba.
Hudson, Lucy Maria, Toronto : Now deceased.
Hume, Annie, Galt : Retired ; married Mr. McDonald.
Jackson, Margaret : Taught school for ten years ; died about seventeen years ago.
Jameson, Hugh Alfred : Was for some time in business in Stratford ; left some years ago for the United States.
Johnston, Phoebe Jane : Teaches in the Toronto Public Schools.
Lavin, Armina, Galt ; Lennon, Bridget Mary, Greenwood.
McCammon Kate: Taught in Kingston for a short time; married Mr. H. Dunn, of Montreal ; now deceased.
McCaully, Ellen : Taught for a time in Toronto ; resides in Buffalo.

McCaully, Mary Jane: Resides in Buffalo, U. S. A.
McKay, Sarah Elizabeth, Belleville.
McKibbon, Archibald: Taught for a time; now deceased.
McLaughlin, Mary, Ancaster; McNeil, Frank, Leeds.
Madge, Walter: Taught in Ingersoll Public School; graduated in Arts in Queen's University; now a Presbyterian minister in California.
Mechan, Mary Matilda Aloysius: See biographical sketches of members of staff.
Miller, Harriett (Mrs.), Toronto.
Moore, Elizabeth: Now Mrs. H. Lloyd of Hamilton.
Neilly, William: Taught till 1881; farmed in Manitoba; became a Presbyterian minister; was drowned in Jack Fish Bay.
Nethercott, Samuel: Taught in Perth County till 1892, eighteen years of the time as Principal of the Mitchell Public and Model Schools; has been for five years Principal of the Woodstock Model School.
Newell, Maria Elizabeth: Taught in Toronto Public Schools from 1872 to 1875; married Mr. Wm. J. Hughes; lives in Toronto.
Ovens, Thomas: Taught in Middlesex till 1881; entered the medical profession; practised at Arkona, and afterwards at Parkhill, where he still lives.
O'Brien, Kate Stanislaus, Wellington; Pettey, Selenia, Northumberland.
Powell, George Kingdon: Taught in Middlesex, Huron and York Counties; has been teaching in Toronto Public Schools since 1877, for many years as Principal; graduated in Arts in Queen's University.
Purkiss, Irene Elizabeth: Now Mrs. John Stewart, living in Manitoba.
Richards, Drusilla: Taught in various Public Schools in Northumberland till 1896.
Ross, Jennie, Oxford.
Rowell, Ada Matilda: Now Mrs. Goldsmith.
Scott, Edward: Taught for a time in Prince Edward County; engaged in farming; now in Ohio, U. S. A.
Scott, Jane Crystalle: Has charge of the Kindergarten in the Town of Dundas.
Shoff, Elgin: Taught till 1875 in Victoria, York and Brant Counties; entered the legal profession and has practised in Toronto till the present time; still takes an active interest in educational work.
Smith, Robert Henry, Mt. Brydges.
Spafford, Alice Adelia: Married Mr. Rutherford, of Colborne, Ontario.
Stalker, John: Taught three years; entered the medical profession; has practised ever since in Strathroy.
Waugh, Fannie R., Listowel.
Wilson, Jasper: Taught three years in Norfolk County; entered the Methodist ministry in 1873; graduated in Arts in Victoria University in 1881.
Wittet, George L.: Taught a short time in Norfolk and Haldimand; entered the Baptist ministry; filled several pastorates in Canada; is now in Immanuel Church, Detroit, U. S. A.

FORTY-FIFTH SESSION.

(January, 1871—June, 1871.)

Acheson, Weir, Perth: Teaching in Waterloo County.
Armstrong, Andrew: Taught six years in Kent County, till his death.
Beaman, William D.: Is in business in the Town of Essex, and Police Magistrate there.
Bowerman, Lydia, Victoria.
Burns, Susan Cooney: Teaching in the Hamilton Public Schools.
Carter, Mary Ann: Taught in the Provincial Model School, Toronto, from 1872 to 1877; resigned to be married to Mr. Wm. Kelly of London died in 1880.

Chapman, Almira Melissa, Pickering.
Christie, Amelia Jane : Taught in London : still lives there.
Clark, Alvina, York ; Clark, James, Addington ; Crossley, Ellen, York.
Davis, Emma Frances, Hamilton : Married.
Duck, Katie Marion : Now Mrs. Edward Benson of Lindsay.
Duggan, Annie Maria, Toronto ; Duggan, Frederick, King ; Dunham, Jonathan, Middlesex.
Ellis, Jessie Christina, Patterson.
Evans, Edward Thomas : Taught in Durham, and afterwards in Parry Sound.
Ford, Adelaide Josephine : Now Mrs. Gough of New York, U.S.A.
Forster, Sarah Catherine : Taught in the Chatham Central School ; married Mr. Christopher Wilson ; removed to Detroit and died there some years ago.
Gardiner, John : Taught a few years ; entered the medical profession ; practised in London from 1878 till his death, which occurred during the Normal School Jubilee Celebration.
Gould, Robert, York : Teaching in Wentworth County.
Hagarty, Sara, Toronto.
Hislop, Thomas : Taught ten years in the Mount Forest Public School, the Ottawa Collegiate Institute and the Haldimand County Model School ; entered the legal profession ; has practised for sixteen years in Detroit, U.S.A.
Hewson, Alfred John, Haldimand.
Holmes, Sarah Sophia : Taught in the Chatham Central School till 1879 ; married Mr. Wadsworth, and now lives at Toronto Junction.
Johnston, John Hatton Deltamore, Montreal.
Kay, Martha : Married a farmer in Georgina, York County.
King, Ellen Andrews, Port Hope ; Kirkland, Mary Robertson, Oneida.
Knight, Silas W. : Taught in Kent County ; retired to a farm near the St. Clair River.
Lean, Marion Elizabeth : Mrs. J. Westington ; deceased.
Linton, Charles Beattie : Taught six and a half years in New Dundee ; was first assistant for twelve and a half years in the Galt Central School ; is now in business in Galt.
McArthur, Nancy : Married ; died ten years afterward.
McBrady, Mary Ellen : Entered the Community of Loretto ; has now charge of the young ladies, preparing for teachers' certificates.
McDonald, Flora : Taught in London ; married Mr. W. J. Carson, now Inspector of Public Schools in that city.
McDonald, Donald, Grey.
McKay, Owen : Taught in Beachburg from 1876 to 1882 ; went into land surveying and civil engineering in Windsor, where he still follows that calling.
McKay, Andrew, Oxford : Taught for a number of years in Oxford County ; entered the medical profession ; is now practising at Woodstock, Ontario.
McLachlan, Archibald Gillespie, Elgin.
McLaren, John Ferguson : Engaged in business in Toronto.
McPhedran, Alexander : Taught from 1871 to 1876 in the Provincial Model School, Toronto ; entered the medical profession, and has practised since 1876 in Toronto ; has taught for some years in the Womens' Medical College ; has been a member of the Toronto University Medical Faculty since 1882.
Mark, Jessie Smith, Grey ; Maguire, Maggie, Lindsay.
Maxwell, David Alexander : Taught in Wallaceburg, Chatham, Cornwall, and Strathroy High School ; was appointed in 1878 Public School Inspector of Essex County and the Town of Windsor ; is a graduate in Arts and Law of Victoria University.

Miller, Andrew Hamilton : Taught a short time ; entered the medical profession ; practised in New Dundee till 1896 ; moved then to St. Thomas, where he still resides.

Mills, Mary, Cathcart.

Moses, Clarke : Taught in Colborne and Caledonia High Schools until 1875, when he was appointed Public School Inspector of Haldimand County ; he still discharges the duties of that office, residing at Caledonia.

Nixon, Samuel : Taught in Halton until 1888 ; is now in business.

Nugent, Matilda : Taught Public Schools in Victoria ; was assistant in the High Schools at St. Mary's and Brockville ; married in 1879 Rev. James Smith, and went with him on a mission to India, where she still lives ; her husband is Principal of a Government School.

O'Boyle, Walter Francis : Taught till 1892 in Ontario and Victoria Counties ; was in that year appointed to a municipal office, which he still holds ; resides in Lindsay.

Peplow, Martha: Taught in Lindsay ; married Mr. Lloyd Wood, Toronto.

Radc'iffe, John, Perth ; Raymond, Charles Peer, Wentworth ; Relihan, James, Perth.

Scobie, Hughina Julia, Hamilton.

Scott, Margaret : Taught three years ; married Mr. Wells of Missouri.

Sefton, Catherine : Married Mr. G. Hodgins, Toronto.

Shapley, Mary: Taught till 1878 as Head Mistress of the Ottawa Central School ; after a short period in the Sarnia High School, she retired owing to ill-health ; died in 1880.

Shillington, Thomas Benjamin : Taught a few years in Carleton and Renfrew Counties ; has been in business seventeen years in Blenheim, Kent.

Smith, Eliza, Peel.

Spence, Francis Stephens : Taught several years in Prescott and Toronto ; went into journalism for a time ; is now Secretary of the Dominion Alliance for the suppression of the liquor traffic ; lives in Toronto.

Steel, Thomas : Taught for a few years ; entered Victoria University and became a Methodist minister.

Stewart, Maggie, Toronto.

Stirton, Annie, Hamilton.

Tennent, David Haskett : Taught near London till 1878 ; entered the legal profession, and has practised ever since in that city.

Warnick, Sarah, Elgin ; West, Alexander Williamson, Perth ; West, Albert, Perth.

Whimster, Christina : Taught in Strathroy Public and High Schools till 1873, when she was appointed to the staff of the Provincial Model School in Toronto ; married Mr. Mansfield in 1875, and has lived for many years in California.

Wilson, George : Taught in Lindsay ; removed to Manitoba ; taught there until failing health compelled him to retire.

Young, Thomas : Taught in Huron County till 1879 ; went to Manitoba and taught there from 1882 to 1889 ; is now engaged in farming and ranching in that Province.

Zealand, Maria Phelp : Taught several years in the Public Schools of Hamilton ; married, and now resides in that city.

FORTY-SIXTH SESSION.

(August, 1871—December, 1871.)

Abbott, William B. : After teaching a few years went into the newspaper business ; then studied Medicine ; is now practising in the Western States.

Amos, William Thomas : Has taught continuously Public Schools in Middlesex County since 1872 ; is now teaching in McGillivray Township.

Anderson, James, Euphrasia ; Armstrong, Martha, Oxford.

Baldwin, Louisa Mary, York ; Barr, William, Perth.
Bastedo, Marian Emily : Teaches in the Hamilton Public Schools.
Battel, Elias, Elgin : Died about the year 1875.
Belfry, William James : Has taught continuously in Public Schools ; is now in Bradford.
Beveridge, John B. : Taught till 1893 in Public Schools in Middlesex and Lambton ; went into business ; is now teaching in the Brandon College, Manitoba.
Black, Priscilla : Taught in Simcoe County till 1875, then in York till 1878.
Black, Margaret, Owen Sound ; Blandford, Ella Matilda, Hamilton.
Blatchford, George : Taught in Durham ; entered the medical profession.
Brown, Abbie A., Pickering.
Buchanan, Christina : Taught in Welland and York Counties ; married Mr Thomas Henry Taylor ; now deceased.
Campbell, Isabella, Toronto ; Campbell, Richard Ginty, Flesherton.
Campbell, Annie : Taught in Welland, Wellington, Wentworth and Halton Counties till 1883 ; married Mr. Charles Campbell ; resides at Corwhin, Ontario.
Carson, William John : Taught in the Central School, London, from 1872 to 1891 ; was Principal of the Model School from 1877 to 1891 ; has since been Inspector of Public Schools for that city.
Colton, John : Taught for a time in Middlesex, and afterwards in London till 1886 ; farmed a few years at Moosejaw, N.W.T. ; is now in the Canadian Civil Service, resident in Winnipeg.
Coulson, Martha, Medonte ; Creighton, Mary Elizabeth, Perth ; Cruickshank, Robert, Simcoe.
Dearness, John : Was Principal of Public Schools in Lucan and Strathroy ; then was appointed Assistant in the Strathroy High School ; has been Public School Inspector of East Middlesex since 1874 ; was for a time a member of the Central Committee and is now a member of the Educational Council ; is lecturer in Biology in the Western University, London.
Donovan, Patrick, Northumberland : Now deceased.
Douglas, John, Wellington ; Duvall, Margaret Ann, Prescott.
Eedy, John W. : Taught in Middlesex until 1885, and a short time in Fingal ; went into journalism in St. Thomas, and afterwards in St. Mary's, where he is still in business.
English, Andrew James : Taught some years in Kent County ; now deceased.
Fergusson, John Bowerman : Taught for a time ; removed to Winnipeg, and engaged in mercantile pursuits ; resides now in Victoria, British Columbia.
French, Sheldon Young, Picton.
Gardiner, William : Is practising Medicine at Toledo, Ohio.
Gillespie, Julia Montgomery : Has taught continuously till the present time in the Picton Public School.
Goldthorpe, Amy Hannah : Taught in Port Elgin ; married Mr. Guthrie in 1875 ; has since the death of her husband taught several years in Toronto Township.
Grant, Margaret : Married Mr. A. E. Wallace of the same session ; now resides in St. Thomas.
Gray, Francis, Durham.
Grier, Rosa Elizabeth : Now Mrs. Blackwell ; resides in Toronto.
Grier, Sarah, Millbrook ; Gwatkin, Sarah, Toronto.
Hall, George : Taught for a number of years in an Indian settlement in North Bruce.
Hands, Jonathan Griffith : Now practising Medicine at Duncans, B.C.
Hanning, Catherine Ann : Taught a few years ; married ; resides in Toronto.
Helliwell, Sarah : Now married ; resides in Toronto.
Henry, Alexander, Durham : Died in 1887.

Heslop, Elizabeth, York.
Hind, William : Now in business in Guelph.
Hodge, Samuel Alexander : Has been in business in Mitchell, Ontario, since 1878.
Hodgins, Frank : Taught a few years in Middlesex and then went into business.
Hoskins, Caroline Cecilia : Taught in Elora ; is now teaching in Chicago.
Hull, John B., Seneca.
Hunter, Margaret Jane : Has taught since 1872 in the Toronto Public Schools.
Irwin, Archibald, Perth.
Jack, Jessie : Taught in Belleville ; now married.
Jackson, Charlotte Fannie : Teaches in the Toronto Public Schools.
Jewitt, Samuel : Principal of the Carlton School, Toronto Junction.
Johnson, Sanford : Taught several years ; afterwards engaged in business.
Jones, Emma Elizabeth : Taught for a time in Waterloo County ; married Mr. William McKenzie ; resides near Galt.
Kennedy, Lizzie, Toronto ; King, Joseph Henderson, Toronto.
Knowles, Elizabeth : Taught a few years in Dundas, Ingersoll, and Brantford ; married Mr. T. Simpson Wade in 1888, and has since lived in Brantford.
Logan, Catharine Bethiah : Married Mr. Geo. Bigelow ; resides at Cornwall.
Lumsden, Louisa : Teaches in the Toronto Public Schools.
McColl, Malcolm Charles : Taught a few years in Canada ; spent some time in California on account of ill health ; died a few years later at his former home, Blenheim.
McDiarmid, Andrew : Taught three years in Haldimand and Elgin Counties ; entered the medical profession ; practised a short time in Ontario, then went to Winnipeg and became one of the founders of the Manitoba Medical College ; now practises and teaches Medicine in Chicago.
McDowall, Sarah Carpenter : Taught some time in Kingston ; ceased teaching many years ago.
McFadden, Moses, Perth ; McFarlane, Elizabeth, Guelph.
McGill, Dugald : Taught Public Schools in Huron, York, and Lambton for twenty-three years ; is now farming in King Township.
McLaughlin, Thomas, Mono Mills.
McLellan, Margaret, N. Easthope : Now married.
McNicholl, Eugene Charles : Now a physician in Cobourg.
McRae, Matilda, Toronto ; McTavish, Mary, Caledon.
Main, Elizabeth Findlay, Hamilton.
Malcolm, George : Taught six years in Durham County ; graduated in Arts in Queen's University ; taught six years in Mitchell, and has taught seven in the Stratford Collegiate Institute where he is still engaged.
Martin, Alice Sophia, Cardwell ; Martin, Fannie, Cardwell.
Mathews, Charlotte Elizabeth : Never taught ; resides in Toronto.
Mills, Lizzie, Prince Edward.
Moir, Andrew : Died in 1873.
Moir, Robert : Graduated in Arts in Queen's University ; taught in Manitoba ; now teaching near Denver, Colorado, U.S.A.
Morrison, Donald, Oxford.
Mulloy, Charles Wesley : Taught a few years ; graduated in Arts in Toronto University in 1884 ; was Head Master in High Schools in Grimsby and Lucan prior to 1896, when he became Head Master in Aurora.
Naismith, Archibald D. : Taught in the Counties of Huron and Perth ; graduated in Medicine, Toronto University, in 1882 ; has practised in Crediton, Staffa and Milverton ; he still practises in the latter place.
Nixon, James Nugent, Simcoe.

Noble, Cynthia Ann : Married to Mr. Wm. Ward, Toronto.
Norman, Annie Eliza : Married Mr. Canniff; resides in Brandon, Manitoba.
Norman, Phœbe Emma : Married Mr. Ruttan; resides at Ruttanville, Manitoba.
O'Connor, Margaret : Married Mr. J. Laidley ; resides at Ernestown, Ontario.
O'Leary, Alice Margaret : Still teaches in Ontario County.
Parker, Michael, Perth.
Preston, Mary : Married Mr. George Sisson, jr., of Bethany ; died recently.
Rice, Amelia, Fonthill ; Rowe, Sarah Jane, Ops.
Scott, Walter Wallace, Prince Edward.
Shannon, John Henry, Caledon : Died in 1876 or 1877.
Sharman, George : Was for a time Principal of the Model School at Athens, Ontario ; now engaged in High School work.
Sharpe, Mary Eleanor, Cavan.
Sims, Amelia : Has taught till the present time in the Toronto Public Schools, of one of which she is Principal.
Slater, James, East Nissouri
Slocombe, Annie : Teacher in the Hamilton Public Schools.
Smith, George : Taught three years in Oxford County ; took an Arts degree in Toronto University in 1879 ; taught for two years in Woodstock College, and now practises Law in that town.
Somerville, Harriett : Taught in Toronto from 1874 till her death in 1881.
Staples, Samuel : Taught several years in Wentworth ; graduated in Arts ; entered the Methodist ministry.
Stewart, Barbara, Belleville.
Thompson, Ada Florence : Taught in Toronto ; married Rev. C H. Shutt ; resides at Scroon Lake, New York.
Thompson, Mary, Toronto.
Tom, John Elgin : Taught in Haldimand County from 1872 to 1875, and was Principal for one year of Georgetown Public School ; was Science Master in the St. Mary's and Strathroy Collegiate Institutes till 1886, when he was appointed to his present position of Public School Inspector for West Huron.
Vandervoort, Elgin Dorland: Taught six years in Hastings County ; entered the medical profession; practises in Deseronto, Hastings.
Walker, Lula Anne, Caledonia.
Wallace, Alexander Eastman : Taught eleven years ; went into mercantile business for five years and afterward into financial business.
Wells, Margaret : Taught six years ; resides in Aurora.
Williams, Samuel Colin : Taught in Aylmer till 1881 ; took up Commercial College work in Rochester, Kansas City, and again in Rochester, where he is Associate Principal of the Business Institute.
Wills, Elizabeth : Taught in several of the Toronto Public Schools from 1872 to 1878.
Wilson, Elizabeth : Taught for several years ; married.

FORTY-SEVENTH SESSION.

(January, 1872 - June, 1872.)

Armstrong, Isabella, Durham.
Beattie, Maggie, Toronto.
Beckett, Jane Wallace ; retired ; resides in Peterboro'.
Bonny, Alfred: Spent some years in mercantile life; entered the Anglican ministry ; is now Rector at Port Colborne, Ontario.
Boswell, Sarah : Taught in South Hastings and Belleville ; married Mr. McPherson ; resides in Belleville.

Bristol, Laura Ann : Married Mr. G. W. Moore, of Toronto.
Burkholder, Annie Julia : Married Mr. H. Glendinning, Dundalk, Ontario.
Cameron, Amanda, Kent ; Campbell, John, Wellington ; Campbell, John F., Elgin ; Challen, Joseph W., Norfolk.
Chapman, George Ferguson : Taught at Waterford and Oakland ; now teaching at Townsend Centre.
Christie, Margaret : Taught several years in Stormont ; married Mr. John Cumming ; lives at Apple Hill, Ontario.
Christie, Mary : Has been a teacher in Winnipeg, Manitoba, for many years.
Chisholm, Wellington P., Hastings ; Clarke, Mary, Peterboro'.
Cobb, Martha : Now Mrs. Machell of Aurora, York.
Coleman, Elizabeth Jane, Whitby ; Collins, Frederick, Durham.
Copeland, George : Retired from teaching many years ago ; farming in Waterloo Township.
Costin, Richard, Oxford ; Coutts, Marian, Grey ; Cowan, Richard, Waterloo.
Davidson, Thomas Usher : Taught for one or two years in Wentworth ; went to the State of New York.
Davison, John Lorenzo : Taught in the Provincial Model School, Toronto, from 1873 to 1884 ; graduated in Arts in Toronto University in 1880 ; entered the medical profession ; practises in Toronto, and lectures in Trinity Medical College.
Devine, Daniel, York.
Dinsmore, Andrew : Taught four years in Huron County ; went into mercantile business in Ontario and afterwards in Michigan ; resides at Imlay City, in that State.
Dodson, William : Taught a few years in Middlesex ; died while studying for the medical profession.
Dolbear, Ransome : Went into mercantile business in London.
Dunphy, James, Oxford.
Ford, Lucy Agnes : Now Mrs. William Lester, Mitchell, Ontario.
Foulds, Victoria : Taught in Glengarry ; married Mr. F. McIntyre ; lives at Martintown, Ontario.
Galloway, Jane, Durham ; Gardiner, Ann Eliza, Leeds ; Gilpin, Martha, Durham ; Graham, Mary Jane, Hastings ; Grandy, Robert, Lifford ; Grant, Catharine, Cayuga ; Goodbow, Alfred, Perth.
Harper, Annie Maria, Grey.
Hart, Edward : Taught till 1876 in Durham and Victoria Counties ; is now practising Dental Surgery in Brantford.
Hart, Peter, York.
Haviland, Harriet : Now Mrs. McMorin, Tyrrell, Ontario.
Holtorf, Agnes Claudine : Died in 1872 shortly after leaving the Normal School.
Hosball, Emma : Taught two years in Welland County ; married Mr. Ira De La Matter, B.A. ; now lives on a farm in Welland.
Isbister, Malcolm : Taught for some time in the Township of Wawanosh.
Jackson, Alfred, Wellington.
Jamieson, Samuel Bell : Taught in Middlesex and Perth ; went to the North-West in 1882, and engaged in farming ; has been since 1889 in the Canadian Civil Service at Regina.
Ketchum, Mary Elizabeth, Orangeville.
Le Feboie, John Matthew, Hastings.
Lovekin, Mary Elizabeth : Taught in Durham County ; married Mr. George White, a farmer ; died about sixteen years ago.
McAlpin, Donald : Taught a few years in Middlesex ; has been in financial business in London for a long time.

McCrea, Maggie, Lanark; McGregor, William, Lambton; McInnes, Margaret, Grey; McKay, Matthew, West Gwillimbury.

McKenzie, Annie McLean, Wentworth : Died in 1880.

McKinnon, James : Was Principal in the Port Elgin Public School ; now deceased.

McMicking, Christina Eleanor : Taught two years ; married, and now resides in Hamilton.

McNeill, Alexander : Taught in Windsor High School ; now engaged in horticulture; resides at Windsor.

McRae, Roderick, Bruce.

McTavish, Alexander A. : Practises Law at Parkhill, Ont.

McTavish, John, Waterloo ; Matheson, Alexander, Elgin.

Maloy, Sarah : Now Mrs. Foy ; teaching in Blythe, Huron.

Minshall, Henry : Now practising Medicine.

Mitchell, Lizzie Bruce, Bayfield.

Moore, Charlotte Elizabeth : Taught in the Hamilton Public Schools ; married Mr. Johnson ; now resides in New York.

Munro, John : Taught in Wellington County and afterwards in Ottawa for many years ; was Principal of one of the City Public Schools when he died in 1897 ; was President of the Ontario Educational Association at the time of his death.

O'Grady, Mary, Wentworth.

Overend, Elizabeth Mary : Taught Public Schools in Ontario and Simcoe Counties till 1876 ; has since that time had charge of the Roman Catholic Separate School in Orillia.

Reid, John, Dundas.

Ritchie, Catherine : Died in 1873 at Brantford.

Russell, Maggie, Oxford.

Sanford, Thomas D., Northumberland ; Shaw, Annie, Orangeville.

Sherry, George James : Taught in Hastings and Northumberland ; now practises Law in Norwood, Ont.

Sinclair, John, Perth.

Smith, Arthur Henry: Taught in Kincardine High School ; went to the North-West in 1880.

Somerville, George Anderson : Taught in a rural school in Ontario, and in Whitby High School ; was appointed Public School Inspector of South Wellington ; went into financial business in London where he still resides.

Sowerby, John, Ontario ; Springer, Amaziah M., Elgin.

Stevens, Edward Abel : Taught as assistant in Athens High School, and as Principal of Renfrew Model School ; has taught fifteen years in Toronto.

Stilwell, Nicholas, Elgin ; Stone, Eliza, Percy.

Sutherland, Donald : Practises Medicine at Cheboygan, Michigan.

Telford, William : Taught six years in Port Dalhousie Public School, then as Principal of the Caledonia Model School, and eleven as Principal of the Walkerton Model School ; is now in business as a journalist in Walkerton.

Thompson, Robert Gilmore, York.

Waddell, William, Waterloo ; Watson, Jane, King ; West, Walter, Thornhill.

White, Mary Agnes : Entered St. Joseph's Convent in 1877 ; died in 1895.

Wicher, Thomas : Taught for a time ; went to the United States ; now deceased.

Wood, James Smith : Taught in Simcoe County, and for five years in the Kingston Model School ; now farming near Elkhorn, Manitoba.

FORTY-EIGHTH SESSION.

(August, 1872—December, 1872.)

Andrews, Mary Louisa : Married Mr. George Welbourne, a teacher ; now resides in Manitoba.

Anderson, John, Waterloo ; Armstrong, Isabel, Durham.

Armstrong, Isabella : Now Mrs. R. Hawley, Dorland, Ontario.

Armstrong, Maria Maud : Now Mrs. H. H. Kittridge, Spokane, Washington Territory.

Asher, James : Teaching in Lincoln County.

Baird, George Meredith : Taught for some years in Kent ; now in business in Blenheim, in that county.

Baird, James Laird : Taught several years in Kent County ; has been an Accountant for fifteen years in Chicago.

Baird, John Robert, Huron.

Ballantine, Catharine, Wentworth.

Barber, Albert : Taught five years at Tyrone, two at Orono and six in Bowmanville ; was for some years Principal of the Cobourg Model School ; now fills a similar position in Brampton.

Barker, Elliott, York ; Bartholemew, Matilda Estella, York ; Bell, Martha, Brant.

Belfour, Harriet Ann : Married Mr. J. H. Madden ; died in 1893.

Bennett, George : Taught many years ; retired, and was accidentally killed in 1894.

Bennett, George James : Taught several years ; went to live in Newmarket ; died there six years ago.

Bickell, David : Became a Presbyterian Minister ; now deceased.

Blanchard, William : Taught for several years in Prince Edward County ; went into farming near Belleville.

Bowerman, Cornelius : Now practising Dentistry.

Cassidy, William : Taught rural schools in Middlesex, Oxford and Wentworth, and in the Model School at Athens ; taught afterwards in the Toronto Public Schools, and took a Medical Course ; died in Japan while on his way to establish a Christian mission in China.

Clarke, Mary, Peterboro' : Now retired.

Cook, Welthia, Hastings.

Culham. Edwin : Now farming in Peel County.

Currie, Nellie Maria, Kent.

Eyres, Sarah Jane : Taught in Durham County ; went to Manitoba and married there.

Farley, Sarah Ann : Taught in Bowmanville for a number of years, removed to New Orleans, U. S. A.

Fletcher, Morris Johnston : Taught in the Provincial Model School, Toronto, from 1874 to 1878 ; spent some time in Manitoba ; returned to Toronto to enter the legal profession.

Foxton, Jane Elizabeth, Leeds ; Freeman, Mary Eliza, Oxford.

Gilfillan, James, Huron.

Graham, Margaret : Married Mr. R. J. Porter ; resides in Picton, Ontario.

Gray, Annie Amelia : Has taught in the Toronto Public Schools since 1877.

Grant, Catharine, Haldimand ; Grundy, Sarah Ann, York.

Gripton, Charles McPherson : Taught at intervals till 1883 in schools in Lincoln, Leeds, Kent and Oxford Counties ; went into financial business in St. Catharines.

Hart, John, Ontario.

Head, Martha : Living retired in Galt.

Henderson, Anson Gaines : Taught in the Villages of Paisley, Ashburn and Brooklin until 1881, when he became a member of the staff of the Whitby Collegiate Institute where he is Commercial Master and Director of physical culture.

Henderson, Maggie Murray, Ontario.

Hicks, William Thomas : Entered the Methodist ministry ; now deceased.

Humberstone, Frederick, York ; Humphries, Jane, Northumberland.

Hunt, Charlotte Jane : Taught some time in Brighton, Ontario.

Hunter, Maggie, York.

Jones, Alfred Edwin, York.

Kirk, David : Practises Medicine in Washington Territory, U. S. A.

Little, Mary : Taught a short time in Guelph ; married Rev. D. L. McCrae, now Presbyterian minister in Collingwood, Ontario.

Living, Anna Maria : Taught in the Ottawa Public Schools, and afterwards in the Collegiate Institute in the same city ; married Mr. T. W. Thompson in 1879 ; resided in Ottawa till her death in 1887.

Lothian, Susannah : Taught many years in Prescott and Glengarry ; married Mr Chauncey Doty of Portsmouth, Nebraska, where she resides.

McCallum, Margaret Scott, Wellington.

McColl, Mary : Married Mr. George Mackenzie ; resides in St. Thomas.

McCullough, William Kenneth : Taught for a time ; went into the Presbyterian ministry.

McCully, Archibald, Oxford.

McEachren, Peter : Taught many years in the Jarvis Street Collegiate Institute, Toronto ; resigned in 1897.

McGuin, Schuyler Francis : Taught for a short time ; went to Bay City, Michigan.

McKay, Christina.

McKay, Christina : Taught one year at Thamesford, five years at or near Kintore, one year at Braemar, and for a short time in the Model School at Madoc ; died in 1889.

McKay, Donald, Oxford.

McKay, John Sutherland : Taught at Thamesford for three years ; graduated from Toronto University in 1881 and from Knox College, Toronto, in 1884 ; was called to a congregation in New Westminster. B.C.; died on March 20th, 1886.

McKay, Angus : Taught for some years in Oxford County ; is now a Presbyterian minister settled at Lucknow, Ont.

McKone, Hugh : Resides at Parkhill, Ontario.

McLeod, Dollina : Taught some years ; married Dr. Galloway of Beaverton.

McMullen, Mary Ann, Leeds : Now deceased.

McMullen, Sarah Charlotte, Leeds.

McNevin, James : Died while Mathematical Master of the Ottawa Collegiate Institute.

McTavish, Duncan A. : Taught in Middlesex till 1877 ; entered the medical profession ; practises in West Bay City, Michigan.

McTavish, Isabella : Teaching in Glencoe.

Mavety, Albert F. : Taught three years in the Public Schools of Frontenac and eight years in the Sydenham High School ; graduated in Medicine from Queen's University in 1886 ; is an M.R.C.S. Eng. ; practises in Toledo, Ohio.

Magwood, James Wilberforce, Perth ; Mavety, Alexander, Frontenac.

Mitchell, Isabella : Now Mrs. (Dr.) McClure, Thorold.

Morrison, Hugh, Oxford ; Murphy, Alexander, Norfolk ; Murphy, Lizzie, York.

Neilly, Samuel A., Simcoe ; Nichol, James, Bruce.

Ogilvy, Ann, Perth.

Poole. William : Taught some time in Carleton County ; superannuated ; resides at Kemptville.

Purdy, Rebecca Maud : Taught in York County ; married.
Rawlings, James Reid, York ; Robertson, Robert Hutchison, Waterlo .
Rutledge, Annie Jane, Hastings : Died in 1873.
Sanderson, Annie Louisa, Simcoe.
Sherwood, William Albert : Taught several years in Oxford ; became a merchant in Brownsville in the same county.
Sloan, Juliana, Prescott.
Smith, Ansley : Practises Medicine in Detroit, U.S.A.
Stewart, Barbara Fergusson, York.
Stillwall, John : Graduated in Arts in Toronto University ; entered the Baptist minisrty ; now President of a teaching institution in India.
Thomson, James, Huron : Now deceased.
Todd, Charles, Simcoe.
Tutt, Hannah, Elizabeth : Teaches in the Brantford Public Schools.
Wallace, Isabella : Taught some years in Peel ; married Mr. James Sharp, and now lives in Sudbury.
Wallace, Mary : Taught some years ; married Mr. Henry Perdue ; lives in Peel County.
Watson, Alexander Thomas : Practises Dental Surgery in Rossland, British Columbia.
Watson, Jane, York : Webster, Jennie, Kent ; Weller, Matilda Caroline, Addington ; Wells, Lizzie, York.
Wood, William Segsworth : Teaching in Haldimand County.
Worth, Margaret : Taught in York County till 1879 ; married Mr. W. B. Poulton of Toronto.

FORTY-NINTH SESSION.

(January, 1873—June, 1873.)

Armistead, Samuel : Has been teaching in Belleville for several years.
Armstrong, George Henry : Taught in Public Schools in York and Brant until 1876 ; has ever since been Mathematical Master of Paris High School.
Bailey, Fannie, Oxford ; Barnard, Mary Jane, Ontario.
Barr, Robert, Taught in Kent and Essex counties ; was for some years on the editorial staff of the Detroit *Free Press* ; is now a well-known *litterateur* ; resides in Woldingham, Surrey, England ; his pen-name was " Luke Sharp."
Bateman, Maria Frances, Middlesex.
Belfrey, Frances : Now Mrs. William Gartley, Toronto.
Blakeley, Elgin Adams : Taught for a few years in Prince Edward County ; was Principal of the Winnipeg Central School until 1888 ; has been since 1889 an official of the Manitoba Department of Education.
Cornor, Mary Margaret Louie Jane : Taught in the Toronto Public Schools from 1878 until 1887 ; now Mrs. Anderson.
Cooper, Margaret : Taught in Bowmanville High School till 1876 ; married Rev. James Fraser, now Presbyterian Minister in Sutton West, Ontario.
Cornforth, William : Taught in Wentworth and Welland, and in the Thorold High School till 1882 ; went into business in St. Thomas where he still resides.
Cowie, Agnes : Taught in Wentworth and Hastings Counties ; married Mr. W. Mackintosh, now Public School Inspector of North Hastings ; lives at Madoc.
Crawford, Peter : Has taught continuously in Kent County since 1873 ; is now in Duart.
Curtis, Smith : Taught in Ontario and Hastings, and in Ottawa ; practised Law for a time in Portage la Prairie, Manitoba ; is now in Rossland, British Columbia.
Davidson, Hadassah, Wellington : Never taught ; now deceased.

Davidson, Alice, York ; Davidson, Sandfield, York ; Davidson, Victoria, York.

Dorland, Solomon Matthews, Prince Edward : Taught in the Provincial Model School, Toronto, from Oct., 1876, until Aug., 1884 ; graduated in Medicine ; is now practising at Rodney, Ontario.

Duncan, William Anderson : Taught several years in Ottawa City, and for a time in the Strathroy and Hamilton Collegiate Institutes ; graduated in Arts in Toronto University in 1882 ; is now a Presbyterian Minister at Sault Ste. Marie.

Dyke, Augusta, Oxford.

Embury, Allan : Taught Public School in Hastings, and in the Collegiate Institutes of Perth and Brockville ; was Principal of the Goderich Model School for five years ; has since 1889 Public School Inspector of the County of Peel.

Featherstonhaugh, Maude, York.

Foy, Joseph : Taught in Public Schools, and for a short time in a High School, in Middlesex until 1883 ; has since followed a mechanical pursuit.

Franklin, Minnie, York.

Graham, Robert Henry, Peel : Entered the medical profession.

Hawkins, Thomas : Taught two years ; is now farming near Exeter, Ontario.

Healy, Isaac William, Oxford.

Hewitt, Margaret : Taught a short time ; married ; lives at Highland Creek, Ontario.

Hewitt, Mary Ann, York.

Hixon, Elizabeth : Went as a Missionary to China ; is now Mrs. Z. C. Beals.

Hughes, Caroline : Taught in Cavan Township for one year ; married Mr. Adam Preston in 1875 ; died at Bethany in 1878.

Hyndman, Elizabeth, Brant : Teaches in Methodist Mission Schools.

Kahler, Louisa Ella : Taught for a time in Chicago ; is now Matron of the Lutheran Church Home in Buffalo, New York.

Law, Amanda, York ; Lawson, Elizabeth Eleanor, York ; Lemon, Elizabeth, Welland.

Linton, Adam Robert : Taught some time in Renfrew County ; graduated in Arts in Queen's University in 1881 ; entered the Presbyterian Ministry, and is now stationed as Pastor at Port Credit, Ontario.

McCamus, David Nathan : Taught three years ; entered the Methodist ministry ; is still on circuit, now at Port Perry.

McClung, John, Grey.

McColl, John Ross : Entered the legal profession ; has since practised in Chatham.

McCreight, Elizabeth Anne : Teaches in the Toronto Public Schools.

McDonald, Donald, Grey ; McIntyre, Agnes, York.

McIntyre, Duncan Archibald : Taught many years ; died in 1885.

McKellar, James, Middlesex ; McNaughton, Catharine, Durham ; Maxwell, Louisa Theresa, Durham.

Meldrum, George Grant : Died many years ago while preparing for the ministry.

Murray, Elizabeth, Hastings.

Murray, Robert W. : See biographical sketches of members of staff.

Nairn, David : Is now teaching in the Central School, Galt.

Ogilvy, Susan, Perth ; Ogilvy, Ann, Perth.

Patterson, Elizabeth Caldwell : Taught a few years ; is now Mrs. S. Marsh, of Elkhorn, Manitoba.

Peacock, Isabella : Still teaching near Delaware, Ontario.

Pearson, Elizabeth Ann : Taught in Bruce and Simcoe Counties till 1879, and in Toronto till 1886 ; married Mr. E. A. Miller ; resumed teaching in Toronto in 1893.

Peregrine, Minerva, York ; Pyne, Katie Maria, Victoria.

Rawlings, James, York.

Riddell, Catherine Cora : Taught in York County till 1875 ; married Mr. Mark Kay, of Georgina, where she still resides ; resumed teaching in 1894.

Rowat, Isaac S. : Is Principal of the Simcoe Public School, and the Norfolk County Model School.

Sellars, Ford : Taught in Huron County ; now practising Medicine in Michigan, U. S. A.

Shepherd, Richard : Now in financial business in St. Mary's, Ontario.

Sinclair, Franklin : Taught in Kent County till his death in 1878.

Sinclair, Samuel B.: Graduated in Arts, with a Bachelor's degree from Victoria University, and a Master's degree from the University of Toronto ; was Principal of Ridgetown Public School and Hamilton Model School ; is now Vice-Principal of the Provincial Normal School at Ottawa.

Smirle, Archibald : Taught in Ottawa City till 1883 when he was appointed Public School Inspector of Carleton County, which office he held till his death in 1897.

Smith, David Leonard, Bruce.

Smith, Janet : Now Mrs. (Dr.) Stewart of Ailsa Craig.

Stinson, Susie Frances, Oxford.

Sykes, Charlotte Elizabeth ; Teaches in the Toronto Public Schools.

Twohey, Maggie Ellenor, Victoria.

Vanderburg, Alice : Never taught : married Mr. B. Tucker, of Allanburg, where she died in 1890.

Watterson, David, Carleton.

Whaley, John : Taught in several schools in York County until 1890 ; now fills a municipal office in North Toronto.

White, Elizabeth, Northumberland.

Wingfield, Jessie : Now Mrs. Lynde, Toronto.

FIFTIETH SESSION.

(August, 1873—December, 1873.)

Allen, Amelia Maria, York.

Alley, Catherine : Never taught ; is now Mrs. John Harney, St. John, New Brunswick.

Baily, Louisa : Taught in Toronto Public Schools ; died in 1889.

Barclay, Alice, York.

Barclay, Catherine Hugh : Taught in Lambton and Essex Counties ; married Mr. Cumming, now Postmaster in Arva, Ontario.

Betts, Susan A. : Taught in Prince Edward and Ontario Counties till 1882 ; married Mr. James Richardson ; taught in Muskoka from 1894 to 1896 ; resides near Aspdin, Ontario.

Blain, Jennie Burgess, York.

Brown, William Greenwood : Taught for a time in Ontario County ; graduated in Arts in Queen's University in 1881 ; was Commercial Master in Galt Collegiate Institute for two years ; was in financial business in London until 1886 ; now in the same occupation in Toronto.

Cameron, Mary Maggie, Ontario ; Campbell, Maggie, York.

Carter, Emma : Taught for a short time in the Strathroy and Sarnia High Schools ; was appointed a teacher in the Provincial Model School in 1877 ; married in 1880 Mr. James Wood of Sarnia ; died in 1882.

Case, Adelaide V. : Taught in Wingham, Ontario, and in Philadelphia, United States ; now Mrs. Marchmont of Alma, Michigan.

Case, Elizabeth B. : Taught in Gananoque, Norwich, Paisley and Wingham, in Ontario, and in Saginaw, Michigan ; is now librarian of a college at Alma, Michigan.

Chapman, Ella, Ontario : Married.

Church, Eliza Jane : Taught in the Toronto Public Schools till December, 1882 ; married Mr. Murray in 1883.

Clarke, Emmeline, Peterboro' : Now deceased.

Clerke, Harvey Show : Taught some time in Ontario County ; entered the medical profession in 1883 ; has practised ever since in Lucan and Thedford, Ontario.

Cooper, Mary Ann : Taught some time in Toronto ; married in 1892 Rev. M. P. Talling, B.A., Presbyterian minister in London, Ontario, and has since resided there.

Cooper, Samuel, Middlesex.

Dean, James H., Norfolk ; Dutcher, Adelia J., York.

Emory, Vernon Hope : Taught a short time ; entered the Methodist ministry ; now stationed in Toronto.

Fisher, Sarah Ann : Taught several years in York County ; married Mr. John Mann ; now lives at Roach's Point, Lake Simcoe.

Fletcher, William Miles : Taught in Wentworth County.

Gibson, Maggie, York ; Greenly, Esther, Perth.

Hamilton, Kate May, York ; Harcourt, Bessie, Peterboro' ; Hart, Herman, Durham.

Hart, William Lindsay : Taught in Stormont, Dundas, and Glengarry, till 1881 ; has since been engaged in mercantile pursuits ; is Postmaster at Grantley, Ontario.

Hellworth, Sarah, York ; Hill, Hortense, Wentworth.

Johnston, Martha Maud, York.

Jones, Edgar : Taught a few years ; became an Accountant in Brantford ; died in Winnipeg in 1880.

Lehman, William : Taught a short time ; now practises Medicine in Toronto.

Lytle, M. A., Simcoe.

McArthur, Mary, Victoria ; McAvoy, Jennie, York ; McCulloch, Maggie, Perth ; McDonald, Eliza, Haldimand ; McDowell, Mary Anne, York.

McIlmoyle, John Donaghue : Was Principal for many years of the Roman Catholic Separate Schools of Peterborough ; now engaged in financial business in Toronto.

McLaughlin, Alice, Cardwell.

McLean, Matilda Mary Eunice : Taught a short time in Toronto ; married Mr. J. H. Taylor ; resides at Todmorden, near Toronto.

McRae, Alexander Archibald, Prescott.

McTaggart, Angus : Now farming at Appin, Ontario.

Martin, Jane : Now Mrs. Joseph Carter, Guelph.

Martin, Robert Thomas, York ; Miller, Thomas, Huron ; Mills, J. M., Victoria.

Mills, Mary Ann : Taught some years ; married Mr. McBean ; lives in St. Catharines.

Mitchell, Rachel : Has taught continuously in the Mount Forest Public and Model School since 1875.

Morden, Eliza Jane, Middlesex ; Morden, S. E., Middlesex.

Newton, Margaret E. : Taught in Toronto Public Schools from 1874 to 1877.

Oxenham, Emma Louisa, York.

Parlow, Edwin D. : Taught in one of the Ottawa Public Schools ; is now Head Master of the Provincial Model School for Boys, Ottawa.

Reeves, Emily Louisa, York ; Rodger, Mary Jane, Shefford P. Q.

Shaw, William G., Lambton ; Smith, Minnie Bloomfield, York ; Staples, Susannah, Victoria ; Stevenson, E. J., Simcoe.

Thompson, Margaret Jane, Durham ; Totten, Jane, York.

Westman, Mary Ann : Teaches in the Toronto Public Schools.

White, W. R., Durham ; Wilson, James Thomas, Wentworth.

Woodington, Harriet : Taught in the Toronto Public Schools.

FIFTY-FIRST SESSION.

(January, 1874—June, 1874).

Arner, Arthur, Essex : Now living in Nova Scotia.
Arner, Martha : Married Mr. E. Grenville, Kingsville, Ontario.
Aylward, Sarah Anastasia, Peterboro'.
Baird, George : Taught fourteen years in Huron County ; died in 1888.
Bannerman, William : Now practising Law in Orillia.
Barnes, Charles A.: Graduated in Arts in Victoria University in 1881 ; has been Public School Inspector for East Lambton for many years ; resides in London, Ontario.
Belton, Minnie, Middlesex.
Bissell, Alice : Married ; lives at Granton.
Blacklock, Mary Elizabeth, Frontenac : Now deceased.
Botts, Sarah Ellen : Married Mr. L. Hawley ; resides at Hay Bay, Ontario.
Brown, James : Taught a short time in Waterloo County ; has taught in Whitby Town since 1876 ; is now Principal of the Model School there.
Cameron, Hugh : Taught in Victoria County ; is now in business in Woodville.
Cameron, Mary, Middlesex.
Campbell, Cassius : Has taught continuously in Ottawa City since 1875, most of the time as Principal of one of the Public Schools.
Campbell, John, Victoria.
Carlyle, Thomasina : Teaches in the Toronto Public Schools.
Carruthers, James Benjamin : Taught in Simcoe County and Barrie Town till 1883 ; has practised Medicine in North Bay from 1886 to the present time.
Case, Thomas Edward : Taught some time ; entered the medical profession.
Chadwick, Charles William : Taught some years in the County of Simcoe ; was Principal for some time of the Stratford Model School ; is Public School Inspector of the Town of Forest ; is engaged in financial business and resides in Toronto.
Cole, Cordelia Elizabeth, Brockville ; Conroy, Annie, Haldimand ; Couen, Susie Jane, Simcoe.
Cowan, Andrew : Taught a few years in Huron County ; now lives in Michigan.
Cunningham, Aiken Walter, Simcoe.
Dales, John Robert : Taught for several years in Oxford and Ontario Counties ; entered the medical profession in 1885 ; has practised ever since in Dunbarton, Ontario.
Dalzell, John Bell : Taught six years in Waterloo County ; has practised Law in Berlin since 1886.
Darrock, Sarah, Simcoe ; Davidson, Jane Hughes, York.
Donnocker, Delbert George : Taught in Oxford Public Schools for several years ; is now a Baptist Minister in one of the Eastern States.
Douglas, Mary A., Peel ; Dygert, Kate, Oxford.
Elliott, Thomas, Durham.
Ferriss, Mary Ann, Essex : Married.
Fisher, Jennie Elizabeth, Halton.
Fletcher, John : Taught in Oxford County till 1879 ; spent some time farming in Manitoba ; resumed teaching in Ontario till 1894 ; now practising Medicine in Kalamazoo, Michigan.
Fox, Mina Elizabeth, Essex : Married.
Freeman, Alice : Taught in Toronto for several years, and gave up teaching to go into literary work ; her pen-name is "Faith Fenton."
Glassford, Mary Emma, York.

Grant, James : Still teaching in Wellington County.
Gray, Anna Maria, York.
Gray, Eliza Rebecca : Taught in the Colborne School till 1877, and in the Toronto Public Schools till 1891 ; has practised Medicine in Owen Sound since 1893.
Hall, Eliza Ann : Now Mrs. E. Johnson of Tilsonburg.
Hendry, Donald, York.
Hicks, Robert William : Taught in Leeds County till 1876, and as Principal of the Prescott Model School till 1880 ; has taught in Parkdale and Toronto, as Principal, since 1883.
Hill, Lucy : Taught some time on Garden Island, near Kingston, then at St. Jacob's ; married Mr. Peterson ; died in 1882.
Hogarth, Jabez B. : Taught four years in rural schools in Oxford County, and over eleven years in the New Durham and Norwich Public Schools and the Guelph and Stratford Collegiate Institutes ; now in business in Norwich.
Hotson, Alexander : Taught in the London Public Schools from 1875 till 1880, and to the present time in the London Collegiate Institute.
Hudson, Celeste : Is now teaching in Ingersoll.
Hunter, James, Oxford.
Irwin, Joseph, Perth ; Ivison, Mary, Victoria.
Jermyn, Hannah Maria, Simcoe.
Langton, Maria, York.
Lee, Archibald : Taught in Ottawa City from 1874 to 1879 ; graduated in Arts in McGill University in 1883 ; entered the Presbyterian Ministry and is now pastor of a congregation in Prince Albert, N.W.T.
Lee, Martha : Taught four years in Brant County ; in 1882 married Dr. J. W. Willmott, of Toronto.
McCrea, Anna Laura, Grenville ; McGowan, Thomas Manson Kinney, Hastings ; McInnes, John, Grey.
McKibbin, John Henry : Taught a few years ; went into business as a druggist ; is now practising Medicine in Kalamazoo, Michigan.
McLean, Margaret Ann, Durham.
Mallon, Kate, York.
Moir, George Ross : Taught about three years ; is now farming in Iowa, U.S.A.
Northcott, Mary Ann : Has taught since 1874 in Belleville.
Norton, Theophilus : Has taught at Glen Williams for the past twenty years.
Ogden, Henry Harrison : Engaged in financial business in Strathroy.
O'Leary, Alice : Entered Loretto Convent ; has taught in Lindsay, Ireland, Guelph and Stratford.
Oswald, Janet, Bruce : Now in Dakota, U.S.A.
Palmer, Frances Louise : Taught at Richmond Hill ; married Dr. Langstaff ; still resides there.
Patterson, George Dean, Durham ; Patterson, Robert, Northumberland ; Pearson, Mary Elizabeth, York ; Pearson, Emily Margaret, York.
Powell, Francis : Taught in Windsor and Teeswater Public Schools, and as assistant master in the Ottawa Collegiate Institute till 1878 ; has practised Law in Toronto since 1885.
Ratcliffe, James : Taught a short time in Ontario County, and some years in the Hamilton Collegiate Institute ; went into business in Chicago, and afterwards in Kansas City where he still resides.
Reynolds, Arthur James : Taught in Durham and York Counties till 1890 ; now farming near Scarboro' Junction, York.
Robinson, Alice Maria, York ; Robinson Georgette, York.
Rose, David : Taught at Port Ryerse, Norfolk County ; is now a physician in Chicago.

Sample, Samuel, Huron; Scarlett, Eva Selina Gertrude, York.
Segsworth, Emma, York ; Shaw, Charles Thomas, York.
Shaw, Kate Ann : Now Mrs. Daniel Clink ; resides in the Kootenay District, B.C., where her husband is a farm instructor for the Government.
Sifton, James, Oxford ; Smith, Maggie Paul, York.
Smyth, Jane : Has taught continuously in the Toronto Public Schools since 1874.
Spence, Margaret : Has taught in the Toronto Public Schools since 1877.
Stalker, Sarah, Elgin.
Stratton, Elizabeth : Now Mrs. Samuel Wright, London.
Sutton, Eleanor : Now living with her parents at Clandeboye, Ontario.
Thompson, Alice Kate, York.
Thorne, Nancy A.: Taught at Port Perry till 1878 ; married Mr. Alexander McRae, then and still Principal of the Port Perry Model School.
West, Robert Walter, York ; Whitfield, Margaret, Millbrook.
Willmot, John W.: Taught three years in York, Ontario and Peel Counties ; graduated in Medicine in 1882 ; is practising in Toronto.
York, John, Carleton.

FIFTY-SECOND SESSION.

(August, 1874—December, 1874.)

Amos, Edwin : Taught some years in Middlesex County ; is now practising Medicine in St. Paul, Minnesota.
Baxter, Sarah Sophia, Ontario ; Bell, Stephen Harvey, Middlesex.
Black, Hugh : Now farming ; clerk of Eramosa Township.
Boyd, Isaac Chapman, York.
Brown, Richard Ellis : Is still teaching in Huron County.
Burns, Maggie Elizabeth, Ireland ; Burton, Margaret, York.
Cameron, Angus : Taught at various places in Bruce County.
Cameron, Wilhelmina, York ; Campbell, Dugald, York ; Cook, Edgar Mason, Hastings ; Cummings, Annie, Hastings.
Davis, Bidwell Nicholas : Taught Public School till 1878 ; graduated in Arts in 1881 in Queen's University ; taught in Chatham High School till 1883, and afterwards as Head Master of the Trenton High School ; has practised Law in Toronto since 1889.
Dickie, William : Now living at Carberry, Manitoba.
Dickson, John Forest, Huron ; Dobbin, Selina Ann, Wellington ; Duncan, Agnes, Ontario.
Egan, Winnifred, Middlesex.
Fisher, Mary McIntosh, Huron ; Foster, Edward, York.
Foulds, Elizabeth : Taught in the Toronto Public Schools from 1877 to 1888 ; married Mr. R. Torrance, Toronto.
Grace, Dora Louisa, Norfolk.
Grace, Julia Maria : Teaches in the Brantford Public Schools.
Hockey, John Edwin : Taught four years ; entered the Methodist ministry ; is still on circuit.
Holmes, Edward, Huron ; Hopkins, Kate Georgina, Hastings.
Hughes, Joseph Henry : Taught a short time ; went into business as merchant and lumberer ; resides at Souris, Manitoba.
Huntsman, Lution Erotas : Taught for some time ; has been many years engaged in farming.
Jack, Alma : Now living in Belleville.
Jameson, Hugh Alfred, York.

Kelly, Simeon, York : Taught a few years ; now retired.
Kemp, John Hunter, York.
Kennedy, Archibald : Now farming in Manitoba.
Kerr, James, Oxford
Lake, Henry : Taught in Durham County ; is now farming in Dakota, U.S.A.
Lang, Helen F. : Taught in rural schools in Kent County, and in the Chatham Public Schools till 1890 ; married Mr. Waterhouse ; resides still in Chatham.
Lennox, John : Taught in Campbellford, Lindsay and Welland High Schools ; died in 1895.
McAree, Annie, Wellington.
McBrady, Eliza Jane : Now Mrs. C. J. O'Neil of Chatham.
McKay, Myra, York ; McKellar, Nancy Jane, Oxford.
Mitchell, Lizzie Bruce, Huron ; Mitchell, Margaret, York.
Neilson, Mary, Haldimand.
Ogden, Millicent Elizabeth, York.
Oliver, Margaret Goldie : Taught some years ; now Mrs. Robb of Seaforth.
Patrick, Thomas : Taught in Middlesex for a few years ; is now carrying on a lumber business in Souris, Manitoba.
Robinson, Asenath, York.
Robinson, John : Now in business in Dakota, U.S.A.
Sanderson, Amy Louisa : Teaches in the Toronto Public Schools.
Shea, Hattie Elizabeth Mary, Northumberland ; Simpson, Marianna, York.
Sims, Florence : Has taught since 1876 in the Toronto Public Schools.
Stuart, Duncan E. : Taught in Mono Mills, in South Dumfries and London ; removed to the North-West and taught the Moose Jaw school for a year ; returned to Ontario to study Law ; is now a member of the firm of Stuart & Ross, and has charge of the London branch.
Stone, George : Taught some time in Public Schools, and afterwards as Assistant Master in Beamsville, Waterdown and Port Perry High Schools ; still teaches in the last named school.
Trotman, Annie : Taught several years ; married ; lives in Ancaster, Ontario.
White, Christopher, Perth.
Yeaman, Sarah Elizabeth, Northumberland.

FIFTY-THIRD SESSION.

(January, 1875—June, 1875.)

Abbott, Elizabeth Ann : Married ; resides in Michigan, U.S.A.
Acheson, John, Grey.
Adair, Alexander Aird : Taught two years ; entered the legal profession ; practised for a time in Bracebridge, Ontario, and since 1890 in Riverside, California.
Allan, Kate Morrison, York.
Anderson, Elizabeth Jane : Taught in the Toronto Public Schools till 1884 ; married ; died in 1892.
Archer, David, Durham : Now practises Medicine at Port Perry.
Archer, Eliza Jane, Lambton.
Bain, William Leckie, Perth.
Baker, Emma Sophia : Taught for some time in Public Schools ; was lady Principal of the Presbyterian Ladies' College, Toronto, from its foundation until 1886.
Baldwin, Janet Alice : Married ; resides in Emerson, Manitoba.
Balfour, James : Now Medical Superintendent of the General Hospital, London, Ontario.

Ballantine, Maria, Wentworth.
Barclay, Isaac Bartlett : Is now teaching the Blackstock School, Durham County.
Barr, Margaret Holmes : Taught two years in the Parry Sound District, and three in the Newmarket Model School ; married, in 1881, Rev. Walter Amos, Presbyterian minister in Aurora.
Bell, Margaret, Kent.
Bessey, James Reid : Farming near Georgetown.
Black, Adam, York ; Booth, William Benjamin, York.
Bourns, Thomas, Leeds : Entered the medical profession.
Brodie, Jessie Crawford, York.
Brown, Elizabeth Margaret, Prince Edward : Married Mr. Call.
Brydon, Robert, Waterloo : Now farming near Galt, Ont.
Burke, Daniel : Has taught for sixteen years ; now teaching near Embro in Oxford County.
Burnside, Ina, York.
Caldwell, Henry James, Carleton.
Campbell, Alexander : Taught two years in St. Catharines Collegiate Institute ; has been Public School Inspector for West Bruce since 1877.
Cathcart, Caroline : Taught three years in Mitchell, and a short time in Northumberland County ; has taught in the Toronto Public Schools since 1881.
Chapman, Edwin Alfred, York.
Climie, Catherine, Perth : Married.
Colgan, Eliza, Simcoe ; Collins, Frederick Charles, York.
Comfort, Etoile : Taught a number of years in St. Thomas ; married ; resides in that city still.
Cook, William Henry, York ; Coolahan, Louisa, York.
Corbett, Louis Christopher : Taught in Middlesex and Perth ; graduated in Arts in the University of Toronto in 1882 ; was Principal of the Arnprior High School for seven years, and has ever since been Modern Language Master in the Sarnia Collegiate Institute.
Craig, Lizzie Helen, York ; Crozier, Susan, York.
Currey, Hannah K. : Taught in Wellington County till 1878 ; has taught in Toronto since 1882.
Devlin, Thomas, Essex : Now deceased.
Devins, Annie, Haldimand ; Dibb, Ruth, Lambton ; Donald, Jessie Jane, Grey.
Donaldson, Elizabeth : Married Mr. William McPhail, Campbellville, Ontario.
Dorssey, Mary Jane, Simcoe.
Duncan, Barbara : Taught in Perth County for several years ; married Mr. A. Robb ; now teaching in Huron County.
Dusty, James, Perth : Resides at St. Mary's.
Elliott, Marion, Wellington ; Emery, Horatio James, Lambton.
Francis, Daniel, Perth : Now at Prince Albert, N.W.T.
Freel, Annie : Taught five years ; retired ; now resides in Hamilton.
Galbraith, Lachlan, Bruce.
Gellatly, Elizabeth : Has taught in the Toronto Public Schools since 1877.
Gibson, Thomas, Durham.
Gillespie, Fanny Leonard : Married William Briden, M.A., Principal of the High School, Ingersoll.
Glass, Matthew James : Taught in London West some years ; now practising Medicine at Poplar Hill, Ontario.
Gould, Bridget, Middlesex ; Graham, Alexander Campbell, Victoria ; Graham, Andrew Albert, Peel ; Graham, Thomas Chapman, Huron ; Grant, William Hume, Halton ; Gray, Annie, York ; Green, Dolly, York.

Green, Thomas Samuel, Ontario: Now in business in Chicago.
Hambly, Louis Elwood: Taught three years in York and Perth Counties; is now in financial business in Toronto.
Harrison, Annie, York; Harvey, William Andrew, York; Hastings, Andrew Orr, York.
Hart, Georgina, Prince Edward: Married Mr. H. B. Bristol; resides at Picton, Ontario.
Head, Martha Jane: Taught a short time; married.
Hendry, Annie: Teaching in the Hamilton Public Schools.
Holmes, Selina Emily: Taught in Kingston as Principal of one of the Public Schools; married Mr. John Renton; resides in Kingston.
Houston, David Walker: Taught several years in South Hastings; now practises Medicine in New York State.
Huff, Samuel: Has taught almost continuously since 1875, fourteen years in Public Schools and nine years in Orillia and Meaford High Schools; is an undergraduate in Arts of Queen's University.
Hurley, Thomas Francis, Kent.
Iles, Isabella: Taught in Strathroy Public School till 1878, and in the Ottawa Collegiate Institute till 1883; has taught in the Toronto Public Schools since 1884.
Irwin, William: Taught till December, 1896, the last eleven years in Flesherton; has gone into journalistic work in the Town of Durham.
Jarvis, Eliza Jane, Huron; Jarvis Maggie, Halton.
Jarvis, Sarah Ann: Married Mr. John Waldie, Ex-M.P.; resides in Toronto.
Johnston, Ada. York.
Johnston, Robert William: Taught a number of years; is now a Methodist minister.
Jones, Sophia Bethany, York.
Kennedy, Eleanor, York; Kenyon, Henry, Lennox.
Kindred, Mary: Now Mrs. (Dr) Kidd, Midland, Ontario.
Leitch, Jane Frue: Taught in Glengarry and Cornwall till 1879; married Mr. E. McDonald of that town; resides now in Chicago.
Leitch, Malcolm Laughlin, Middlesex.
Lingham, Bessie, Hastings; Littlefield, Elizabeth, York.
Lough, William Romaine: Taught many years in Public Schools, and for a time in Clinton High School; has been for the last fourteen years Principal of the Clinton Model School.
Ludlow, Richard, Grey: Practises Dentistry in Petrolia.
McCanzie, Duncan, Hastings; McCanzie, James, Hastings.
McCracken, Thomas: Taught in Simcoe County; practices Medicine in Kansas; lives at Topeka.
McCredie, Emily: Died over twenty years ago.
McCordie, Alma, Elgin.
McDowell, Isabella: Taught in several Halton schools till she married Mr. John Murray, ten years ago; now lives on a farm near Milton.
McDougald, Sarah, Bruce; McGill, Robert, Huron; McGowan, Robert W., Huron; McGregor, Mary, Lambton; McKague, Samuel Robert, York; McKay, William, Huron; McKenzie, James, Hastings; McKenzie, Duncan, Hastings. McLaren, Helen Buchanan; McLean Mary E., Brant.
McLellan, Hattie: Taught in the Grimsby High School two years, and five in the Ottawa and Toronto Provincial Model Schools; went to California and taught four years; married Mr. Randolph of Los Angeles, where she still resides.
McMullen, Emma, York.
McNevin, James, Ontario: Taught for a time; now deceased.
McPhail, Sarah Ann, Ontario; McKay, John, Oxford.

McTavish, Christina : Now teaching in Mountain, Dundas County.
McWilliam, John : Taught in Oxford and Kent Counties till 1878 ; entered the Medical profession ; practised for a short time in Scotland, and has ever since done so in Thamesford, Ontario.
Manderson, Georgiana, Wellington ; Meldrum, Anna Pencil, Wellington.
Merrifield, Martha Priscilla, Grenville ; Milady, Thomas, Lambton.
Miller, Emma Noletta : Now Mrs. Marlatt, Aylmer, Ontario.
Miller, William Rome : Still teaching ; resides at Goderich.
Mossacar, Marana Emma Matilda, Halton ; Munro, Catharine, Middlesex.
O'Reilly, Mary Ann, Victoria ; Orr, Maggie Antoinette, Northumberland ; Orr, Mary Ann, York.
Parker, Thomas : Taught in Northumberland County till 1879, and has since taught in the Toronto Public Schools, much of the time as Principal.
Pascoe, Richard, Durham.
Pettit, Hiram : Taught two years in Elgin and Hastings ; has since been engaged in farming.
Ptolemy, Henry : Taught several years in Wentworth ; practises Medicine in Michigan, United States.
Pyne, Albert Roberts, Haldimand.
Rae, James William : Taught a number of years in Durham County ; entered the Presbyterian ministry ; is now pastor of the congregation at Toronto Junction.
Read, Frank Allen, Grenville ; Reilly, William George, Simcoe ; Richardson, Henry, York ; Robinson, Edward Bravender, Ontario.
Robson, Lizzie, York ; Robinson, Thomas Harvey, York.
Scott, William : Teaches in Oxford County.
Scott, T. Ann B., Wellington.
Schofield, Jennie Louise, York ; Shaw, William Alexander, York ; Shea, Bridget, Middlesex ; Shore, Margaret Jane, Cardwell.
Silcox, Fannie, Elgin : Taught in Elgin County ; married.
Sims, Stephen Henry, Brant.
Sprague, William Edward : Taught in South Hastings, Belleville and Cobourg ; now practises Medicine in Belleville.
Springer, Mary Elizabeth, Elgin.
Stevenson, James McGregor, Middlesex : Never taught ; has been farming since 1875.
Stuart, Alexander : Taught in the Morrisburgh and St. Mary's High Schools till 1877 ; entered the legal profession ; has practised for many years in Glencoe, Ontario.
Stinson, Mary Jane, Wellington ; Sutherland, Della, Hastings ; Sutherland, Jeffrey Talbot, Elgin.
Symons, William Henry : Taught in various schools in Durham and Victoria Counties till 1885 ; entered the medical profession and has practised for the last twelve years in the State of New York.
Terry, Robert Irwin : Teaches in Whitchurch, near Sharon, York County.
Trusler, Emma, Lambton.
Trusler, Jane : Married Mr. Twiss ; resides at Glencoe, Ontario.
Van Camp, Loretta Anne : Taught three years in Petrolea ; Married Mr. T. L. Adams in 1878 ; still lives in Petrolea.
Van Amburgh, Luther Elliott, Elgin.
Walsh, Hattie Amelia, Durham ; Warwick, Amelia, York ; West, Edward, Middlesex ; West, Minnie, York.
Westland, Bertha F. : Now Mrs. Sammons of Pennsylvania, U.S.A.
White, Robert, Peel.

Wightman, George Easton : Now teaching in Colchester Township, Essex.
Wilkinson, Sarah : Taught in Waterdown, Palmerston, Stratford, Port Dalhousie and West Toronto Junction until 1890 ; married Dr. J. W. McLaughlin, now Registrar of Durham ; resides in Bowmanville.
Willoughby, Mary Ann, Simcoe ; Windrum, Maggie, Oxford ; Wright, Anna, Hastings.
Young, James Alfred : Was Principal of the Fergus Public School till 1882 ; went into business for two years in Toronto and ever since in Thamesford, Ontario.

FIFTY-FOURTH SESSION.

(August, 1875—December, 1875.)

Alexander, Margaret Laing : Taught in Brantford ; studied Art ; married Mr. J. K. Fairbairn ; resides in Toronto.
Armitage, John R. : Has not taught since 1875 ; farmed for a time ; is now in business in Lucan.
Badgeley, Philip, Hastings ; Badgeley, Thomas Vincent, Hastings ; Barr, Annie Carrick, Oxford ; Barr, William, Kent.
Bate, Jane : Taught several years in Wellington County ; now teaching in Guelph.
Beneteau, Eli Celestin : Now a farmer in Essex County.
Blackwell, Jennie, York.
Bolton, Eliza : Taught primary classes in Morpeth, Listowel and Toronto ; has for a number of years been Directress of Kindergarten Training in the Provincial Normal School at Ottawa.
Borrowman, Marion : Married Mr. William Church ; resides at Mt. Julian, Peterboro'.
Breer, Edward, Middlesex.
Brown, Clara Louise, Addington : Now superannuated.
Brown, Jennie, Peterboro' ; Brown, Mary, York ; Brown, William, York.
Bruce, Edward W. : Taught thirteen years in Public Schools, part of the time in Toronto ; was four years Assistant Master in one of the Toronto Collegiate Institutes ; is now Principal of one of the Toronto Public Schools.
Burke, Alexander, Oxford.
Campbell, Duncan, Wellington ; Campbell, John, Huron ; Carpenter, Mary Elizabeth, Halton.
Carter, Hannah : Taught in London Public Schools from 1876 till 1895, when she died.
Chisholm, Teresa, York ; Clendinning, Ruth Jane, York ; Clendinning, Martha Ann, York.
Coatsworth, Nettie : Now Mrs. William Ramsay of Toronto.
Cole, Eleanor, Leeds.
Cornell, Daniel Birt : Taught in Ridgetown and Amherstburgh as Principal of Public School, and Mitchell as High School Assistant till 1881 ; now practises Medicine in Saginaw, Michigan.
Cowan, William Edward : Taught a short time in Halton and Lambton ; is now a druggist in Deloraine, Manitoba.
Chisholm, Angus Downie, Middlesex ; Cunningham, Carrie Eliza, Simcoe.
Curlette, Margery : Taught in rural schools and in the Brantford Ladies' College till 1887 ; was Lady Principal of a Ladies' College in Atlanta, Georgia, for five years ; taught vocal language to deaf and dumb pupils in Belleville and Montreal till 1896 ; now Lady Principal of the Toronto Presbyterian Ladies' College.
Currie, Margaret Strang, York.
Curtis, Sophia Jane : Teaches in Newcastle, Ontario.

Demill, Amelia : Now Mrs. Duggan, Denver, Colorado.

Dix, Mary Ellen, Victoria ; Donoghue, Daniel, York ; Dowe, Mary Ida, York.

Drury, Victoria : Taught in London from 1876 till her marriage to Mr. Walter Morgan in 1882 ; resides in London

Duck, William Brock : Entered the medical profession eighteen years ago ; practises in Preston, Ontario.

Dunlop, Lilla Stuart : Married Mr. Stephen Nearse ; resides at Hillier, Ontario.

Edgar, Mary: Now Mrs. Thompson, Watford, Ontario.

Edwards, Margaret Stephen : Taught almost continuously in Strathroy till 1893 ; married Dr. E. G. Edwards ; resides in Grand Rapids, Michigan.

Emerson, Mary Elizabeth, Hastings.

Field, Sarah Eliza, Lincoln.

Flavelle, Margaret : Taught for some time ; married, in 1891, W. S. Milner, M A., now Associate Professor of Classics in University College, Toronto.

Foster, Helen Margaret, York.

Freel, Ellen : Taught several years ; now lives retired in Toronto.

Freeman, Joseph, Perth.

Fuller, Charles H.: Taught in Amherstburg ; engaged in financial business ; resides at Ruthven, Ontario.

Gillies, Margaret Jane, Perth ; Gfroerer, George Sebastian, Bruce ; Greer, Sarah, Durham.

Greenwood, William John : Taught for some time ; graduated in Arts in Victoria University in 1886 ; taught for a few years in the Whitby Collegiate Institute ; has been for the last five years on the staff of the Whitby Ladies' College.

Halfey, Elizabeth Mary, Simcoe.

Hale, Agnes : Taught schools in Middlesex till 1880 ; married in that year ; died in 1887.

Hea, Charles Henry : Taught some time in Kent ; went to the United States.

Head, Gilmour, Brant.

Hicks, Orrin Stanley : Taught in Tweed for a time, and has taught in Bayside, Ontario, sixteen years.

Holterman, Christina : Taught in the Toronto Public Schools from 1884 to 1886 ; now Mrs. Culver of Brantford.

Home, Elizabeth, Simcoe ; Horner, Selina, Perth.

Horsburgh, Mary : Married Mr. Robertson ; now resides in Portage la Prairie, Manitoba.

Hughes, Sarah, York.

Hunt, Martha Elizabeth : Was a teacher in the Provincial Model School in Toronto from January, 1879, to December, 1882 ; now deceased.

Hunter, Margaret Stephen, Halton.

Ireland, Edwy Schuyler, Northumberland.

Jordan, John, Wellington.

Knowles, Robert : Taught several years ; became a farmer ; died at Lynedoch in 1882.

Laimon, Jeanne, Wentworth ; Lawson, Mary Elizabeth, York ; Liles, Hettie Louise, York ; Lowrie, Eliza Ann, Perth ; Lyon, Emily Medora, Oxford.

Loney, George Albert B. : Practises Law in the United States.

Lowe, Mary Ida, York.

Lyons, Robert Alexander : Taught near Georgetown ; now a merchant in Glen Williams, Ontario.

McArthur, James, Elgin ; McAvoy, Jennie Clara, York.

McCreadie, Samuel Nelson, Hastings : Taught in the Provincial Model School, Ottawa, from September, 1881, to August, 1883 ; now deceased.

McDiarmid, Ellen, Brant ; McDougall, Duncan, Victoria ; McFadyen, Archibald, Victoria.

McGrath, Matthew Francis : Practised Medicine ; now deceased.

McIver, John, Bruce.

McJanet, Elizabeth : Taught in the Toronto Public Schools till 1879 ; married Mr. John Imrie ; still resides in Toronto.

McKay, Angus, Oxford ; McKay, Donald, Oxford ; McKellar, Daniel, Elgin.

McKellar, Eliza : Taught some years in Halton County ; married Mr. McLaren ; is now in the United States.

McTavish, Mary, Oxford.

Mains, Thomas : Now resides in Watford.

Marquis, Kate Mabel : Has retired from teaching ; resides in Brantford.

Marshall Robert Gilray : Practises Law in Chicago, United States.

Meade, Letitia : Taught in Halton until 1887 ; entered the medical profession ; married Mr. Sirs ; resides at Cargill, Ontario.

Miller, Abigail : Married ; went to the United States.

Montgomery, Esther Munro, Lincoln.

Moray, Charles W. : Entered the medical profession ; practising in Kingston, Michigan, U.S.A.

Mowbray, James, Huron : Died many years ago.

Munro, Donald C. : Taught several Public Schools in Waterloo, Perth, and Wellington ; went into journalistic work for a time, and afterwards took charge of the Indian Industrial School at Regina, which he conducted till his death.

Munro, George : A clergyman of the Disciple denomination, Hamilton.

Murch, Thomas : Teaches in Hullett, County of Huron.

O'Brien, Alice Agnes, Wellington ; O'Brien, William James, Hastings.

Park, John : Taught for five years in York County ; has practised Medicine for thirteen years at Saintfield, Ontario.

Potter, Mary Ann, Hastings : Now deceased.

Powell, Matilda, Perth.

Rankin, Mary Lavina : Taught seven years in Halton, York and Durham Counties ; married Mr. Jacob Snider ; resides in Toronto.

Ray, Emma, Northumberland ; Reid, Thomas, Simcoe.

Ridley, Jennie : Taught for some time ; married Mr. Alexander Drake ; resides in Toronto.

Ritchie, Maggie, York ; Robertson, Annie, Bruce.

Ross, Mima : Taught in Oxford County, and in the Institute for the Blind at Brantford ; married Mr. R. W. Murray, now a teacher in the Provincial Model School, Toronto.

Ross, Roderick, Kent : Died in 1876.

Sams, Elizabeth Yates : Has taught in the Toronto Public Schools since 1876.

Scott, Elizabeth Kennedy, Simcoe ; Sinclair, Archie McCollum, Perth ; Smith, Fanny Mordaunt, Peel.

Spence, Mary Frances : Taught in the Toronto Public Schools from 1877 to 1889 ; now Mrs. (Dr.) Reid.

Stevenson, John, York ; Sutherland, Della, Hastings.

Taylor, Thomas Hugh, Wellington.

Walker, Carman Gould, Northumberland.

Watts, Mary Lobb : Has taught almost continuously since 1875 in rural schools ; is now teaching near Coboconk, Ontario.

Webster, John Dickson : Taught nine years in Brant County ; graduated in Arts in Toronto University in 1894 ; has entered the medical profession.

Weeks, William James : Entered the medical profession ; practised in Thorndale till 1893, and now practises in London, Ontario.

White, James F. : Taught the Roman Catholic Separate School in Lindsay for some years ; was appointed the first Separate School Inspector in 1882, which position he still holds.

White, John Wesley : Taught a short time ; went into financial business, and then entered the legal profession ; has practised in Chatham since 1886.

Wilkinson, George, Waterloo : Now deceased.

Wilkinson, John : Never taught ; is now farming in Waterloo County.

Wilson, Samuel Lount, Waterloo.

Winter, Charles Ambrose : Taught in Waterloo County for some years ; has long been in mercantile and financial business in Preston, Ont.

Wynne, John B. : Taught in Middlesex and Lambton for nearly ten years ; was a druggist in Brigden, Ontario, till 1897 ; is now in the same business in Leamington.

Zufelt, Florana Augusta : Now Mrs. Lamb ; resides in the United States.

IX.

MEMBERS AND EX-MEMBERS OF THE STAFF.

Members of the teaching staff of the Toronto Normal and Model Schools from 1847 until 1897. Those whose names are printed in italics are, at present, on the staff; those marked with an asterisk are deceased.

Adair, Miss Mary : Kindergarten Assistant, Sept., 1892—Sept., 1893.
Adams, Miss Annie : Teacher, Model School, Oct., 1871—Aug., 1878.
Adams, Miss M.: Teacher, Model School, Jan., 1863—March, 1865; Second Head Mistress, Girls' Model School, March, 1865—Dec., 1866.
*Archibald, Chas., M.D. : Teacher, Model School, Jan., 1868—Sept., 1869.
Armstrong, Wm. : Drawing Master, Jan., 1864—March, 1884.
Barron, F. W., M.A. ; Second Master, Normal School, May, 1857—July, 1857.
Bell, D. C. : Professor of Elocution, Nov., 1880—Dec., 1882.
Bell, Robert : Teacher, Model School, Feb., 1848, for the Session.
Bentley, J. : Drawing Master, Nov., 1857—May, 1859.
Campbell, Alex. R. : Teacher, Model School, Aug., 1859—May, 1864.
Carlyle, Jas., M.D. : Fourth Head Master, Boys' Model School, Dec., 1858—Aug., 1871 ; Mathematical Master, Normal School, Sept., 1871—Dec., 1893.
*Carter, Miss Emma : Teacher, Model School, Oct., 1877—Aug., 1880.
*Carter, Miss Mary : Teacher, Model School, Sept., 1872—Sept., 1877.
Casselman, A. C. : Drawing Master, Jan., 1892.
Caulfeild, Miss M. K. : Teacher, Model School, Sept., 1887.
Clare, Samuel : Writing Master, Aug., 1867—Dec., 1884.
Clark, Miss Clara J. : Teacher, Model School, Aug., 1865—April, 1869.
Clark, Mrs. Dorcas : First Head Mistress, Girls' Model School, Nov., 1852—March, 1865.
Clark, Miss Helen M. : Teacher, Model School, April, 1855—March, 1865.
*Clarke, J. P. : Music Teacher, Feb., 1848—June, 1848.
Clarkson, Charles, B.A. : Seventh Head Master, Boys' Model School, Sept., 1882—Dec., 1886.
Cody, Miss Helen : Kindergarten Assistant, Sept., 1894.
Colles, W. H. G. : Teacher, Model School, March, 1878—Dec., 1878.
Cooper, Thos. : Music Teacher, July, 1856—Nov., 1857.
Coulon, Alphonse : Drawing Master, Oct., 1859—Dec., 1863.
Craig, F. J. : Writing Master, Nov., 1854 April, 1855.
*Cullen, Mrs. Martha : Third Head Mistress, Girls' Model School, Feb., 1867—Jan., 1884 ; died 1884.
Davey, P. N., M.D : Teacher, Model School, Jan., 1879—Aug., 1884.
*Davies, Rev. H. W., D.D. : Second Master, Normal School, Aug., 1866- July, 1871 ; Third Principal, Normal School, Aug., 1871—Dec., 1884 ; died March 20th, 1895.
Davison, John L., B.A., M.D. : Teacher, Model School, Jan., 1873—Aug., 1884.
*Dearnlay, C. R. : Instructor in Drill and Calisthenics, May, 1877—March, 1884.

*Disher, John C., M.D.: Teacher, Model School, Oct., 1858—May, 1864 ; died in 1864.
Dorland, Solomon M., M.D.: Teacher, Model School, Oct., 1876—Aug., 1884.
Fletcher, M. J.: Teacher, Model School, July, 1874—Jan., 1878.
Fotheringham, David : Teacher, Model School, Sept., 1856—Feb., 1858 ; Third Head Master, Boys' Model School, Feb., 1858—Sept., 1858.
Fripp, H. G. R.: Teacher, Normal School, Nov., 1852—May, 1853.
Gillmayr, Miss Natalie : French Teacher, Oct., 1887—April, 1893.
Glashan, J. C.: Teacher, Model School, May, 1864—Dec., 1867.
*Goodwin, Major H.: Instructor in Drill and Calisthenics, Nov., 1852—Oct., 1853 ; Jan., 1854—Feb., 1877.
Graham, Mrs. F. T.: Teacher of Elocution, Oct., 1878—Oct., 1880.
*Hagarty, Miss Kate F. : Teacher, Model School, Jan., 1875—Aug., 1890.
Hailman, Miss Bessie E.: First Kindergarten Director, Sept., 1885—March, 1886.
Hart, Miss C. M. C.: Second Kindergarten Director, April, 1886—Aug., 1892.
Hickok, Samuel S. : Music Master, Nov., 1857—May, 1858.
Hind, H. Youle : Second Master, Normal School, Nov., 1847—Oct., 1852.
Hind, Wm. : Drawing Master, Nov., 1851—Nov., 1857.
Hughes, Jas. L.: Teacher, Model School, April, 1867—Aug., 1871 ; Fifth Head Master, Boys' Model School, Sept., 1871—May, 1874.
*Hunt, Miss M. E. : Teacher, Model School, Jan., 1879—Dec., 1882.
Johnson, Miss Emma : Kindergarten Assistant, Jan., 1888—Aug., 1888.
Johnston, Miss Catharine : Teacher, Model School, Nov., 1852—April, 1855.
Jones, Miss L. H. : Teacher, Model School, July, 1869—July, 1873.
Kirkland, Thomas, M.A.: Science Master, Normal School, Aug., 1871—Dec., 1884 ; Fourth Principal of the Normal School, Jan., 1885.
Knox, Miss Agnes : Teacher of Elocution, 1891 and 1892.
Laidlaw, Miss Jean R. : Kindergarten Assistant, Sept., 1891—Aug., 1892.
*Lewis, Richard : Teacher of Elocution, Oct., 1882—Dec., 1884.
Livingstone, John : Teacher, Model School, April, 1855—Oct., 1855.
*Lowey, Charles : First Head Master, Boys' Model School, Feb., 1848 ; died Aug., 1848.
Lusk, Charles H., M.D.: Teacher, Model School, Aug., 1864—Feb., 1867.
Masson, Eugene Albert : French Teacher, Oct., 1893.
Meehan, Miss M. : Teacher, Model School, Jan., 1883.
Mencilley, Miss J. : Teacher, Model School Sept., 1878—Dec., 1878 ; Sept., 1880 —Aug., 1887.
Mills, Miss Hattie B., B.A. : Teacher, Model School, Sept., 1896.
Mitchell, Mrs. Kate H.: Teacher of Domestic Economy, Jan., 1897.
Moore, R.: Teacher, Model School, May, 1858—Oct., 1858.
Montizambert, Miss Louisa H.: Teacher of Scientific Sewing, Aug., 1897.
Morris, James : Teacher, Model School, Oct., 1858—June, 1859.
Murray, R. W.: Teacher, Model School, Jan., 1887.
Macintyre, Miss Mary E.: Kindergarten Assistant, Sept., 1890—Aug., 1891; Third Kindergarten Director, Sept., 1892.
*McCallum, Archibald, M.A.: Second Head Master, Boys' Model School, Oct., 1848 —Feb., 1858.
McCausland, Miss C. E.: Teacher, Model School, March, 1868—Oct., 1871.
McFaul, J. H., M.D.: Drawing Master, Feb., 1884—Dec., 1891.
McIntosh, Angus : Teacher, Model School, Sept., 1884—Dec., 1886 ; Eighth Head Master, Boys' Model School, Jan., 1887.
McKenzie, Miss L. P.: Kindergarten Assistant, Sept., 1889—Aug., 1890.

MacKenzie, Miss Wilhelmina : Teacher of Calisthenics, Sept., 1896.
McLellan, Miss Hattie : Teacher, Model School, Sept., 1884—Dec., 1887.
McLurg, James, M.D.: Teacher, Model School, Sept., 1884—Aug., 1887.
MacMurchy, A.: Teacher, June, 1857—Sept., 1857.
McPhedran, A., M.D.: Teacher, Model School, Aug., 1871—Sept., 1876.
Ormiston, David, M.A. : Teacher, Model School, Nov., 1855— Aug., 1857.
Ormiston, Rev. Wm., B.A., D.D.: Second Master, Normal School, May, 1853—May, 1857.
*Paige, Robert George : Music Master, Nov., 1854—Oct., 1855.
Parr, T.: Instructor in Drill and Calisthenics, April, 1884.
Porter, T. M.: Teacher, Model School, Sept., 1888.
Preston, S. H.: Music Master, Aug., 1882.
Purslow, Adam, B.A., LL.D.: Teacher, Model School, May, 1858—Sept., 1858.
Robertson, J. H.: Music Master, Jan., 1848, for the session.
*Robertson, T. Jaffray, M.A.: First Principal of the Normal School, July, 1847—Oct., 1866 ; died 1866.
Robins, S. P., M.A., LL.D.: Teacher, Model School, May, 1852—Nov., 1854
*Rock, Warren : Teacher, Model School, Nov., 1854—July, 1856.
Rose, Miss Ada E.: Teacher, Model School, Sept., 1888—Aug., 1892.
Rose, Miss Martha : Teacher, Model School, Jan., 1888—Aug., 1894.
Ross, Miss Mary M.: Kindergarten Assistant, Sept., 1888—Aug., 1889.
Ross, Miss Sara M.: Teacher, Model School, Sept., 1892.
Russell, Miss Nellie : Teacher, Model School, Sept., 1891—Dec., 1891.
Sangster. J. H., M.A., M.D.: Teacher, Model School, Jan., 1849—May, 1853 ; Second Master, Normal School, Jan., 1858—Oct., 1866 ; Second Principal of Normal School, Oct., 1866—July, 1871.
Scott, Miss M. T.: Fourth Head Mistress, Girls' Model School, Feb., 1884.
Scott, Wm., B.A.: Teacher, Model School, Oct., 1869—May, 1874 ; Sixth Head Master, Boys' Model School, May, 1874—Sept., 1882 ; Vice-Principal of Normal School, Jan., 1894.
*Sefton, H. F.: Music Master, May, 1858—Dec., 1882 ; died 1882.
*Shenick, Miss Henrietta : Teacher, Model School, April, 1855—Dec., 1862.
Sinclair, Arthur H., B.A.: Teacher, Model School, Sept., 1887—Sept., 1888.
Stacey, J. Samuel : Writing Master, Nov., 1849—July, 1852.
Strachan, Alex. R., M.D.: Writing Master, July, 1858—Sept., 1861.
Strachan, H. G.: Writing Master, Sept., 1861—July, 1867.
Stuart, Miss Alice: Teacher, Model School, Sept , 1890.
Sutherland, Miss C. F.: Teacher, Model School, Sept., 1895—Aug., 1896.
Townsend, Wm.: Music Master, May, 1848—April, 1850.
*Tupper, Elon : Music Master, Jan., 1853—Nov., 1854.
Turnbull, Miss Jessie : Teacher, Model School, Aug., 1865—April, 1868.
Walsh, Patrick : Music Master, Sept., 1850—Oct , 1852.
Watts, Walter A.: Second Master, Normal School, Nov., 1857 -Nov., 1858.
Whimster, Miss Christina : Teacher, Model School, Aug., 1873—Dec., 1874
Wood, Miss Jeannie: Teacher, Model School, Oct., 1889.

X.

GENERAL PROGRAMME AND OFFICERS.

Sunday, October 31st.

THE METROPOLITAN CHURCH, - - 7 P.M.

Sermon by REV. E. H. DEWART, D.D., a member of the first Toronto Normal School Class. Subject: "The True Elements of Individual and National Progress and Stability."

The members of the Convention will assemble in the school-room of the church at 6.45 p.m. and proceed together to the section of the church allotted to them.

Monday, November 1st.

1. NORMAL SCHOOL (PRINCIPAL'S LECTURE ROOM), - 2 P.M.

Unveiling of Portraits:—(1) THOMAS JAFFRAY ROBERTSON, M.A., First Principal—David Fotheringham; (2) JOHN HERBERT SANGSTER, M.A., M.D., Second Principal—Rev. R. P. McKay, M.A.; (3) REV. HENRY W. DAVIES, M.A., D.D., Third Principal—Charles A. Barnes, B.A.; (4) PAST HEAD MISTRESSES OF GIRLS' MODEL SCHOOL—Mrs. Nasmith, Miss Mary Caven; (5) PAST HEAD MASTERS OF BOYS' MODEL SCHOOL—Frank Rolph, C. Hodgetts, M.D.

2. PUBLIC HALL OF EDUCATION DEPARTMENT, - 3 P.M.

Reminiscences:—(1) Mrs. Catharine Fish; (2) William Carlyle; (3) David Ormiston, M.A.; (4) Rev. Mungo Fraser, D.D.; (5) Mrs. Georgina Riches; (6) Joseph H. Smith; (7) A. S. Allan.

3. PUBLIC HALL AND MUSEUM OF EDUCATION DEPARTMENT, - 8 P.M.

Conversazione.—Conductor, S. H. Preston. 1. Part Songs, (*a*) "Home," (*Volkslied*), (*b*) "'Tis the Last Rose of Summer," Normal School Choir; 2. Song, "The Kerry Dance," (*Molloy*), Miss Marie Wheeler; 3. Song, "The Bay of Biscay," (*Davy*), Mr. Rechab Tandy; 4. Duet, "Maying," (*White*), Miss Marie Wheeler, Mr. Rechab Tandy; 5. Song, "Good Night," (*Hawley*), Miss Laura L. Phœnix; 6. Song, "Mona," (*Adams*), Mr. Rechab Tandy.

Promenade.—Music: D'Alesandro's Orchestra.

Tuesday, November 2nd.

1. PUBLIC HALL OF EDUCATION DEPARTMENT, - - 2 P.M.

Educational Addresses:—(1) THE HISTORY OF THE TORONTO NORMAL SCHOOL, Thomas Kirkland, M.A.; (2) THE SCHOOL OF THE TWENTIETH CENTURY, James L. Hughes; (3) PROTESTANT EDUCATION IN QUEBEC, S. P. Robins, M.A., LL.D.; (4) WHERE DO WE STAND EDUCATIONALLY AS COMPARED WITH FIFTY YEARS AGO?—J. H. Sangster, M.A., M.D.

2 ROSSIN HOUSE - 7.30 P.M.

Banquet.
Music: Glionna-Marsicano Orchestra.

OFFICERS:

President,
Hon. G. W. Ross, LL.D.

Vice-President,
Thomas Kirkland, M.A.

Chairman of Executive Committee,
James L. Hughes.

Secretaries:

Wm. Scott, B.A.   Angus McIntosh.

Committee:

Wm. Houston, M.A.	W. F. Chapman.
J. S. Deacon.	M. J. Kelly, M.D., LL.B.
J. Dearness.	J. H. Smith.
J. C. Glashan.	J. A. McLellan, M.A., LL.D.
R. W. Doan.	S. B. Sinclair, M.A.
R. Alexander.	A. Barber.
D. Fotheringham.	A. C. Casselman.
S. H. Preston.	R. W. Murray.
T. M. Porter.	W. H. Elliott, B.A.
Mrs. J. S. Arthurs.	Mrs. G. Riches.
Miss A. Shenick, B.A.	Miss M. T. Scott.
Miss Macintyre.	Miss M. K. Caulfeild.
Miss M. Meehan.	Miss A. Stuart.
Miss J. Wood.	Miss S. Ross.
Miss E. Cody.	Miss H. B. Mills, B.A.

Committee on Biograhical Sketches:

Messrs. Houston, Kirkland, Scott, McIntosh and Casselman.

www.ingramcontent.com/pod-product-compliance
Lightning Source LLC
Chambersburg PA
CBHW020912230426
43666CB00008B/1418